Employment and Work Relations in Context Series

Series Editors
Tony Elger and Peter Fairbrother

Centre for Comparative Labour Studies,
Department of Sociology,
University of Warwick

The aim of the Employment and Work Relations in Context Series is to address questions relating to the evolving patterns and politics of work, employment, management and industrial relations. There is a concern to trace out the ways in which wider policy-making, especially by national governments and transnational corporations, impinges upon specific workplaces, occupations, labour markets, localities and regions. This invites attention to developments at an international level, tracing out patterns of globalization, state policy and practice in this context, and the impact of these processes on labour. A particular feature of the series is the consideration of forms of worker and citizen organization and mobilization in these circumstances. Thus the studies address major analytical and policy issues through case study and comparative research.

HISTORY OF WORK AND LABOUR RELATIONS IN THE ROYAL DOCKYARDS

Edited by Kenneth Lunn and Ann Day

MANSELL
London and New York

First published 1999 by
Mansell Publishing Limited, *A Cassell imprint*
Wellington House, 125 Strand, London WC2R 0BB, England
370 Lexington Avenue, New York, NY 10017-6550, USA

© Kenneth Lunn, Ann Day and the contributors 1999

All rights reserved. No part of this publication may be reproduced or transmitted in any form or by any means, electronic or mechanical, including photocopying, recording or any information storage or retrieval system, without permission in writing from the publishers or their appointed agents.

British Library Cataloguing in Publication Data
A catalogue record for this book is available from the British Library.

ISBN 0-7201-2349-6

Typeset by BookEns Ltd, Royston, Herts.
Printed and bound in Great Britain by Bookcraft (Bath) Ltd.

Contents

Notes on Contributors   vii
Preface and Acknowledgements   ix

    Introduction   xi
    Kenneth Lunn and Ann Day

1   From Impressment to Task Work: Strikes and Disruption in the Royal Dockyards, 1688–1788   1
    Roger Knight

2   Government and Community: The Changing Context of Labour Relations, 1770–1830   21
    Roger Morriss

3   The Changing Nature of the Dockyard Dispute, 1790–1840   41
    Philip MacDougall

4   Class Rule: The Hegemonic Role of the Royal Dockyard Schools, 1840–1914   66
    Neil Casey

5   The Dockyardmen Speak Out: Petition and Tradition in Chatham Dockyard, 1860–1906   87
    Mavis Waters

6   Trade Unionism in Portsmouth Dockyard, 1880–1914: Change and Continuity   99
    Peter Galliver

CONTENTS

7 Continuity and Change: Labour Relations in the
  Royal Dockyards, 1914–50   127
  Kenneth Lunn and Ann Day

8 Neither Colonial nor Historic: Workers' Organization
  at Rosyth Dockyard, 1945–95   151
  Alex Law

9 The Way Forward? The Royal Dockyards since 1945   179
  Kenneth Lunn

Index   193

NOTES ON CONTRIBUTORS

Roger Knight is the Deputy Director of the National Maritime Museum. Following his PhD on the 'Royal Dockyards in the American War of Independence', completed in 1972, he has written a number of articles on the dockyards in the eighteenth century. He also published a volume in the Portsmouth Record Series, *Portsmouth Dockyard Papers, 1774–1783* (1987).

Roger Morriss received his BA from the University of Southampton and his PhD from the University of London. He joined the National Maritime Museum in 1979, where he became, in succession, Head of the Manuscripts Section, Head of Naval and Mercantile History, Research Curator and Head of Adult and Higher Education. He left the Museum in 1995 and is currently an Honorary Research Fellow at University College London and in the Centre for Maritime Historical Studies, University of Exeter. He has published *The Royal Dockyards during the Revolutionary and Napoleonic Wars* (Leicester University Press, 1983), *Nelson: The Life and Letters of a Hero* (Collins and Brown, 1996) and compiled the *Guide to British Naval Papers in North America* (Mansell, 1994). His biography of Sir George Cockburn (1772–1853), *Cockburn and the British Navy in Transition*, was published by the University of Exeter Press in 1997.

Philip MacDougall has a particular interest in social and maritime history, much of his work concentrating upon the lives and working conditions of those who served the Navy either on board ship or within the dockyard complexes. His published works include *The Chatham Dockyard Story* (1981, 1987) and *Royal Dockyards* (1982, 1989) together with a number of related articles that have appeared in *Mariner's Mirror* and *Archaeologia Cantiana*. A former tutor at the University of Kent, his PhD thesis considered changes in naval administration that took place in the 1830s.

NOTES ON CONTRIBUTORS

Neil Casey was brought up in Portsmouth and now lives in Plymouth where he lectures in sociology at the University College of St Mark & St John. He has published a number of articles on social aspects of dockyard history. Other research interests include the sociology of language and the sociology of sport.

Mavis Waters was born in Medway, educated at South Shields Grammar School, Oxford University (1950) and the University of Essex (1979) and has published several articles on dockyard history. She retired recently from York University, Ontario, Canada.

Peter Galliver graduated in Modern History from St Peter's College, Oxford, in 1975. Following postgraduate study at Lancaster and Southampton, he was awarded an MPhil. for his study on the Portsmouth Dockyard workforce. His great-grandfather was a shipwright in Portsmouth Dockyard, his grandfather a labourer and his father an Inspector of Shipwrights. He also had several great-uncles and uncles who served in the Dockyard. He is currently Head of History at Ampleforth College.

Kenneth Lunn is Reader in Social History at the University of Portsmouth. Much of his recent work has focused on a comparative study of work and labour relations in the Royal Dockyards. In conjunction with Ann Day, the research has generated a number of articles and a forthcoming book on the topic.

Ann Day is Research Associate in Local History at the University of Portsmouth. She has worked as a research assistant with Kenneth Lunn on the recent history of British naval dockyard towns. As part of this research, she has been responsible for the establishment of an oral history archive consisting of over 300 interviews with dockyard employees, including women workers.

Alex Law is a Lecturer in Sociology at the University of Abertay, Dundee. He worked as a dockyard fitter/turner for thirteen years, first at Portsmouth Dockyard and latterly at Rosyth. His doctoral thesis (1997) at Edinburgh University was on the restructuring of state, capital and labour relations in the military industry in Scotland.

Preface and Acknowledgements

The origins of this volume began with a study of the political economy of Portsmouth at the beginning of the twentieth century and then moved on to an examination of industrial relations and labour culture within Portsmouth Dockyard. A comparative study of some of the other Royal Dockyards in Britain followed. Further impetus was given by co-operative research projects involving the University of Portsmouth, Portsmouth Naval Base Property Trust and Portsmouth Royal Dockyard Historical Trust. Amongst other things, this produced a major oral history archive of interviews with dockyard men and women, some of whom first entered the yard in the 1920s. The celebration of 'Dockyard 500' in 1995, the five-hundredth anniversary of the construction of the first dry dock in Portsmouth (and effectively the beginnings of the Dockyard), saw a series of events in the Dockyard heritage area and a major exhibition on the history of the yard. As part of the festival, a conference was held, entitled 'A Job for Life?', on the history of labour in the Royal Dockyards. It was from this conference, and the support which it engendered, that these essays have emerged.

In bringing the volume to fruition, a number of acknowledgements and votes of thanks are due. Peter Goodship, of the Naval Base Property Trust, deserves recognition for his encouragement of the various stages of the research projects, as do his staff for their support of these ventures. Fergus Carr, Head of the School of Social and Historical Studies, has provided consistent recognition of the importance of this collaborative work and enabled both academic and financial viability. All the speakers at the original conference, and the members of the audience, many of whom were ex-dockyard workers, helped to stimulate the kind of enthusiasm which sustained the production of the volume. The contributors to this collection, who responded to our strictures on submission dates and on word length with admirable restraint, and engaged in constructive

PREFACE AND ACKNOWLEDGEMENTS

dialogue on the contents of their chapters, can be genuinely thanked for their spirit of co-operation and shared commitment. The series editors, Tony Elger and Peter Fairbrother, offered both the opportunity to publish and helpful comments on the overall direction of the study, whilst Veronica Higgs at Mansell eased us through the process as painlessly as possible. Our thanks go, too, to the many workers and ex-workers interviewed, who told us far more about labour relations in the dockyards than could have been gleaned from any written sources.

Kenneth Lunn
Ann Day

INTRODUCTION

Kenneth Lunn and Ann Day

Histories of the shipbuilding and repair industry in Britain have focused almost exclusively on the private sector.[1] From time to time, the occasional glance at the state-controlled yards has been offered, usually for comparative purposes, but there is no comprehensive study of work and labour relations in the Royal Dockyards. Indeed, it could be argued that, until fairly recently, the history of industrial relations in Britain has also largely been concerned with the private sector. Recent material, which has identified the public sector as a significant dimension, tends to concentrate on the last quarter of the twentieth century, understandably since this is where the battleground of labour relations has now been established.[2]

Solid historical studies of the Post Office[3] and the growth of the white-collar sector of public service unions[4] have opened up the possibilities of producing a more rigorous and wide-ranging analysis of work and industrial relations within both the local and national state sector. However, even in this consideration, the focus has been on the service sector, with little or nothing on the industrial worker. One of the major sectors of state industrial employment was the Royal Dockyards and their comparative neglect has been a somewhat puzzling omission. The sheer size of their enterprise suggests their importance to the economy of Britain and certainly to that of dockyard towns. Nor should the scale and significance of their technological contribution be ignored. The Block Mills in Portsmouth Dockyard contestably provided the example of the first mass production techniques[5] and have led some commentators to argue that the Industrial Revolution was born not in the textile factories of Lancashire but in Brunel's Block Mills. Whilst this clearly over-simplifies a very complex debate, its symbolic argument is important.

In addition, little has been written about the nature of industrial relations within the dockyards. What exists has tended to lack an analytical approach and to concentrate on the celebratory aspects of dockyard work. In order to understand more effectively some of the forces that have helped determine the work processes and the sets of values and attitudes which were associated with them, a wider field of study is required, examining what might be called the processes of control over work relations, the kind of detailed consideration which has recently been suggested as vital to the general history of industrial relations.[6] Existing work has been inclined to adopt a somewhat deterministic note on the politics of dockyard towns[7] and dockyardmen have been 'written off' as deferential, even subservient and distinctly non-militant. A more productive approach would be to identify and investigate the specific elements of dockyard employment which might explain some of these characteristics. The consequences of employment by the state (or, as it was articulated, by the Crown) as well as being subject to quasi-military discipline obviously has importance in determining employer–employee relations. Contact with the employer over questions of pay and conditions was, until the end of the First World War, conducted largely through the submission of petitions by individuals or by groups of workers to the Lords of the Admiralty. The very powerful sectional and trade distinctions within the dockyards were also significant defining characteristics, as was the division between 'established' workers, those who seemed to have guaranteed employment and pensions, and 'hired' men, who lacked this security. The reinforcement of these work divisions was apparent within the wider community, through residential patterns, social and cultural hierarchies and models of consumption and leisure. Education, as Casey's chapter argues, was also a powerful ideological force, gearing young boys not simply for the educational challenges of a dockyard apprenticeship, but inculcating within them a more abstract set of values which were part of a dockyard 'ethos' – a sense of discipline and deference which, it is suggested, produced a workforce amenable to the specific requirements of the British state. Yet, in identifying these features, what is being developed is not merely a study of dockyard work culture but a general model for the analysis of industrial and work relations in any setting. Thus, what might be considered as a very narrow and specialized field of study has some wider significance in the history of work and labour.

To date, little of this approach has been seen in any work on the Royal Dockyards. Much of the published material on the yards concentrates on the ships and the buildings, rather than on the men and women who built, repaired and maintained the fleets. Publications from dockyard historical societies and similar organizations offer more relevant material and repay detailed examination.[8] The academic literature reveals similar gaps and lack of analysis. The best work has concentrated on the eighteenth and nineteenth centuries,[9] whilst the most recent attempt at an overview of two hundred years from 1714 has the title *A Management Odyssey* which indicates very accurately its focus.[10] What is necessary, therefore, is an over-arching approach which builds on the better earlier writings and offers a more dynamic model of labour relations. Whilst it is essential to recognize the strengths of tradition which often dominated work in the yards, traditions which Haas has described as a 'very heavy burden, inherited from the distant past and sanctioned by long usage',[11] there are also distinct patterns of change. What this collection of essays attempts to provide is both a sense of the continuities in the work within the yards and the ways in which distinct changes have occurred.

Perhaps the most obvious area on which to comment is the impact of changing technology on the dockyard workforce. Here it is important to identify ways in which old craft skills, and in particular, craft status, was maintained or adapted through a considerable number of years. Given the constraints of building in wood, particularly on length, shipbuilding techniques remained relatively unchanged until the nineteenth century, although clearly there were degrees of mechanization and refinements of manufacture over the previous centuries. The major shifts were initiated with the change from wood to iron. Within the private yards, this saw the rise of different skills and the emergence of new groups of workers to claim the status of skilled workers. However, within the dockyards the hierarchy of workers remained much the same, as shipwrights made the transition from workers in wood to workers with iron.[12] The reasons for the adaptation and continued status of the role of shipwright within the Royal Dockyards, in contrast to that in the private sector, remain unclear. Having been identified over the centuries as key workers, there seems a reluctance on the part of the Admiralty to dispense with this position, as demonstrated by the preservation of the promotion route through the shipwright trade until well into the twentieth century.

As a consequence, the advancing technology in naval shipbuilding brought with it constant pressure from the emerging trades for adequate recognition, riveting and welding being two prime examples. Within the dockyard system, these trades were still relatively downgraded in the first half of the twentieth century compared to workers in private yards. Their inter-trade rivalry was a significant feature of twentieth-century dockyard relations and often became institutionalized through the trade union-based negotiating system. Galliver's chapter in this volume highlights this trend from the late nineteenth century, and for the years after 1945 Law's study emphasizes the sectional conflicts which were a dominant feature of labour relations at Rosyth. The employment of women workers during the two World Wars also posed a challenge to the conventional hierarchies of craft and skill, albeit temporarily, as Lunn and Day indicate. What also emerges is that technological changes brought into the dockyards recruits from outside, often unencumbered by the yard traditions, and several of the essays here provide clear evidence of this.

It is, therefore, apparent that dockyards were never the totally insular institutions which many commentators have suggested. Whilst they clearly had particular systems for the recruitment and retention of workers (and there were family traditions of dockyard employment), it is surely misleading to suggest, as Haas does, that employment was 'virtually hereditary'.[13] As Knight's work has indicated, even in the eighteenth century there was an interchange of workers between private yards and the Royal Dockyards, as the comparative situation of pay and conditions altered to favour one or the other. Thus, whilst it was possible to identify generations of dockyardmen who undoubtedly became steeped in the traditions of that particular service, there was, in addition, a regular pattern of outside labour, bringing in different values and ideas. No doubt these were often subsumed into and by the dominant ethos of the dockyard, but they could also help to challenge or reshape it. Both Knight and Morriss give indications of the possible influence that 'outside' ideas might have had on industrial activity and in its politicization. By the 1880s and 1890s, with an influx of workers from other areas and with some experience of emerging trade union representation and confrontation with employers, as Galliver indicates, increasing unease with the effectiveness of the petition system led to concessions by the Admiralty and the eventual introduction of the Whitley system. This, too, was not without its critics and pressure from the newer workers.

Recruitment in the inter-war period may have drawn in shipyard workers and others with a more radical political background. Law's study of Rosyth reveals the potential strength of trade unionism within the

Rosyth yard, because of its location close to the militant Fife coalfield. It was also the case that Rosyth, only opened in 1916 and then closed in 1926 until the Second World War, lacked a firmly established and localized dockyard culture.

Augmenting the impact of labour migration from outside, there was also significant inter-yard movement, both within Britain and abroad. Whilst many aspects of yard work and management were constant, there were variations in approach and attitudes towards work and labour relations and these too helped to reshape particular cultures. Thus, what is being uncovered is a persistent sense of challenge and adaptation throughout some 250 years, with a consistent pattern of recruitment into, and movement from, the yards. These movements provided counter-balances to the apparent solidity of dockyard labour relations.

All this draws attention to the dynamic processes of labour negotiation within dockyard history. From the eighteenth century, what is displayed in vivid terms is a 'moral economy' discourse which clearly articulated both the sense of service which was part of the dockyard culture but also the extent to which perceived transgressions could result in fierce resistance from dockyardmen. Nowhere is this better illustrated than in Knight's discussion of the controversy over 'chips', the accepted form of wage supplement in the shape of surplus wood. Here, official attempts to limit the amount was not simply deemed miserly but also as an additional enforcement of authority which overstepped the legitimate territory negotiated by the workforce. In some circumstances, it could lead to confrontation, as Knight describes. Other issues which could unleash the strike weapon in the eighteenth century included the question of the allocation of apprentices and pay, particularly when, as the century progressed, rates outside the dockyard were significantly higher. Indeed, this grievance on pay differentials between dockyards and the private sector was to be a continuing facet of labour relations. The Admiralty claimed that they paid the prevailing rate for the district and that other benefits, such as continuity of employment and, later, pensions, compensated the workforce. What Knight's material suggests, therefore, is the construction of a very clear sense of legitimate and illegitimate industrial behaviour and the emergence of a set of values which, if transgressed, could provoke militant response.

Morriss's study further supports this line, indicating as it does the significance of outside agencies in influencing the dockyard culture and helping to construct traditions of resistance, as well as the processes whereby such alternative views were subsumed by the dominant culture and by Admiralty authority. As an indicator of both the powerfulness of dockyard management and of the unwillingness of workers to conform unquestioningly to that authority, Morriss's work is a very effective reminder of the processes of negotiation which took place within the dockyards and their communities.

In contrast, MacDougall presents evidence from the mid-nineteenth century of a trend towards rejection of the strike weapon and a commitment to petitioning, albeit through a more coherent and organized approach to the latter. Here, his emphasis is on the recognition by the workforce on the futility of striking, revealing as it did the uneven distribution of power and the financial disasters which seemed to present themselves as a consequence of the withdrawal of labour. Thus, as MacDougall suggests, it was a pragmatic choice by dockyardmen. However, this was not simply a return to self-effacing petitions but ones based on a degree of concession by the Admiralty over some key issues. They were also part of a process of inter-yard communication, one which sought to identify common grievances and to construct a more effective lobby for their solution. In this sense, MacDougall sees the period not necessarily as one of de-politicization but as one in which a rethinking of political and industrial strategies occurred; strategies which were shaped by the tightening of Admiralty control but also which sought to respond to that control by new forms of organization linking dockyards. Waters's work on petitioning tends to support this theme, examining the ways in which, towards the end of the century, the language and substance of petitions were an assertion or, in the light of Knight and Morriss, a reassertion of a strong sense of 'moral economy'. They can be seen as attempting to reclaim a degree of autonomy in a period towards the end of the nineteenth century when, as Haas has indicated, both technological change and Admiralty attempts to improve its administration and control were beginning to take effect.[14]

As MacDougall, Waters and Galliver suggest also, it was this reorganization of workers, through inter-yard contact over common grievances and petitioning, which eased the emergence of the logic of trade union representation and a burgeoning desire to dispense with the archaic forms of 'negotiation' with the Admiralty and management. In particular, Galliver notes the mounting clamour for formal trade union recognition within the bargaining process and the influence exerted by the growth of trade unionism outside the yards. There had been a tendency for established men in particular to ignore the support which unions might have offered, feeling instead that their privileged position was protection enough. However, as there came a tightening of administrative control and, in the early 1900s, discharges from the yards seemed to threaten the concept of 'a job for life', so the demands for trade union support grew. Galliver's analysis of the immediate pre-First World War years reveals the extent to which this challenge had developed and the pressures upon the Admiralty to agree to an increasing role for unions in the dockyards and therefore to change in the formalized systems of negotiation. Here again, the importance of seeing the dockyards as part of a wider industrial and political framework is emphasized.

In addition, it was the circumstances of the First World War which helped to bring about what seemed like a fundamental change. General unease at the national system of industrial relations sparked off government planning for reconstruction after the war and, consequently, as Lunn and Day demonstrate, the Whitley system of representation and negotiation was put in place in many sectors of the economy, including the Civil Service and the dockyards. After initial resistance, the system was heralded as more democratic than petitioning and an indicator of a new era in dockyard industrial relations. In this volume, however, questions are posed about the extent to which Whitleyism significantly changed the mind-sets of both sides. Clegg has suggested that the introduction of the Whitley system promoted trade union growth and centralized political power within the unions.[15] This was probably the case within the dockyards and, in some ways, could be seen in a positive light. There is, however, another perspective which sees in the inter-war years a growing disenchantment both by formal union representatives and by rank-and-file, and a continuation of the Admiralty attitudes of the previous era. Petitions were accepted or rejected by the Admiralty at will; Whitley-style negotiations seemed to replicate this approach, even if some kind of spurious defence had to be offered in place of the curt 'Petition Dismissed' of the former period. Other attempts by Admiralty and dockyard officials to undercut the official status of trade unions were a fairly constant feature of these years and, together, they offer a less rosy view of the new form of labour relations in the yards.

This is reinforced by Law's study of Rosyth, which concentrates on the particular nature of that dockyard's labour force and on the variety of responses as political and economic circumstances changed in the post-war period. He notes the persistence of 'lobby' politics, a continual feature of dockyard negotiation over the centuries, alongside more militant forms of industrial action, often learnt through association with non-dockyard tactics and political culture. His comparison of Rosyth's responses to cutbacks and threats of privatization with those of the English dockyards seems to indicate very different political cultures but this is clearly an area which deserves much greater consideration.

What emerges, then, from this discussion of forms of labour negotiation is a varied pattern. Whilst it is possible to identify an underlying trend of passivity, deference and pragmatism on the part of workers, this is not the only feature. A strong sense of the limits to authority, of legitimate control and the abuses of what may be termed the dockyard 'moral economy' produced responses which drew on other traditions of radicalism and challenge. Some of these were part of the dockyard tradition itself; others drew on or adapted forms of resistance from outside the yards. Labour relations were a mix of the traditional and the new, evolving and reacting both to new Admiralty initiatives and to the broader political and economic dynamics of the British state and industrial structures. No single static model can do justice to these forms of labour attitudes.

Thus, as has already been suggested, the politics of the dockyard workforce are also deserving of a more analytical scrutiny. For too long conventional notions of conservatism and reaction have simplified, indeed caricatured, a very complex set of ideas and ones which varied from one yard to the next. For the twentieth century, distinctions between political cultures in Devonport, Chatham and Portsmouth have been noted[16] and to this list could be added the singular dimensions demonstrated at Rosyth, as indicated by Law. Looking back to the eighteenth and nineteenth centuries, we can also identify forms of political radicalism, within dockyard communities if not within the dockyards themselves. This is not to deny the significant influence of the dominant patterns of authority which helped shape those dockyard work cultures and the cultures of the communities. There was a particular 'edge' to education, certainly from the middle of the nineteenth century, which helped to reinforce a set of values which made for an ordered and ultimately subservient workforce. This is the essence of Casey's argument here about the role of dockyard schools. It is supported, from a rather different political perspective, by Haas, who has argued that the dockyard schools produce 'an unhealthy degree of inbreeding'.[17] Their argument, that recruitment and training reinforced the narrow range of dockyard labour by mainly opting for sons of dockyardmen as apprentices, seems, however, to ignore the other external forces which reacted against that narrowness.

Other chapters, by Knight, Morris, MacDougall and Waters, have all suggested degrees to which dockyard workers sought to define their own particular identities and to make sense of the highly politicized forms of authority which were part of their everyday world. Given the types of constraint which they were operating against, forms of resistance were as noteworthy as the processes of accommodation and subservience. Above all, what these essays draw out are the processes of negotiation, albeit ones within an uneven set of power relations, between dockyardmen and Admiralty authorities. To reduce this to formulaic pronouncement about the politics of dockyard towns, as inevitably dominated by state control and military concerns, and to see the work culture of dockyardmen as equally inevitably shaped by these forces, is to lack a historical understanding. That these were frequent features is not in dispute: that they were always so deterministically apparent is contested. Collectively these essays begin to provide some ideas about the need to look more closely at the ways in which the distinctive and dynamic relations of job control and authority emerged and re-emerged throughout the history of the dockyards.

In conclusion, there seems to be a fundamental point in the study of labour relations which has been largely ignored by existing work. Too frequently, the emphasis has been upon the particularities and the peculiarities of the dockyard system and its distinctive ideological constructions. What has been suggested here is that a wider frame of reference and a comparative approach, which looks both at other examples of state sector employment such as the Post Office and the Civil Service, and at the private sector, can only aid an understanding of dockyard culture. Whilst accepting wholeheartedly the critique in Knight's essay of Haas's ahistorical evaluation of the 'efficiency' of the Royal Dockyards, the opposite view sometimes advanced of the uniqueness of the dockyards is also untenable, at least in an academic sense. In effect, each industry and each unit of production, each working community, is unique. A case for the particularities of coalmining could equally be made, with its isolated, single-industry communities, its highly specialized and status-ridden work and its peculiar hierarchies of authority and control. This does not, however, prevent comparative work, looking across regions at differences within the industry, changes through time and evaluations of work and community vis-à-vis other industries and sectors of the economy. In effect, these essays are seeking to draw the history of dockyard labour relations into the mainstream of labour and social history. That different dimensions of political, cultural and economic control are at play, and that diversities of workplace strategies emerge, is thus recognizable but does not detract from the overall importance of applying this more challenging theoretical approach. This does not hide the particularities of the dockyards, but makes them more understandable. This collection of essays therefore sets out to create an agenda for that more sophisticated way of assessing work relations in the Royal Dockyards.

Notes

1. See, for example, E. Lorenz, *Economic Decline in Britain: The Shipbuilding Industry, 1890–1970* (Oxford, Clarendon Press, 1991); A. Reid, 'The division of labour in the shipbuilding industry, 1880–1920, with special reference to Clydeside', unpublished PhD thesis, University of Cambridge, 1980; A. Reid, 'Skilled workers in the shipbuilding industry 1880–1920: a labour aristocracy?', in A. Morgan and B. Purdie (eds), *Ireland: Divided Nation, Divided Class* (London, Ink Links, 1980), pp. 111–24; S. Pollard and P. Robertson, *The Shipbuilding Industry, 1890–1914* (Harvard University Press, Cambridge, Mass., 1979). The British Shipbuilding History Project, a co-operative venture involving the National Maritime Museum, the University of Newcastle upon Tyne and the University of Glasgow, should add to this literature.
2. See, for example, P. Beaumont, *Public Sector Industrial Relations* (London and New York, Routledge, 1992); R. Fryer, 'Public service trade unionism in the twentieth century', in R. Mailly, S. Dimmock and A. Sethi (eds), *Industrial Relations in the Public Services* (London, Routledge, 1989), pp. 17–67; P. Fairbrother, *Politics and the State as Employer* (London, Mansell, 1994).
3. M. Daunton, *Royal Mail: The Post Office since 1840* (London, Athlone, 1985).
4. See, for example, G. S. Bain, *The Growth of White-collar Unionism* (Oxford, Clarendon Press, 1970); H. Parris, *Staff Relations in the Civil Service: Fifty Years of Whitleyism* (London, George Allen and Unwin, 1973); K. Prandy et al., *White-collar Unionism* (London, Macmillan, 1983); R. Hyman and R. Price (eds), *The New Working Class? White-collar Workers and Their Organizations* (London, Macmillan, 1983).

5. See S. Osterholm, 'The blockmills', *The Journal* (Portsmouth Royal Dockyard Historical Trust), **4** (Summer 1996), 4–6.
6. D. Lyddon and P. Smith, 'Editorial: industrial relations and history', *Historical Studies in Industrial Relations*, **1** (March 1996), 7–8.
7. See, on this theme, M. Pugh, *The Tories and the People, 1880–1935* (Oxford, Blackwell, 1985); D. Tanner, *Political Change and the Labour Party* (Cambridge, Cambridge University Press, 1990). For a more generalized discussion of community and political links, see N. Kirk, ' "Traditional" working-class culture and "the rise of Labour": some preliminary questions and observations', *Social History*, **16**(2) (May 1991), 203–16.
8. See, for example, *'The Last Cast-off: A Dockyard Community Remembers: A Collection of Memories of Working Life in the Chatham Dockyard* (Gillingham, Arts in Medway, 1990); *The Times of Our Lives* (Gillingham, Arts in Medway, 1990); B. Patterson, *'Giv' 'er a Cheer Boys': The Great Docks of Portsmouth Dockyard 1830–1914* (Portsmouth, Portsmouth Royal Dockyard Historical Society, publication no. 5, 1989); E. Lane, *The Reminiscences of a Portsmouth Dockyard Shipwright 1901–1945* (Ryde, private publication, 1988); E. C. B. Lee, *Shipwright Apprentice 1922–27* (Portsmouth, WEA Local History Group, 1993).
9. See, for example, R. Knight, *Portsmouth Dockyard Papers 1774–1783: The American War* (Portsmouth, Portsmouth City Council, 1987); R. Morriss, *The Royal Dockyards during the Revolutionary and Napoleonic Wars* (Leicester, Leicester University Press, 1983).
10. J. M. Haas, *A Management Odyssey: The Royal Dockyards, 1714–1914* (Lanham, Maryland, University Press of America, 1993).
11. *Ibid.*, p. 194.
12. D. Dougan, *The Shipwrights: The History of the Shipconstructors' and Shipwrights' Association 1882–1963* (Newcastle, Frank Graham, 1975).
13. Haas, *A Management Odyssey*, p. 193.
14. *Ibid.*, p. 193.
15. H. A. Clegg, *A History of British Trade Unions since 1889: Volume II, 1911–1933* (Oxford, Oxford University Press, 1987), p. 207.
16. For some evidence of different political patterns, see K. Lunn, 'Labour culture in dockyard towns: a study of Portsmouth, Plymouth and Chatham, 1900–1950', *Tijdschrift voor social geschiedenis*, **18**(2/3) (July 1992), 275–93.
17. Haas, *A Management Odyssey*, p. 192.

1

FROM IMPRESSMENT TO TASK WORK: STRIKES AND DISRUPTION IN THE ROYAL DOCKYARDS, 1688–1788

Roger Knight

> Why such impress of shipwrights, whose sore task
> Doth not divide the Sunday from the week?
> (*Hamlet*, Act 1, scene 1)

The hundred years from the accession of William III saw a rise in British naval power which brought England from a contender on the fringes of Europe to the centre stage. The Navy itself became a central institution in British political and economic life.[1] This was brought about by the commitment of the Hanoverian state to a capital-intensive war economy, a notable feature of the historiography of recent years.[2] A substrand of these great themes was the expansion of the English shipbuilding capacity, and at its heart was the remarkable growth of the royal dockyards. At the beginning of this period the yards were essentially units of workers employed only in war or emergency, and impressed in a real crisis. By the middle of the eighteenth century, six of the largest industrial establishments of the day competed in the skilled labour market, in particular for shipwrights, caulkers and ropemakers. It is the contention of this chapter that, once in the market, the government was unable and, to a certain extent, unwilling to compete effectively, and that this large workforce was well organized in maintaining its standard of living in the ups and downs of a war economy.

Thus the yards developed labour relations problems which we would recognize today, with aggressive penal state legislation, violence, troops, lock-outs, prison and, of course, negotiation. At the beginning of every war or mobilization from 1729, when the Admiralty needed every effort to get fleets to sea, the skilled workforce extracted every concession it could through well-timed action. From the beginning of this period, the state enforced discipline and in emergencies forced trained shipwrights to work in the royal yards through its powers of impressment. During the middle of the century there was a period of rough balance, and a testing of strength; and finally there was a period dominated by the government's introduction of an incentive, payment-by-results, system. This was the 'task work' brought in by the Admiralty and Navy Boards just before the American War of Independence when the country was faced by strategic demands which by now were worldwide. The reaction of the Admiralty was to spread incentive pay throughout the yards and finally to the aristocrats of labour, the shipwrights. This system was resisted for nearly fifteen years. Finally, in 1788, the shipwrights of the last yard, Plymouth, gave up the struggle and accepted task work.

Supply and Demand

For the first 25 years of this period, until the peace after the Treaty of Utrecht, work stoppages seem to have been insignificant. There had been stoppages in the 1660s and 1670s over lateness of pay and this aggravation was to continue throughout the eighteenth century, especially at Plymouth.[3] Though there were associated demands for an increase in wages, their cause was simply the delay in paying the wages. Throughout King William's war, the workforce 'remained, largely in the background, as a constant problem to their superiors ... generally hampering the pace of administration, but never actually stopping it ...'[4] This meekness was essentially caused by the fact that the government was prepared to override the market and use its powers of impressment. It seems to have been used to its greatest extent in the 1690s, and at least on five occasions between 1704 and 1706.[5] But at some point after the Treaty of Utrecht the government no longer used its impressment weapon. It is not clear why there was this change of heart, and it may have been linked to an awareness that the country was losing shipwrights abroad. It seems likely that it was a political rather than economic decision, for the Admiralty and Navy Boards must have been sorely tempted to use impressment during the shortages in the coming years.[6]

The first outward sign of the new supply and demand struggle came with the ropemakers during the 1720s, particularly in the Thames yards, culminating in a prolonged strike at Woolwich, Chatham and Portsmouth in the summer of 1729, just at the time of a mobilization against Spain.[7] Ropemakers had a physically wearing and dangerous task. The men were paid by how much they produced (task work) and lives depended upon teamwork, and it bred an independence and toughness notable even in the yards. In 1721 a 'confederacy' of journeymen ropemakers had already negotiated with the 30 or so merchant ropegrounds on the Thames a comprehensive agreement specifying the number of men per task and wage rates and, perhaps most importantly, restricting the number of servants a merchant ropemaker could take on.[8] The mid-1720s was a slack time for both naval and merchant shipbuilding, and the number of qualified ropemakers grew smaller to the point where one merchant ropemaker complained that business was lost to Holland. The Navy Board had tried to increase complements but no men came forward. When a mobilization came, there was bound to be trouble. Hemp rope did not store well, and rope could not easily be put in reserve in quantity, so that mobilizations put very heavy pressure on ropemakers. Trouble was anyway brewing, and was predicted by the Clerk of the Ropeyard, Richard Maddocks, in a letter to the Surveyor of the Navy in May 1729, which is worth quoting at length because of its mix of old naval discipline and awareness of market forces:

> In June last, the ropemakers were reduced to a single day's task, several made application to your honourable Board for their discharge with success, others without, who absconded the Service here, went and worked in the private ropegrounds in and about London; upon which complaint was made to the Board, whereupon by warrant of the 25th October 1728 they were mulct Two for One [fined], notwithstanding that they still persisted in their disobedience, insulted the Foreman, and myself escaped not, and I much fear are yet quite ripe to put in execution disturbance (if not mutiny) upon any little occasion, they are being as I have observed a perverse and obstinate set of people, but why they should be so, is to me surprising when I well know they have not only good encouragement, but also good usage, and I cannot comprehend but their evil carriage may or must arise from the scarcity of men that seems at this time to be of the Ropemaking trade, for those since discharged hence as above said not one spinner applied to be entered here til the last week in March and then but four, and they I suppose for fear of being imprest which hath oft happened before now, for at such times they do offer their service but none hath since.[9]

When the Navy Board ordered nine additional servants to be entered to the ropeyard clerical officers at Woolwich yard on 18 July, the ropemakers announced their intention to strike and the Board discharged the ringleaders. The strike spread within days to the other naval ropeyards at Chatham and Portsmouth, and the Board 'ordered all the Deserters to be made run on the Books of the Yard, according to the usage of the Navy' and brought in journeymen ropemakers from as far as Newcastle, Bristol, Cornwall and Devon, including seven from Ireland. There was further trouble on 19 August, when the yard porter was knocked down and the culprits were sent before the justices at the Quarter Sessions. In the end, the Board broke the strike; ropemakers drifted back to work, although there was further trouble between the local men and the Irish. The mobilization did not develop into war, pressure on the authorities for output lessened and thus the advantage of supply and demand passed to the authorities. For once the merchant ropemakers were on the side of the Navy Board.[10]

Generally the navy competed unsuccessfully against the merchant yards for labour. From three-quarters of the way through the seventeenth century, it was never able to match merchant yard wages. Although there were large variations in wage rates, pay in the merchant yards in the south of the country, except possibly in the west of England, compared very favourably with the 2s.1d. a day which was set for the royal yards as early as 1650.[11] Other skilled trades received slightly less, while those without an apprenticeship, such as riggers and sawyers, were paid 1s.6d. The value of unskilled labour was set at one or two pence over or under a shilling. These rates lasted with minor variations for 150 years, but by the time of the American War of Independence shipwrights in private yards on the Thames were earning 3s.6d a day.

Since the problem of supply and demand was clearly understood by the Navy Board, why could the government not seek to increase the numbers of skilled workmen? Parliament could not be persuaded to increase wages, but why did the authorities not take steps to introduce more apprentices?[12] There were shortages of every type of skilled men at different times through the century, especially shipwrights, although in the first half of the century, overall, the yards managed to get the number they wanted in the 1739–48 and Seven Years Wars. By the time of the American War there were real difficulties, particularly at Portsmouth and Plymouth. The number of shipwrights actually fell as the war progressed, while smiths, joiners, sailmakers, riggers and ropemakers were in short supply at various times.[13] Early dockyard Standing Orders of 1711 and 1732 established a proportion of one apprentice to every six shipwrights and one to every five caulkers, and the situation had improved even on that level by the time of the 1739–48 war.[14] Mainly because the dockyard officers' hold over the apprenticeship system was very strong, for it was an important source of their authority and of their income, the administrators in London did not persist in reform and expansion. 'Had apprentices been given to the most deserving shipwrights,' remarked Thomas Fitzherbert, MP for Arundel, in the debates at the end of the American War of Independence, when British naval power had reached a very low point, 'it would not only have rewarded the old, but encouraged the young; and we might have then had double the number of shipwrights we had at this time.'[15]

This failure to increase the number of apprentices has recently been described as one of the two 'greatest administrative follies of the whole period'. Over the century it is remarkable how low the shipwright population managed to keep itself, contrasting to the steady and continuing rise of unskilled labour. 'The most astonishing statistical fact is that, notwithstanding the increase in ships and tonnage, the shipwrights employed in the royal dockyards hardly changed: 3100 in 1743, 3200 in 1772, 3300 in 1781, 3100 in 1792, and 3300 in 1804.'[16] Some went abroad, in spite of legislation which was passed to prevent it in 1718, 1750 and 1765, and there is no doubt about the influence of English shipwrights in Holland and Russia.[17] One of the undercurrents of the 1775 strike was the fear of American agents at Woolwich, enticing shipwrights to the colonies, an activity which interested the Home Office.[18] From early in the century it was to the North American colonies that an out-of-work shipwright would turn, especially from the 1720s which was a particularly difficult period for shipbuilding. 'We have good reason to believe,' the Thames merchant yards petitioned in 1724, 'the number of shipwrights in Great Britain is diminished one half since 1710. This diminution is chiefly owing to the great number of ships built annually in Your Majesty's plantations, but particularly in New England.'[19] The abundance of shipbuilding timber and the opportunity for riches in a freer economy attracted the shipwrights and sent the tonnages from the colonies higher and higher through each decade of the century.[20]

The naval authorities had few advantages in influencing the supply and demand balance, and when it mattered most, at the beginning of a war, they were especially vulnerable. 'The authorities talked of discipline but yielded to market realities and the shipwright's organised pressure.' This is not only the opinion of an historian, but also of the contemporary MP, Thomas Fitzherbert. The British weakness at sea did not arise, he said in the debates in 1782, 'from neglect in the particular officers, but it was owing to the want of shipwrights'.[21]

Reward and Privileges

To this unchanging rate of 2s.1d. a day, overtime or 'extra' was invariably added. Throughout most of the century it was used by the Navy Board to add to the basic pay; hardly surprising in view of the slow inflation in the eighteenth century. The Commission of Naval Enquiry noted disapprovingly in 1804 that overtime was rather 'to add to their daily wages, than on any account of any extra exertion being required'.[22] Every year, in April when the daylight hours became longer, the Board sought the Admiralty's permission to work the men extra. This made a total of thirteen hours a day. In an emergency, the men worked a 'tide' of one-and-a-half hours (for which they received just under a third of a day's pay) or a 'night' of five hours, which earned a full day's pay. As a result there was considerable variation in the income of men between peace and war, and between winter and summer. For instance, shipwrights at Deptford who earned £35 a year in 1774, four years later, at the height of activity, were earning £52 (see the seasonal and annual breakdown in Table 1.1). In general, the system was costly and troublesome. Men were working when they were not wanted, and when effort was really needed far too much was asked of them; the futility of men working seventeen hours a day, even for the short period of an emergency, was realized even then.

The second way in which workmen customarily supplemented their wages was the collection of chips, the waste wood which fell from the adzes of the shipwrights, and which by jealously-guarded custom they were allowed to take out of the yard under their arm. More wood could be carried on the shoulder, which was therefore forbidden, and when the shipwrights carried out the chips on their shoulder it became a symbol of resentment against authority, and has passed into the language to describe a resentful person.[23] Friction between the workforce and the authorities was often expressed through trouble over chips; for instance, when the women who were allowed into the yard on Wednesdays and Saturdays to collect chips were prevented from having free access to the yard at Portsmouth in 1771, they rioted in protest.[24] It was a problem for the naval administrators of any age or of any country, for chips (called *stelle*) in seventeenth-century Venice or the *droits de copeaux* in Toulon at the end of the *Ancien Régime* posed just as much a problem for the authorities as they did in eighteenth-century England.[25] As a supplement to the men's wages, it was of considerable value in the coal-less south of England, but it was always subject to a large amount of abuse, and the wood provided cover for higher-value and illegal stores to be secreted from the yard.[26] A steady stream of Navy Board standing orders through the century tried in vain to regulate the custom. In fact, throughout the century the shipwrights were keen to have this abolished, in return for cash, and in this they were generally supported by the Navy Board. It was finally commuted for cash in 1801.[27]

Perhaps the most striking weakness in the whole system was the way in which apprentices were allotted and then trained. The only way to become a shipwright was through a seven-year apprenticeship and both management and the men ensured that men taken on were properly qualified; if not, the other shipwrights tied the imposter to a piece of wood and carried him out of the yard, a rough custom known as 'horsing'. But not only was the apprenticeship system ineffective as a means of augmenting the supply of labour by the second half of the century, it also provided a means of augmenting income on an inequitable basis, since servants were allocated to officers rather thaN to working men.[28] The yard officers held the indentures, and therefore the wages, of most of the servants, and consequently the chance of a workman obtaining an apprentice was far too slim to encourage a good skilled man to join or stay in the yards. In early 1779 the Navy Board reported that out of 703 apprentices of all trades in the yards, 121 belonged to officers, 202 to petty officers, 165 to carpenters of ships and only 135 out of several thousand ordinary artificers had the benefit of a servant. This was no way to train a skilled workforce; by the mid-century there was an overriding concept of an indenture as a piece of property. Some apprentices had no masters at all, since officers were frequently transferred from yard to yard; often they would take their apprentices with them, but this was not always possible. Not surprisingly, this situation was harshly criticized by the Commission on Fees and Perquisites in 1786, when it recommended that no officer on a salary should have a servant.[29]

The third major feature of the working life of a shipwright in the royal yards was relative security of tenure. Of all aspects of dockyard management, this depended upon the management by the dockyard officers, but there was a reluctance to dismiss workmen who had given a lifetime of service to the yards and men were kept on until well past their useful working life. Some jobs where experience counted rather than strength were available, such as cabin-keepers or trennel (or treenail) mooters, but they were in short supply. By the mid-century the workforce had grown to the point where reform was clearly needed and in 1764 Lord Egmont, as First Lord of the Admiralty, introduced superannuation. The scheme was limited to quartermen, shipwrights and caulkers of thirty years' service, although those who had been disabled were exempt from this rule, and was to be awarded only to one in 50 of the workmen. Two-thirds of the income was to be paid as a pension. In the 1771 visitation to the yards, Lord Sandwich found that many men were kept on in the yards 'out of compassion' and he extended the scheme to include one in forty, including yard labourers, ropemakers and sawyers.[30]

Although these schemes went some way to eliminating inefficiency, by limiting the number of pensions to a fixed and inadequate proportion of the workforce, the number of men who received pensions each year was dependent on the death rate of those who had already received them. Those who received pensions were lucky and few. However, the government reply in the propaganda battle at the time of the 1775 strike, from a printed pamphlet amongst Lord Sandwich's papers, perhaps summarizes best of all the London administrator's view of the working conditions of the dockyard workforce:

> In the King's Yards the shipwright is paid winter and summer, wet and dry; in the merchants, his employment is uncertain, and in bad weather he is rung off and an abatement is made from his wages while he is absent; if hurt, he receives no pay; when old or incapable of labour, he is left to the parish. With all these advantages on the side of the service in the King's yards, which are great comforts to a labouring man, it will, I believe, besides be found, that at the year's end the shipwright's earnings will be more than that in the merchant's service, unless they are all paid by task work.[31]

Control and Resistance

From the 1720s, a clearly understood supply and demand struggle between the authorities and the workforce was fought through demand for employment and consequent price movements. At the beginning of every war, the workforce held the whiphand. In the Chatham disturbances at the beginning of the Seven Years War a shipwright, William Large, stated: 'I do not value staying in the yard, as there is enough work in the merchant yards.'[32] Conversely, at the end of the American War, the Plymouth Resident Commissioner reported to the Navy Board that shipwrights were leaving Plymouth for London: 'I am informed the reason they give for leaving the yard is that every article of provision ... is so dear that they cannot exist on a single day's pay'.[33] When the pressure was on during a war, the authorities moved very carefully; in 1781, in the middle of the American War, it was the opinion of the hardened, risk-taking Controller of the Navy, Charles Middleton, that 'we dare not contest a single point of duty with either shipwrights, caulkers or ropemakers at this time'.[34]

It was therefore unfortunate that in 1739, as the outbreak of hostilities was having its impact on prices, the Navy Board should choose the moment to suppress the collection of chips. It was badly timed. The immediate cause was the fining and discharging, for alleged laziness, of a number of shipwrights at Chatham. The next day 200 shipwrights did not report for duty. It soon emerged that dissatisfaction over chips (in other words, income) was the real cause, though there was also grievance that extra work had been unfairly allocated.[35] The Navy Board capitulated with some speed, much to the horror of the Resident Commissioner who was fearful for future discipline. At Woolwich, three months later, and not at such a strategically critical time, the Admiralty Board had time to collect its wits and broke the strike, and a number of shipwrights were discharged. The smiths of both Deptford and Woolwich combined to petition and struck briefly, after which the Navy Board approved of their demands. There were disturbances in 1742, and troops were called to Deptford and Woolwich in 1744; the following year there was again a serious strike in the ropeyards.[36] At the beginning of the Seven Years War there was an intense strike at Chatham over chips, involving the prolonged use of troops, when the Admiralty pressganged the ringleaders into ships at the Nore, which were about to go on foreign service, while there were sporadic outbreaks of trouble for the next three years.[37]

However, the most serious of all the dockyard strikes throughout the century was that of June to August 1775, brought about by the introduction of task work, when the most effective shipwright gangs were paid by the task set rather than by a simple day rate.[38] Although the effect of the strike on the conduct of the war is difficult to measure, it delayed mobilization, when speed in dealing with the rebellion in America was everything. Within ten days of the first trouble at Chatham in June, work had stopped at every yard except Deptford; although Sheerness continued working, the shipwrights there 'remained as ill-disposed as the rest'.[39] Troops had to be called in at Woolwich and twelve men were indicted at Maidstone Assizes. Although Lord Sandwich and the Admiralty Board soon withdrew any compulsion to work in the new way, there was still sporadic and significant unrest until August.

Thus the only radical government change in dockyard pay in well over a century was defeated by strike action in a couple of weeks, and it took another thirteen years before task work was fully accepted by all the yards.[40] It illustrated very definite limits upon government control and discipline administered by the Navy Board, Resident Commissioner and yard officers. Industrial discipline was inextricably mixed with abuses and petty crime, and always authority was up against the great solidarity of dockyard communities, and the difficulty of bringing successful charges against wrongdoers was considerable.[41] The most successful Resident Commissioners were those who had political connections with the area, and who used other means than the authority of their office; there were always sea officers who did not understand the limits of their powers away from their quarterdeck. For instance, Philip Vanbrugh, the Resident Commissioner at Plymouth throughout the 1739–48 war, who had come ashore from the command of a ship, wrote to the Navy Board complaining that he had caught a woman stealing a bolt and had ordered her to be whipped, 'but found difficulty in getting a person to inflict the punishment on her'. The Board wrote back hastily, 'upon former inquiries of Council learned in the law, we have been assured, that none but Justices of the Assize, or the Bench at a Quarter Sessions of a County inflict Corporal Punishment'.[42]

The dockyard workforce, led by the shipwrights and backed by the communities, developed a growing sense of their importance through the century. William Shrubsole, a shipwright from Sheerness, wrote in 1770:

> As to the right of any other artificers in the dockyards, which can pretend to be of that importance to the nation as the shipwright? It is very true, that all are very useful in their places, but the first place belongs to the shipwright. They set the great wheels of commerce and war in motion ... without which the pulse of civil policy would stand still.[43]

Motivation and Incentive

Historians have themselves laboured with the problem at the heart of dockyard labour relations, that of motivation and incentive. Sidney Pollard commented in 1960 that the dockyards' 'discipline compounded of civil service and armed service practices, and absence of any direct profit motive, fit badly into our concept of "management"'.[44] Direct and usually unfavourable comparison with the practices and productivity of private shipyards has been made from early in the eighteenth century to the present day, and recently the issue has been more clearly defined by the appearance of two interpretations from each side of the political spectrum. In the blue corner, as it were, is a lifelong study by J. M. Haas, who published, in 1994, *A Management Odyssey: The Royal Dockyards, 1714–1914*. Though judicious when he analyses specific issues, Haas's overall verdict on the quality of management and the energy and motivation of the men is damning, stemming from his underlying premise that an organization that has no basis of profit and loss cannot be efficient. He views the dockyards rather like a management consultant, providing a remorseless analysis of management and accounting weaknesses, providing little in the way of contemporary social and political context to explain why things were the way they were. Peter Linebaugh, in the red corner, is the opposite in every sense. In a provocative and idiosyncratic essay, 'Ships and Chips', as part of *The London Hanged: Crime and Civil Society in the Eighteenth Century*, he tries to analyse and understand the worker's role and what it was like to be subjected to the control of the management structure, making the necessity of 'incessant labour' even harsher.[45]

Neither of these historians gets to the heart of the dynamic which drove the yards through the pre-industrial age. The workforce was answerable to a sub-naval discipline, as well as a rigorous peer-group pressure, and was vulnerable to an extraordinarily inflexible pay system which could take no account of food scarcity and prices. There was also the anxiety of living under constant credit because of late wages. 'Every shipwright that takes up his money on usury or by assignment (and it is almost impossible to avoid it),' wrote William Shrubsole in 1770, 'suffers a loss of almost forty shillings a year, which is upwards of three weeks pay.'[46] Yet these organizations had very positive elements. They were intensely patriotic, with strong religious traditions and with a growth in nonconformism coinciding with a growing confidence in themselves later in the century. They were communities which knew right from wrong, high quality from sloppy work. There was only one way to do a job, and that was to the highest standard, as specified by the standing orders from the Navy Board. They did not identify with speed and price, although much could be achieved in emergencies. One private Thames ropemaker remarked in 1729 that royal yard ropemakers whom he employed were quite good, though many found it strange at first, 'for in merchant's business they are not confined to a prescribed method in spinning or other services, so that at their first coming they are estranged to our accurate managements'.[47]

It was also, as Linebaugh emphasizes, a life of incessant labour, wearing and, in part, dangerous. Those engaged in close work, such as sailmakers, often had their 'eyesight much impaired', and constant exposure to the weather resulted in many cases of rheumatism and asthma. Accidents took their toll: 'lost a leg launching a mast' and 'lame by a scald by falling into the boiler' were among the applications for superannuation.[48] One apprentice had

> several escapes from sudden and violent death. Once, he fell from the side of a ship, then on the stocks, and was preserved by a scaffold, at some distance from the ground. At another time, he fell headlong from the side of a wharf into a dock, among several boats and lighters. Had he struck against any of them, he must have been instantly killed; but he fell between them into the water.[49]

Even Lord Sandwich, who knew as much about the administration of the Navy as anyone, was bewildered by the shipwrights' rejection of his task work proposals. Under pressure to increase productivity as the scale of British overseas commitments grew ever greater after the successes of the Seven Years War, to him such a move seemed logical for the men as well as for the country. Between the devil and the deep blue sea, he had as little chance of persuading them as he had of persuading Parliament to increase wages, unable as it was to understand inflation, and he was convinced that the merchant yards would always be able to take as many young shipwrights from the market as they wanted:

> If the trade of this country is to go on, the merchants will, and always must give more money for shipbuilding than the Crown. The increase of wages without the increase of work in the dockyards would be exactly so much money thrown away, as the merchants' would rise in proportion.[50]

As in our own day, the advantages of the private sector seemed overwhelming except to those who were working in a precedent-led and complex organization, which over the generations had developed its own rules. In these 100 years between 1688 and 1788, the relationship of the dockyard workforce to the state was dominated by a steady need for greater productivity, particularly from the mid-century; and the government's power over its employees loosened and it lost its key sanction in the early years, that of impressment. The merchant yards, more flexible and speedy, built more and more tonnage for the Navy, while the dockyards continued to perform their maintenance function. The cost of having an active and expanding private sector setting examples and taking the best young men was an often stormy relationship between the skilled men in the dockyard and the London administrators. And, as in our own day, tough, skilled work breeds inward-looking communities, fiercely defending a jaded and underfunded apprenticeship system which defined that community and gave it both status and bargaining power. Close-knit communities enabled them to act effectively in spite of the Combination Laws. Here, well developed in the early eighteenth century, were the collective values of the industrial nineteenth century, which E. P. Thompson noted 30 years ago: 'the definite moral code, with sanctions against the blackleg, who were the "tools" of the employer or the unneighbourly, and with an intolerance towards the eccentric or individualist'.[51]

Whatever charges can be laid at the dockyards in the eighteenth century, in the final analysis, and over the whole period, they created in part, and were wholly responsible for maintaining, an overwhelmingly successful British fleet; and any judgement on the administrators, yard officers and the workforce must be seen in the context of British state and society, and in comparison with the great antagonist, France. The French yards never developed beyond the stage of impressment and forced labour, for when their galley fleets were suppressed in 1748 they put their convicts to work at Brest, Toulon and Rochefort to meet the demand for labour brought about by the mid-century escalation in the scale of naval warfare. Together with much lower and later yard wages, as well as the power of the French yards to conscript shipwrights from private yards, the lethargy of convict labour eroded motivation and energy to a far greater degree than in England.[52] Yet the British nearly fell into the same trap, pursuing what appeared to be a simple solution to the shortage of labour. In 1752 a Bill 'to change the Punishment of Felony ... to Confinement and Hard Labour in His Majesty's dockyards' was laid before Parliament by Lord Barrington, a member of the Board of Admiralty. The convicts were to be 'kept separate, and distinguished by Habit, Chains and other Marks of

Table 1.1 *Representative Sample of the Wages of a Working Shipwright*

	Days	Nights	Tides	Full wages
DEPTFORD				
Lady Quarter				
1774	77	0	0	£8–0–5
1778	76	0	73	£11–3–4
Midsummer				
1774	78	0	51	£9–14–4
1778	78	1	94	£14–12–5
Michaelmas				
1774	79	0	53	£9–17–8
1778	79	0	155	£13–1–5
Christmas				
1774	79	0	0	£8–4–7
1778	77½	0	100	£13–19–7
			Total: 1774	£35–17–0
			1778	£52–16–9
PORTSMOUTH				
Lady Quarter				
1774	77	0	0	£8–0–5
1778	76	0	104	£11–3–4
Midsummer				
1774	77½	0	51	£9–13–4
1778	77½	58	38	£15–16–0
Michaelmas				
1774	79	0	53½	£9–18–0
1778	78½	63	28	£15–12–3
Christmas				
1774	79	0	0	£8–4–7
1778	78	0	154	£12–18–9
			Total: 1774	£35–16–4
			1778	£55–0–4

Comparison of wages between winter and summer, and between day work and task. Deptford shipwrights were working by task by 1778. *Source*: PRO ADM 42/564, 568, 1290, 1294, Yard Pay Books. Based on a representative sample of twenty shipwrights from each yard.

Servitude from the Artificers and Labourers'.[53] It was indeed fortunate for Britain's naval prowess that this Bill failed, for the ability of any European country to harness skilled shipbuilding labour, public and private, by the state or in the market, was the single most important factor in creating and maintaining an effective fleet in eighteenth-century Europe.

Notes

1. D. A. Baugh, 'The eighteenth-century Navy as a national institution', in J. R. Hill (ed.), *The Oxford Illustrated History of the Royal Navy* (Oxford, Oxford University Press, 1995), pp. 120–1; M. Duffy, 'The foundations of British naval power', in *The Military Revolution and the State, 1500–1800* (Exeter, University of Exeter, 1980), pp. 49–85; R. J. B. Knight, 'The building and maintenance of the British fleet, 1688–1815', in M. Acerra, J. Merino and J. Meyer (eds), *Les Marines de guerre européennes, XVII–XVIII siècles* (Paris, Press de l'Université Paris-Sorbonne, 1986), pp. 35–50.
2. J. Brewer, *The Sinews of Power: War, Money and the English State, 1688–1783* (London, Unwin-Hyman, 1989) has been enormously influential, but for a longer view on military spending see P. K. O'Brien, *Power with Profit: The State and the Economy, 1688–1815* (London, University of London, 1991).
3. See D. C. Coleman, 'Naval dockyards under the later Stuarts', *Economic History Review*, vol. VI (1954), p. 145. Lateness of pay went on through the century. For instance, the Christmas quarter pay of 1774 for Plymouth, ready for transport by the middle of March 1775, was delayed further by a muddle over shipping, for while the money came by road to Portsmouth, the roads were not considered secure enough to Plymouth. By 8 April it was still at Portsmouth, and there was further delay until the Admiralty ordered another ship. The wages could not have reached Plymouth until May at the earliest, so Plymouth Dockyard workers yet again had five months' credit to find (NMM ADM B/189, 22 Mar. 1775; ADM A/2690, 10 Apr. 1775; PRO ADM 106/2592, 8 Apr. 1775).
4. J. Ehrman, *The Navy in the War of William III, 1689–1697* (Cambridge, Cambridge University Press, 1953), p. 98.
5. R. D. Merriman (ed.), *Queen Anne's Navy* (London, Navy Records Society, 1961), p. 105; also N. Macleod, 'The shipwrights of the Royal Dockyards', *Mariner's Mirror*, **11** (1925), 281–2.
6. For the most perceptive analysis of this situation see D. A. Baugh, *Naval Administration, 1715–1750* (London, Navy Records Society, 1977), pp. 265–7. Professor Baugh's work has provided the framework for this article for the earlier part of the century, and his advice over many years has been most valuable.
7. For the timing of the mobilization against Spain see J. Black, *British Foreign*

Policy in the Age of Walpole (Edinburgh, John Donald, 1985), p. 7. The details of the strike are in a gathering of reports and letters to the Navy Board, NMM ADM A/2179, September 1729.
8. See Baugh, *Naval Administration*, pp. 281–3, who prints the document in full. The document is dated 1 August 1729 and contains an enclosure of 1721 which is the 'agreement' referred to here.
9. NMM ADM A/2179, 19 May 1729.
10. A. J. Marsh, 'The local community and the operation of Plymouth Dockyard, 1689–1763', in M. Duffy et al. (eds), *The New Maritime History of Devon* (London, Conway Maritime Press in association with the University of Exeter, 1992), p. 206; NMM, Vaughan Collection, VAU/D/3, 14 May 1745. Notably, the ropemakers were not supported by other workers, and the trouble was still rumbling on into the next year; see Baugh, *Naval Administration*, p. 287.
11. Baugh, *Naval Administration*, p. 266. In comparisons between merchant and royal dockyards, it should be borne in mind that merchant yards built 74-gun ships and usually much smaller ships on slips and had no need of heavy capital expenditure on docks; they did no maintenance on naval ships, although a little was done during the French Revolutionary wars.
12. *Reasons Humbly Offered for a Bill for the better breeding of shipwrights* (London, 1709) demonstrates the current concern over design and building standards.
13. D. A. Baugh, *British Naval Administration in the Age of Walpole* (Princeton, Princeton University Press, 1965), p. 323; R. Middleton, 'The administration of Newcastle and Pitt: the departments of state and the conduct of the war, 1754–1760' (unpublished PhD thesis, University of Exeter, 1968), pp. 138, 142.
14. Baugh, *British Naval Administration*, p. 323.
15. *Parliamentary Register*, V, 255, 23 January 1782. Fitzherbert was the contractor for the teams of horses used in Portsmouth and other yards.
16. Baugh, 'Navy as a national institution', p. 129; R. J. B. Knight, *Portsmouth Dockyard Papers 1774–1783: The American War* (Portsmouth, City of Portsmouth, 1987), pp. xxxvii–xxxix; see also the diverging graph of shipwrights to the total number of artificers in Plymouth yard in R. Morriss, 'Industrial relations at Plymouth Dockyard, 1770–1820', in Duffy et al., *The New Maritime History of Devon*, p. 216.
17. C. R. Dobson, *Masters and Journeymen: A Prehistory of Industrial Relations 1717–1800* (London, Croom Helm, 1980), p. 99. Under the Act of 22 Geo. II, c.60, enticement of artificers was a crime punishable by a fine of £500 and twelve months imprisonment for each worker enticed. See J. R. Bruijn, *The Dutch Navy of the Seventeenth and Eighteenth Centuries* (Columbia, South Carolina, University of South Carolina Press, 1993), p. 170, for English shipwrights in Holland; for Samuel Bentham's service as a shipwright in Russia see I. R. Christie, *The Benthams in Russia, 1780–1791* (Providence, R. I., and Oxford, Berg, 1993), pp. 7–20.

18. See H. Bates van Tyne, 'A British strike in 1775', *Michigan Alumnus Quarterly Review*, **45** (1938–9), 157–64.
19. Quoted in R. Davis, *The Rise of the British Shipping Industry in the Seventeenth and Eighteenth Centuries* (Newton Abbott, David and Charles, second impression, 1967), p. 67.
20. *Ibid.*, pp. 66–8; J. A. Goldenburg, *Shipbuilding in Colonial America* (Charlottesburg, Virginia, The Mariners Museum, Newport News, Va., by the University Press of Virginia, 1976), especially ch. IV, 'Colonial shipwrights'; B. Bailyn, *Voyagers to the West* (New York, Vintage Books, Random House, 1988), p. 254.
21. Baugh, 'Navy as a national institution', p. 128; *Parliamentary Register*, V, p. 254, 23 January 1782.
22. Parliamentary Papers, *Reports of the Commissioners appointed to Enquire into any Irregularities, Frauds or Abuses ... in the General Naval Departments*, 1803–4, vol. III, p. 17. After comparative stability up to the 1740s, the underlying increases in wheat prices and the cost of living were particularly marked in the 1750s and 1760s. As a result, all the dockyard workers could do was to petition for an increase in wages (which they did three times in the 1770s), while other craftsmen's wages increased; see E. W. Gilboy, *Wages in Eighteenth Century England* (Cambridge, Mass., Harvard University Press, 1934), pp. 10, 12, 23, 95, 104–9. For the upward shift in wheat prices at this time see P. Deane and W. A. Cole, *British Economic Growth, 1688–1959* (Cambridge, Cambridge University Press, 1964), p. 91; R. Brown, *Society and Economy in Modern Britain 1700–1850* (London, Routledge, 1991), p. 66.
23. PRO ADM 106/2537, 'An alphabetical digest of the copies of the standing orders of the Navy Board to the yards between 1658 and 1765 inclusive': 31 Aug. 1739: 'Shipwrights to be allowed to bring [chips] on their shoulders near to the dock gates, there to be inspected by the officers', but by an order of 4 May 1753 chips were only allowed to be carried under one arm. Hence the best illustration of the "chip on the shoulder" is the 1756 strike at Chatham. The yard officers reported to the Navy Board that one angry shipwright had exclaimed: ' "Are not the chips mine? I will not lower them." Immediately the main body pushed on with their chips on their shoulders, crowded and forced the Master Shipwright and First Assistant through the gateway, and went out in a riotous manner, saying now is our time, and when out of the yard gave three huzzas' (NMM ADM B/153, 17 June 1756: the letter is printed in J. B. Hattendorf, R. J. B. Knight *et al.*, *British Naval Documents, 1204–1960* (London, Navy Records Society, 1993), pp. 528–9).
24. See Dobson, *Masters and Journeymen*, p. 184, quoted from *Lloyd's Evening Post*, 3–6 September 1771. Also P. Linebaugh, *The London Hanged: Crime and Civil Society in the Eighteenth Century* (London, Penguin Books, 1991), pp. 378–84, for a fresh, powerful passage: 'chips became associated with some deeply-held working-class ideas of freedom and slavery' (p. 381). For further details on chips see M. Slade, *The History of the Female Shipwright; to whome the*

government has Granted a Superannuated Pension of Twenty Pounds per Annum during her Life: written by Herself (London, 1773), pp. 89, 105.
25. R. C. Davis, *Shipbuilders of the Venetian Arsenal* (Baltimore, Johns Hopkins University Press, 1991), pp. 120–1, 160–2; M. Crook, *Toulon in War and Revolution: From the Ancien Régime to the Restoration, 1750–1820* (Manchester, Manchester University Press, 1991), p. 46. The Dutch, on the other hand, allowed no timber out of their yards, as noted by Yeoman Lott, *An Account of Proposals Made for the Benefit of His Majesty's Naval Service* (London, 1777), pp. 5, 16; nor did the Dutch East India Company shipyards in Holland, which had *spaanderrapers* (chip collectors). See J. R. Bruijn *et al.*, *Dutch-Asiatic Shipping in the 17th and 18th Centuries* (The Hague, Martinus Nijhoff, 1987), vol. 1, p. 29.
26. See R. J. B. Knight, 'Pilfering and theft from the dockyards at the time of the American War of Independence', *Mariner's Mirror*, **61** (1975), 215–25.
27. PRO ADM 106/2537: 1662 'wholly forbid, but lawful ones once a week'; 1667, 1669, 1698, 1699, 1739, 1753, 1759; also in 1758, see R. Middleton, 'Administration of Newcastle and Pitt', pp. 140–1. An eloquent case for the ending of the chips system was made by Yeoman Lott (1777), and also by 'W. S.' (William Shrubsole), *A Plea in Favour of the Shipwrights belonging to the Royal Dockyards . . .* (Rochester, 1770), p. 2.
28. PRO ADM 106/2509, Standing Orders to the Yards, no. 172, 4 Aug. 1783. For the ending of the custom see R. A. Morriss, *The Royal Dockyards during the Revolutionary and Napoleonic Wars* (Leicester, Leicester University Press, 1983), p. 93.
29. NMM ADM B/198, 5 Jan. 1778; Parliamentary Papers, *Reports of the Commissioners appointed to enquire into the Fees, Gratuities, Perquisites and Emoluments, which are or have been lately received into the Public Offices . . .*, Sixth Report, 1786–8, 1806 (309), vol. VII, pp. 307–8. The Commission recommended that 'the indentures of all apprentices run so as that they may not become the property of the person to whom they are indented or their heirs, but to be turned over to their successors in the yard' (p. 308).
30. PRO ADM 106/2537, 14 Jun. 1765; PRO ADM 7/659, Sandwich's 1771 Visitation, fos. 75, 95. See J. M. Haas, 'The royal dockyards: the earliest visitations and reform, 1749–1778', *Historical Journal*, **13**(2) (1970), 200–1; Clive Wilkinson, 'The Earl of Egmont and the Navy, 1763–6', *Mariner's Mirror*, **84** (1998), 425.
31. NMM SAN/F/5/9. This is printed in Hattendorf *et al.* (eds), *British Naval Documents*, p. 535. By a Standing Order of 1774 the Navy Board limited a workman's absence to a week, or, in the case of sickness, a month; any exceptions to this were to be submitted to the Board (PRO ADM 106/2508, no. 665, 22 July 1774).
32. NMM ADM B/153, Navy Board to Admiralty, 18 June 1756. Large was described as one of the ringleaders and was pressed into the *Royal Sovereign* at the Nore, a ship about to go on foreign service.

33. PRO ADM 174/117, 11 Oct. 1782, Plymouth Commissioner to the Navy Board.
34. Middleton to Lord Sandwich, draft, not sent, of (?) February 1781, printed in J. K. Laughton (ed.), *Letters and Papers of Charles, Lord Barham*, vol. II (London, Navy Records Society, 1910), p. 29.
35. For a detailed description of the strike see B. M. Ranft, 'Labour relations in the Royal Dockyards in 1739', *Mariner's Mirror*, **47** (1961), 281–91.
36. Baugh, *Naval Administration*, pp. 264, 304, 305.
37. NMM ADM B/153, Navy Board to Admiralty, 18 June 1756; B/155, 30 Apr., 1 May 1757; B/160, 21 Oct. 1758; B/161, 9 Jan. 1759. There had been attempts to petition the throne for an increase in pay in 1765, 1769 and 1770; an Order-in-Council was needed to alter the wages.
38. For a description of the task work system and an analysis of the causes see J. M. Haas, 'The introduction of task work into the Royal Dockyards, 1775', *Journal of British Studies*, **8** (May 1969), 44–68; it is clear from the sample of wages in Table 1.1 that the men were quite correct in predicting that they would suffer from task work in real terms, which Haas cannot believe. For a corrective to Haas's views, see Knight, *Portsmouth Dockyard Papers*, pp. xliv–xlvi; also Morriss, 'Industrial relations at Plymouth Dockyard, 1770–1820', pp. 218–19.
39. PRO ADM 7/662, Sandwich's 1775 Visitation notes, fo. 63.
40. Morriss concludes from his study of Plymouth that '... the workforce at Plymouth increased by 29 per cent between 1780 and 1801, the yard's annual wages bill enlarged in the same period by 105 per cent. Consequently, although more labour was exacted through piecework, financially the artificers in Plymouth dockyard were certainly better off employed that way than they were on day rates, and better paid, too, than workers in nearby merchant shipyards' ('Industrial relations at Plymouth Dockyard, 1770–1820,' p. 219).
41. Marsh, 'The local community'; Knight, 'Pilfering and theft'.
42. NMM, Vaughan collection, VAU/F/9, 19 Feb. 1740/1. Vanbrugh was Commissioner at Plymouth from 1 Feb. 1739 until his death on 22 July 1753; this incident was early in his time at Plymouth, which was marked by ill-health. At Portsmouth Sir Richard Hughes (Feb. 1754 to Aug. 1773) and Sir (later Viscount) Samuel Hood (26 Jan. 1778 to 5 Nov. 1780) were the most effective of all the Commissioners, precisely because they had these local connections.
43. Shrubsole, *A Plea in Favour*, p. 15.
44. Quoted in Dobson, *Masters and Journeymen*, p. 183 n, from Pollard, *The Genesis of Modern Management* (1968 edn), p. 104 n.
45. J. M. Haas, *A Management Odyssey: The Royal Dockyards, 1714–1914* (Lanham, Maryland, University Press of America, 1994); Linebaugh, *The London Hanged*.
46. Shrubsole, *A Plea in Favour*, p. 19. When the wages were again late in 1778,

Commissioner Ourry at Plymouth reported to the Navy Board that the workmen's 'creditors have raised 3d in £ discount' and money was 'so scarce here [that] they cannot get it at any rate to subsist their families' (PRO ADM 174/116, 28 July 1778).
47. NMM ADM A/2179, Navy Board to Admiralty, 23 Sep. 1729.
48. NMM POR/D/21, Portsmouth Dockyard Officers to the Navy Board, 14 Apr. 1778; POR/D/22, 4 Aug. 1780.
49. W. Shrubsole, *Christian Memoirs ... with a life of the Author* (London, 1807, 3rd edn), p. xx.
50. J. Fortescue (ed.), *Correspondence of George III* (London, Macmillan, 1927–8), vol. V, p. 351, Jan. 1782. For a perceptive view of Sandwich's options at the time see N. A. M. Rodger, *The Insatiable Earl: A Life of John Montagu, Fourth Earl of Sandwich 1718–92* (London, HarperCollins, 1993), pp. 149–54.
51. E. P. Thompson, *The Making of the English Working Class* (London, Penguin, 1968 edn), p. 463.
52. See J. Pritchard, *Louis XV's Navy: A Study of Organisation and Administration* (Kingston and Montreal, McGill-Queen's University Press, 1987), pp. 108, 112; M. Crook, *Toulon in War*, pp. 14, 45–6.
53. See J. M. Beattie, *Crime and the Courts in England, 1660–1800* (Princeton, Princeton University Press, 1986), pp. 522–4.

2

GOVERNMENT AND COMMUNITY: THE CHANGING CONTEXT OF LABOUR RELATIONS, 1770–1830

Roger Morriss

Labour relations in the Royal Dockyards and other naval establishments were shaped by more than immediate issues. The Board of Admiralty and its subordinate Navy and Victualling Boards were influenced by prevailing attitudes in government towards their employees. Likewise, artificers and labourers were influenced by feelings in their local community towards government. Administrative innovation, war and peace, economic ideas and doctrine affected attitudes on both sides. This chapter examines the changes in this administrative context, with the aim of revealing how they influenced both the tenor of management and the personality of the workforce in the civil departments of the Royal Navy in the late eighteenth and early nineteenth centuries.

Communities of Common Interest

A distinguishing feature of employment in the naval departments was the existence of other like communities similarly subject to, or affected by, Admiralty policies. The main dockyards in England – at Deptford, Woolwich, Chatham, Sheerness, Portsmouth and Plymouth – in some cases had victualling and ordnance yards nearby, directly administered by different boards but nevertheless observing similar terms of employment. There were also other smaller naval depots around the coast of the British Isles – at Deal, Leith on the Firth of Forth and at Kinsale on the southern coast of Ireland – and small naval bases abroad at Gibraltar, Port Royal in Jamaica, Antigua in the Leeward Islands and at Halifax, Nova Scotia.[1] Other small yards were formed in the course of the wars, for example at Milford Haven and Minorca. Men in these small and foreign yards had little bargaining power and were vulnerable to victimization so did not usually join in large-scale combinations. But when grievances developed common to the major dock or victualling yards, their employees would join together to represent their interests. In consequence these employees and their dependants, including those in the smaller yards at home and abroad, all formed what can be regarded as one national community of interest.

For the resident of a dockyard town in the eighteenth century, employment in a naval establishment represented access not only to the inconceivably vast resources of government finance, but to an independent source of income. So much was the value of that employment, apprentices, artificers and clerks paid handsome 'premiums' to gain their places in the yards. By 1770 few places, if any, were sinecures and few postholders were pluralists. But almost all posts in the dockyards, victualling or ordnance yards provided the opportunity of making money from other sources apart from the government wage or salary, the rates of many of which had been established in the seventeenth century.[2] Officers had their premiums from the entry of subordinates; clerks had their fees for conducting business with contractors; some, too, acted as agents for men at sea; artificers had their chips and the earnings of apprentices.[3] Income from a source separate from government granted its own independent status and was valued for that. Government employees were privileged and not uncommon beings.

Establishment in a government post also represented opportunity for self-improvement. Apprenticeship to a yard artificer, or, even better, an artificer officer, was not only a passport into a government yard but, with the right master, patronage into a supervisory position as a leading man, quarterman, measurer or foreman.[4] Promotion invariably required large payments to the retiring man from all those benefiting from his departure: even after 1764, when one pension was carried on the books of each dockyard to every 40 men, the aged had to be encouraged to abandon their sources of income. But promotion meant not only higher rates of official payment but greater choice in the work available, the different forms bringing different perquisites.[5] Clerks and junior yard officers could gain further promotion by moving yards; after all, the form of employment was generally similar in like establishments.[6] Some took positions as clerks or carpenters' mates on board ships. Regular periods of war in the eighteenth century offered years of greater opportunity. Ships needed pursers, and the small refitting yards abroad required skilled men of every description. One Portsmouth shipwright, Edward Churchill, who chanced his career to the sea, served as carpenter for twelve years in eight different naval vessels between 1782 and 1796, before filling a succession of posts as Master Shipwright at yards serving the Mediterranean fleet on Corsica, Elba, Lisbon, Minorca and Gibraltar, then returning to the same office at Plymouth and Milford.[7]

Yet there were factors that persuaded men to rest content in a dockyard or victualling yard. Once established they were unlikely to be discharged except for misconduct. Although peace-time reductions removed some artificers, often those least capable of performing a fair quota of work, and the temporary extra clerks, tenure was otherwise generally assured.[8] Men past their prime, incapable of earning the high wartime wages offered by private employment, tended to settle down.[9] As they became older, not only had they the advantage of an attendant surgeon and a chance of superannuation, but relations and friends in a workforce tended to co-operate and share work and earnings, supporting those past their prime.

The Pressures of Government Employment

In return for these advantages, government employees acceded to a range of pressures which shaped and guided their conduct. Least stated but everywhere assumed was Royal allegiance. It was everywhere ritually observed and unconsciously imbibed. Ships of war in harbour celebrated royal occasions like the King's birthday with long gun salutes. Vessels carrying Royal representatives bore the Royal standard.[10] Everywhere flags and commissioned and warrant officers demanded respect. Unlike officers in the Navy, artificers in general did not take oaths of allegiance but were soon reminded of their duty on deviating from it. In 1803 oaths of allegiance to the Crown had to be sworn by members of the dockyard volunteer defence corps who were reported to the Admiralty when they refrained from doing so.[11] In 1805 Richard Baker, a joiner at Plymouth, was 'run' on the books of the yard and blacklisted from ever again entering a Royal yard 'for being concerned in uttering seditious expressions'.[12]

It was the same with religion. Common artificers were expected to conform to the practice demanded by the Crown. Until 1828 the Test and Corporation Acts of 1661 and 1673 prohibited dissenters from holding posts in government, the judiciary or the armed services. Officers receiving their commission from the Admiralty or warrant from the Navy Board first had to obtain a sacrament certificate, testifying to their receipt of Holy Communion from a minister, and witnessed by a warden, of the Church of England.[13] Catholics appointed to a post by mistake — even that of cook in a ship — were relieved of their employment.[14]

Most dissenters in dockyard towns were non-conforming Protestants, but they were equally distrusted by representatives of government. At Plymouth, where Wesley made four preaching visits between 1747 and 1782, both on his first and last visits soldiers under a lieutenant disrupted his addresses. His congregations at Portsmouth were 'serious'; at Chatham 'lively, loving'; and at Deptford in 1787 wishing passionately to separate from the Church of England. That summer at Sheerness, a chapel was completed without charge 'during vacant hours' by dockyard carpenters, shipwrights and labourers, including 'those who do not pretend to any religion'.[15] The more radical nonconformists at Plymouth in 1797 formed there a branch of the Methodist New Connexion, which adopted proposals for more democratic organization.[16] The political content of nonconformist religion was not lost on artificers. Not surprisingly, the wording of petitions began to include religious terminology like the word 'brethren'.[17]

The spread of dissenting religion was resisted by the authorities in dockyard towns. In 1793 unguarded expressions in a sermon delivered at Plymouth by the dissenting minister, William Winterbotham, resulted in his trial at Exeter for sedition.[18] At Sheerness in 1801, Commissioner Coffin refused permission for the minister of a congregation at Blue Town to visit the inhabitants of the hulks which formed part of the yard foreshore, maintaining that 'the increase in methodists may not be countenanced by government'.[19] Even in 1818 new yards like Pembroke were deemed to require their own chapel to combat the growth of dissenting meeting-houses outside the yard.[20] In 1819 the second clerk to the Timber Master was dismissed from Woolwich Dockyard for circulating literature associated with Deism.[21] As late as 1842 the chaplain of a dockyard was threatened with removal on account of his Puseyite propensities.[22]

Not surprisingly, political as well as religious consciences were expected to be governed by government. Contracts, pensions and places of profit under the Crown were customarily identified with political subservience.[23] They had always been used to reward Members of Parliament who voted for the King's ministers, while contracts, jobs and advancement at the outports had conventionally been used as a means of persuading constituents to vote for government candidates in elections.[24] By 1770 the patronage available to the Crown had been reduced. Many government office-holders, like the commissioners for sick and wounded seamen, and the prize commissioners and sub-commissioners at each major port, had been excluded from holding a seat in Parliament.[25] Even so, through the votes they commanded, about 25 to 30 boroughs were directly controlled by the Treasury, Admiralty and Ordnance departments.[26] The Admiralty controlled six, including Plymouth, Portsmouth and Rochester, with Queenborough, near Sheerness, shared with the Ordnance Board.[27] Economical reform after 1780 excluded categories of 'profiteers', like contractors, from holding seats in Parliament, and disenfranchised revenue officers who could 'influence' constituents.[28] Thereafter, Parliament was regularly supplied with accounts of offices tenable with a seat in the House of Commons.[29]

However, regulatory measures only marginally affected the influence government had over the political conduct of an employee. It was sufficient for government candidates in Admiralty boroughs to be dispatched to canvas votes with no more than the recommendation of the ministry.[30] Thus at Chatham in 1761, 'the Commissioner ... sent for all the freemen of Maidstone employed in the dockyard and acquainted them he had received orders from the admiralty to direct them to vote for Mr Northey'.[31] In Admiralty boroughs before 1832 the electorates were relatively small – 600 at Rochester, 200 at Plymouth, 150 at Queenborough, 100 at Portsmouth – but all consisted of freemen nominated by borough corporations with which the government worked, and they usually shared the nomination of candidates.[32] The number of government yard employees who were voters was much smaller than the electorates: at Plymouth in 1831, for example, only three worked in the dockyard. Nevertheless the unenfranchised did exert their influence at hustings, and government had means of making its intentions felt with these men as well as with voters.

Practices exposed later, though under new, wider franchises, reveal what happened in Admiralty boroughs. At Chatham in 1835, the commanding officer of the marine barracks could and did intimidate opponent voters, for example by threatening to close slop-sellers' shops, and by refusing them admission to government property to sell their wares.[33] In consequence, even artificers indifferent to a government candidate felt obliged to vote appropriately to 'protect' themselves. At Plymouth in 1852 it was acknowledged that political influence was paramount in appointments of all kinds. It was generally believed that a candidate or his agents were perfectly entitled to obtain, or promise to obtain, a dockyard situation for electors who supported him. It was a belief sustained by the ability of candidates to achieve this end; at Plymouth in 1852, 25 out of '30 to 40' applications for entries on behalf of voters succeeded.[34] At Chatham in 1853, candidates' agents encouraged those voters amenable to the government candidate with promises in aid of a son, of a pension, or of a seafaring relative in need of entry to Greenwich Hospital.[35] It was not unknown for money to change hands, sometimes paid directly in gold coins or in 'bets' on the outcome of an election.

So decided was opinion in government that places depended on the appropriate voting of office-holders and their relatives, even long-established administrators could be threatened with 'retirement' for not ensuring their connections voted appropriately.[36] By comparison with private employment, tenure in a government yard was secure. Nevertheless large-scale peace reductions at the termination of hostilities reinforced the artificers' sense of dependence upon their political masters. Numerous wars throughout the eighteenth century meant workforces were regularly reduced at the termination of hostilities. The discharge of aged and infirm artificers from the dockyards in 1802 cleared 1100 men from the six main yards.[37] Nothing could have been better calculated to weaken any sense of security of tenure.

The Physical Struggle for Control

Perhaps in resistance to these pressures, dockyard employees, like seamen, possessed a deep sense of their independence. Their skills represented their freedom from restraint. In theory at least, they were physically mobile. Almost half the artificers in Plymouth Dockyard in 1746–82 – about 43 per cent – had been trained outside the yard;[38] other yards had probably a similar proportion of outside origin. Being skilled, it was natural for them to assume they might move back to merchant yards where their services were in demand. The most skilled, the shipwrights, were the most confident.[39]

Yet age and family commitments meant even they were limited in their ability to shift elsewhere. Threats to remove their labour, like that of government in wartime to discharge large numbers of men, were principally bargaining ploys. In consequence, behind the rhetoric government developed an increasing array of measures that resisted the artificers' rights to assert their physical independence. These ranged from writing to merchant builders under contract with the Board to forbid the entry of men leaving the King's yards[40] to prosecution for emigration.[41] In 1801 the First Lord of the Admiralty, on the advice of the Admiralty Solicitor, directed that artificers who had been discharged from the dockyards and intended to emigrate to France should be allowed to commit themselves so as to provide proof for their conviction.[42]

Under such discouragement, there was every incentive for artificers to remain within the royal yards to fight for their requirements. However, there they had to be even more prepared to face intimidation. In 1794 Charles Middleton, the Comptroller of the Navy Board between 1778 and 1790, observing that combinations were most common in wartime, wanted their leaders made liable to charges of treason and those supporting them liable to sedition.[43] They were already liable to a charge of conspiracy but, as elsewhere, excessive punishment of leading workmen could be counter-productive in undermining the co-operation of surviving artificers.[44] From 1799 government yard artificers became liable to the more general Combination Laws. But in the event, when the dockyard combination of 1800–1 did break down into local rioting, more precise measures, aimed selectively at individual trouble-makers, were deemed most effective in making examples of the culprits.

One method of punishment employed by Commissioner Lecras, new to Plymouth dockyard in 1783, was to discharge a man then impress him straight away.[45] However this method had no long-term currency. Freedom from impressment in a naval town was an absolute essential to government yard artificers. In 1790, following the impressment of one artificer, 'a large mob consisting principally of shipwrights belonging to Deptford Yard' went to the press rendezvous at the Ship in Launch in Deptford, found the lieutenant in charge, and 'with horrid imprecations threatened him and his gang with death and tore down his colours which they carried off in triumph'.[46] In 1801 a Sheerness yard boatman was impressed by Commissioner Coffin which resulted in the latter being threatened with his life for an hour by the whole yard workforce until he agreed to the release of the man.[47] The Navy had the reputation of being scrupulous in observing regulations relating to impressment. Nevertheless, during wartime, blanket protections against impressment were occasionally lifted. The potential of being subject to impressment, possibly a victim of punitive sanctions, accordingly prepared every government employee of a seafaring town to resist the danger.[48]

Living in the shadow of government power, dockyard artificers were deeply conscious of their liability to subjection to martial law. To those who worked on board ships, in contact with naval officers, this had a particular meaning. Marooned afloat, they could be subject to tyranny at the whim of any young midshipman. Complaints of such treatment occurred at every dockyard. At Plymouth, on board the *Diomede* in 1782, a shipwright was beaten by an officer and an apprentice threatened with flogging for stepping on the foot of a 'young gentleman'.[49] Similar treatment resulted in an appeal for protection from a gang working on board the brig *Sylph* in Plymouth Sound in 1800.[50] The fear of martial law lived on. In 1827 five artificers from the same yard, having volunteered to serve at Fernando Po, petitioned against being placed under martial law, having 'always been treated as mechanics and civilians'.[51]

Such fears survived because the threats remained. Consciousness of them was kept alive from working 'cheek by jowl' with the Navy, and because the communities of government employees in naval towns had long memories, sustained by custom and oral tradition. Linked by wage rates and prices, they had more in common with inland inhabitants, who came to their aid in rioting, than with the navy. Moreover, these communities had immediate power over individuals. Intimidation was not exclusive to government, and was often more rough and ready. Strike breakers were stoned and informants forced to flee in fear of their lives.[52] Hence, throughout the eighteenth century, local communities were able to maintain their claims to take chips and to 'horse' artificers with flaws in apprenticeship indentures, even though the Admiralty and Navy boards disapproved of both practices.[53]

The Enhancement of Central Controls

Local values sat uneasily with those of central government. In the lower ranks of the large yards patronage often had family connections. Sir Charles Middleton, Comptroller of the Navy Board between 1778 and 1790, observed that the officers had 'so many relations and dependents [sic] ... in the dockyards ... that they never lose an opportunity of supporting them when in their power'.[54] Support was of course reciprocal. It involved conniving at, or co-operating in, malpractice. By the end of the eighteenth century, long-established yard officers were beginning to run the yards as they wanted. In 1802, when asked why he did not expose the malpractices of an officer at Chatham as they happened, Thomas Grant explained 'that he was afraid that if he had done so, some opportunity would have been taken of making a complaint against him for some alleged fault and he should have been dismissed'.[55]

Inevitably, where local authority and community values were more important than a standard centralized code of conduct, the greater national interest tended to be ignored. In the late eighteenth century, holders of office in government were regarded as self-servers. It was a view that prevailed until at least 1813.[56] For administrators at the Board of Admiralty and the Navy, Victualling and Ordnance Boards, the need to ensure local practice conformed where possible to central demands placed great importance on the appointment of loyal and obedient men to local positions of trust. Former sea officers were used as commissioners at the Boards and to oversee the dockyards not only because they had experience in naval matters and were accustomed to wielding authority but because they subscribed to the notion of being 'gentlemen'. As such, they were supposed to possess honour, which conveyed a sense of honesty, at least between equals.[57] From the time of the American War of Independence, the growing demands of managing great public concerns were deemed by some to require men inculcated with a sense of public service of a higher order than that which arose from purely personal breeding and interest. In 1788 Sir Charles Middleton, an evangelical, classified men rising from the ranks of the dockyard artificers not only by their age and abilities but by 'how far they are such as fear God and hate covetousness, their moral character, actions, dispositions, whether married or single'.[58] He fought a battle with Lord Sandwich, First Lord of the Admiralty, to gain control of senior yard appointments but without success.[59]

As both Sandwich and Middleton understood, political control of administrative practice was indispensable to the imposition of government will on artificers possessed of a sense of their own independence. It was all the more essential in the late eighteenth century when the degree of central control over earnings was little more than approximate. Sandwich's attempt in 1775 to introduce into the Royal Dockyards piecework for shipwrights for the sake of increased productivity is already well documented.[60] Employed in all six main dockyards from 1788, the scheme was gradually adopted because the pricing of pieces of work brought increased earnings to the artificers. However, neither the Board of Admiralty nor the Navy Board were aware that the higher earnings were virtually assured by the vested interest of the quartermen who measured the work and of the senior officers in the earnings of their apprentices working with the gangs. The officers indulged in creative accountancy to ensure that artificers invariably earned the highest rates of pay permitted.[61] As a result, earnings for shipwrights rose progressively. The average daily earnings of a shipwright at Plymouth doubled between 1790 and 1803. Those of other trades like caulkers, joiners, sailmakers, masons and bricklayers, scavelmen and labourers went up too, the more skilled commanding the higher increases.[62]

These increases in earnings cushioned the families of tradespeople employed in government dockyards from the late-eighteenth-century inflation until its height was reached with the bad harvests of 1799–1800. Then, when prices far exceeded earnings, the old claim for higher basic rates of pay which had been agitated in 1775, before the introduction of piecework, re-emerged. These basic rates had been established as far back as 1690 in the case of shipwrights, 1693 for caulkers and sailmakers and 1696 for bricklayers. As a result, within a local context of food rioting, petitioning for higher basic rates of pay involved all the workers in government yards.

Inevitably, the combination needed to achieve these petitions was regarded with distrust. The French Revolution had injected political content into every disorder; the rising in Ireland confirmed that insurrection could happen in Britain. The mutinies in the fleet three years earlier raised the spectre of dockyard artificers combining with seamen; indeed the report of artificers signalling to ships in harbour at Plymouth in April 1801 led immediately to the removal of guns from the gun wharf. The failure to achieve a response from petitions by the end of March 1801 contributed to confrontations of artificers with the local magistracy and military forces at Plymouth and the riot against Commissioner Coffin at Sheerness. These coincided with a late grant of an 'extra ration' according to the size of artificers' families. But in May 1801 a Navy Board committee toured the six main dockyards to eject the leading committee men and rioters. In all 340 men were discharged that summer.[63]

This experience was followed in 1802 by the discharge of over 100 Thames and Medway yard caulkers for refusing to go to the merchant yards to refit East India Company ships stranded there by a strike of merchant yard artificers. These discharges, combined with the peace reduction of 1100 men in 1802, reduced the whole dockyard workforce by about 10 per cent. Inevitably, morale suffered, for these moves removed both the most spirited leaders, those who, from long service, represented past practice, and those cherished among them as invalids. The impact of the peace reduction can be judged from the response the Navy Board committee making the discharges received at Deptford: it 'experienced much abuse from the enraged families of the workmen', and only 'with some difficulty escaped from worse treatment'.[64]

The Reform and Standardization of Terms of Employment

The combination and discharges of 1801–2 formed a watershed in the collective experience of government yard employees, for it coincided with the abolition of extra unofficial emoluments in government naval establishments. From 1801 officers and clerks lost their fees and perquisites, while artificers had their chips commuted to an extra daily payment. In the dockyards chips had long been regarded as a cover for embezzlement.[65] When wage payments were paid two or three quarters late, dragging families regularly into debt, chips and embezzlement provided a form of immediate recompense. But from 1805 another innovation, subsistence money, provided a weekly payment of a proportion of each artificer's earnings.[66] This militated against artificers slipping into a cycle of debt. Eight years later, improvements in the methods of calculation of earnings permitted the introduction of *all* earnings weekly.[67] From 1812 the old seventeenth-century rates of pay and allowances were anyway consolidated into a new single scale of payment,[68] and from December 1814 pensions were made available to artificers after 20 rather than 30 years' service, a provision that was extended to the victualling yards and naval hospitals as well as the dockyards.[69]

Before the early nineteenth century, such regulations had never been applied to all departments of the Navy simultaneously. However from 1805 they were extended by a process of comparison and example through the work of the Commissioners for Revising and Digesting the Civil Affairs of the Navy. That year, this Commission replaced Lord St Vincent's punitive Commission for Inquiring into Irregularities, Frauds, Abuses practised in the Naval Departments, established in 1802, following hard on the heels of regulations abolishing chips and unofficial payments.

The Commissioners of Naval Revision pursued the principle of establishing one equitable wage or salary to each worker. The process inevitably affected labour relations, for the abolition of unofficial payments undermined the sense of independence of working men. Also, points of dispute were referred to the existing Commission, which gave a long-term dimension to negotiations. Moreover these were undertaken within an atmosphere of increased emphasis on the priority of public concerns over private interests: the principle stemming from the growing middle-class movement in Parliament and a wish to adapt government departments to the new methods of management becoming dominant in industry and commerce throughout the country.[70] The movement focused on the office-holders in the central London departments of government who were first called 'civil servants' about 1812.[71] But the changing terms of employment, associated with the changing view of government employees, also affected artificers and clerks in all the naval towns around the coasts.

Although these years brought a new ethos to work in government naval establishments, labour relations remained important to the preservation of artificers' interests. The outbreak of war again in 1803 saw a revival of bargaining by government workforces. But points were fought only by single departments or trades in yards, not by the whole workforces of all the major yards. The Navy Board, short of labour, tended to concede the majority of claims.[72] These however tended to concern only the hours of work or comparability of pay.[73]

One principle the artificers in the dockyards managed to maintain was their egalitarian belief in helping one another. In 1802 Lord St Vincent had been scandalized to learn that old and young men received similar amounts of pay.

> It was well known to those who are acquainted with dock yards that the young and able men preferred making the sacrifice of what their vigour enabled them to earn in favour of their aged relations and friends, expecting in turn to receive the same indulgence when the decline of their strength should require it; and upon this principle the earnings of the old men appear higher in proportion to the actual labour.[74]

The same equalizing principle motivated the shipwrights in 1804 to oppose their enforced shoaling or classification into gangs of unequal abilities: the separation of the best workers, who produced the greatest output, from those of middling or poor abilities. Hence, in 1804 the Plymouth shipwrights resisted an order for shoaling on the grounds that it was 'injurious and dangerous':

> although nature has not formed every man with equal talents yet in every

department on a stage of work every man has a proportionable part so that every man strives to be equal with his sidemate; but this new mode will tend to make every company enemies to each other when we consider the great differences it may make in our wages, as some jobs are more lucrative than others.[75]

Workforce opposition and Navy Board ambivalence on the subject ensured that a full trial of shoaling by ability was postponed, by the recommendation of the Commission of Naval Revision, until the end of the Napoleonic War.

For the Board of Admiralty the recommendations of the Commissioners of Revision became their guide and policy. In setting wage rates, the Commissioners made them lower than those in private industry, arguing that artificers did not attach sufficient importance to stability of government employment. Partly in consequence, in 1814 the Board of Admiralty was inclined, for example, to discharge victualling yard bakers who compared their own earnings unfavourably with bakers in London.[76]

Laissez-faire and Rationalization

Guided by the recommendations of the Commission, the naval boards were themselves beginning to feel a sense of responsibility towards their workers and this operated in their favour once peace resumed. The years following the Peace of Vienna in 1815 saw the workforces in the dockyards consciously maintained as the Navy Board attempted to reduce ships to the Ordinary in a state of good repair. There were over 14,700 in the six main yards at the end of 1814, and still over 12,000 in 1822. Numbers were consciously maintained in spite of financial reductions by the expedients of reducing working hours or pay.[77] Awareness of the role the yard workforces had played in the war injected labour relations with marked mutual respect.[78] Even in 1821 a committee of the Navy Board inspecting the dockyards specifically stressed the need to achieve economy 'in the manner least irksome to the labouring classes':

looking back to the useful and valuable exertions of the people of the yards, particularly of the shipwrights and artificers during the war, it is due to them, after feeling so lately the importance of their services in a time of need, that their interests should not be lightly regarded the moment after the emergency is passed.[79]

Nevertheless the post-war years were difficult for most communities of government workers and there were repeated references to indigence. High prices coincided with the first years of peace and the Commissioners of Naval Revision had recommended a reduction of wage rates in peacetime, and even reductions of winter rates upon those of summer months. The Navy and Victualling Boards were sympathetic. The latter opposed the introduction of lower winter wages in the victualling yards in December 1816; while the former consistently forwarded to the Admiralty petitions from yard artificers describing their distress.[80]

However, Admiralty policy was to deliberately decline to assume responsibility for the welfare of artificers outside the yards. Because the families of seamen and marines often followed the men to the ports where they became 'burdens' on those parishes, the Admiralty did make occasional payments to the enlargement or rebuilding costs of poor houses, for example at Plymouth and Sheerness.[81] But otherwise it abided by a policy of not contributing to the poor rates of parishes in which their establishments lay, except for the houses of their yard officers.[82] In 1817 parish officials at Plymouth attempted to have the officers of naval establishments take parish apprentices, and took their appeal to the Devon Quarter Sessions. The Attorney and Solicitor General was forced to acknowledge that officers in naval establishments were liable to take apprentices, but, rather than submit to the inconvenience, recommended them to submit to a ten pound penalty imposed by an Act of 1698 for failing to take them.[83] The following month, however, owing to the poverty of artificers in 1817, the Admiralty Board agreed to give orphans priority over the sons of yard employees and naval officers in regulations governing the admission of yard apprentices.[84]

A major concern of parish officials in 1818 was the lack of employment opportunity available in naval towns compared to that which they had enjoyed during the war.[85] The concern contributed to an allegation that the morality of artificers had declined with the reduction in their working hours. It was an allegation everywhere refuted.[86] Rather, witnesses testified to the sobriety and steady good conduct of government yard employees. Weekly payment, freedom from debt, self-respect and aspirations, made most employees models of pecuniary discretion. Many subscribed to friendly societies which, at Plymouth, from 1817, along with individual savers, deposited subscriptions in a dockyard Provident Institution. This took £17,421 from 3724 deposits in 22 months, of which 2093 were less than five shillings. A pension society for widows, orphans and aged artificers was also founded there in 1819 which quickly had a thousand subscribers paying up to £25 weekly.[87] A dockyard pension society had also come into existence at Portsmouth by 1820.

These employees of government needed all their resources through the trade slumps of the 1820s. Reductions of the workforce in the royal dockyards increased in scale. By 1830, numbers had been reduced to 7220, and would be cut to 6000 by the Whig government.[88] But employment elsewhere was difficult owing to over-capacity in the post-war shipbuilding industry. Those who remained in employment were so vulnerable to discharge that militant action became unthinkable. Co-operation with the merchant yard shipwrights in their strike of 1825 was impossible; instead the Navy Board co-operated with the merchant builders to help break the strike.[89]

By 1830 the workforce of the government had been reduced to a state of relative impotence compared to the militancy it had revealed in the eighteenth century. Its conduct was prescribed by the ethic of public service which demanded reliability and responsibility, not to mention an element of gratitude for the consideration with which employees were treated; for, after all, they did enjoy regular weekly payment as well as provisions for injury and old age. Consequently, in contrast to the increasingly radical language and union activity of working men elsewhere in the country, artificers and labourers in government service were obliged more to acknowledge the advantages in their terms of employment than to demand further improvements.[90] Yet it was an attitude that left them vulnerable to even more ruthless government policies. When the Whigs came to power in 1830, the dockyard workforce was unable to resist experimental work doctrines like that of shoaling (that is, classification by ability) or prevent the abolition of the costly system of superannuation for artificers.[91] Subjected and subdued, the workforce in the civil departments of the Navy had been both inculcated with a pacifying doctrine and reduced to the role of an emasculated factor of production.

Notes

1. R. A. Morriss, *The Royal Dockyards during the Revolutionary and Napoleonic Wars* (Leicester, Leicester University Press, 1983), pp. 4–5.
2. H. Richardson, 'Wages of shipwrights in HM dockyards, 1496–1788', *Mariner's Mirror*, **33** (1947), 265–74.

3. For instances of officers holding agency business, see J. S. Bromley, 'Prize Office and Prize Agency at Portsmouth 1689–1748', in J. Webb, N. Yates and S. Peacock (eds), *Hampshire Studies* (Portsmouth, Portsmouth City Records Office, 1981), p. 185. For all forms of perquisites taken in the dockyards, see the *6th Report of the Commissioners appointed to inquire into Fees, Gratuities, Perquisites and Emoluments which are, or have been lately, received in the several public offices*, 1786–8, Commons Reports, 1806(309), VIII.
4. For an apprentice who rose by moving from yard to yard see the career of George Boddy, Public Record Office, ADM 1/4379, 11 Feb. 1805.
5. For discussion by one contemplating paying his predecessor to leave office, see M. E. Matcham (ed.), *A Forgotten John Russell: Being the Letters to a Man of Business, 1724–1751* (London, Edward Arnold, 1905), p. 269.
6. Work in a dockyard could be tedious especially for copy clerks. But a dockyard worker's own view of his employment is a rare survival. For one of these rare records, see J. Field, 'The diary of a Portsmouth dockyard worker', *Portsmouth Archives Review*, (1978), 40–66.
7. National Maritime Museum ADM BP/50C, enclosure in 12 June 1830.
8. For tenure in the ordnance yards at the beginning of the 18th century see H. Tomlinson, *Guns and Government: The Ordnance Office under the Later Stuarts* (London, Royal Historical Society, 1979), p. 81.
9. A list of the 'incapable men' discharged from the six main dockyards in 1802 is given in *Further Papers presented to the House of Commons respecting Ships of War, Timber, Visitation of the Dockyards etc.* Accounts and papers presented to the House of Commons, 1805 (193), VIII.
10. NMM ADM BP/45, 27 May 1825.
11. PRO ADM 106/1917, 30 Oct. 1803; ADM 106/223, 1 Nov. 1803.
12. PRO ADM 106/2237, 28 Sep. 1805.
13. See the sacrament certificates for 1683 and 1745 in NMM MS82/163.
14. NMM ADM BP/20B, 15 July 1800.
15. P. L. Parker (ed.), *John Wesley's Journal* (Pitman, London, 1902), 150–462.
16. E. P. Thompson, *The Making of the English Working Class* (Pelican Books, Harmondsworth, 1968), p. 48n.
17. NMM ADM B/190, 5 July 1775.
18. G. S. Veitch, *The Genesis of Parliamentary Reform* (1913, reprinted 1965), p. 272.
19. PRO ADM 106/1844, 14 Oct. 1801; ADM 106/2228, 15 Oct. 1801.
20. NMM ADM BP/38B, 23 Sep. 1818.
21. PRO ADM 106/3576, 18 Nov. 1820.
22. NMM PLL/6M, 6 Mar. 1842.
23. The Victualling Board do not appear to have been influenced by considerations of electoral and political expediency in 1701–13; see P. K. Watson, 'The Commission for victualling the Navy, the commission for sick and wounded seamen and prisoners of war, and the commission for transports, 1702–14', unpublished University of London PhD thesis, 1965,

pp. 110–11. But the *Gentleman's Magazine* alleged in 1742 that the distribution of frigate-building contracts 'were jobb'd away to the several ports where votes and interests were not wanting'; see No. 846, 11 September 1742, quoted in M. Acerra, J. Merino and J. Meyer (eds), *Les Marines de guerre européennes, XVII–XVIII siècles* (Presses de l'Université de Paris-Sorbonne, Paris, 1986), p. 40.

24. For example, in 1755 the former Navy Board and Admiralty Commissioner, John Phillipson, was able to influence a shipyard owner at Harwich by having a 20-gun ship contract awarded to his yard; at the same time he ordered 'Mr Slade the builder [Master Shipwright] at Deptford, not to suffer young Pulham to be promoted in the Yard, unless his father will ask it as a favour of Mr Phillipson'. See L. Namier, *The Structure of Politics at the Accession of George III* (London, Macmillan, 1965), p. 366.
25. Bromley, 'Prize Office and Prize Agency', pp. 169–99; Watson, 'The commission for victualling the Navy', p. 385.
26. B. Kemp, *King and Commons, 1660–1832* (London, Macmillan, 1957), pp. 51–7, 92–5.
27. See Namier, *The Structure of Politics at the Accession of George III*, p. 141; and N. A. M. Rodger, *The Wooden World: An Anatomy of the Georgian Navy* (London, Collins, 1986), p. 329.
28. J. Steven Watson, *The Reign of George III, 1760–1815* (Oxford, Oxford University Press, 1960), pp. 246–6.
29. See for example NMM ADM BP/37A, 10 Mar. 1817.
30. Matcham, *A Forgotten John Russell*, p. 305.
31. Namier, *The Structure of Politics at the Accession of George III*, p. 115.
32. L. Namier and J. Brooke, *The History of Parliament: The House of Commons 1754–1790* (3 vols, London, HMSO, 1964), vol. I, pp. 258, 297–9, 313–5.
33. The Chatham Election Petition, PP 1835 IX (215), pp. iii–xii.
34. Minutes of evidence taken before the Select Committee on the Plymouth Election Petition, PP 1852–3 XVIII (751), pp. 1–91, 258–65.
35. Chatham Election Petition, PP 1853 LXXXIII (255), p. 449.
36. For a mid-eighteenth-century example of intimidation of artificers at Woolwich, see Rodger, *The Wooden World*, p. 330. In 1820 Sir George Cockburn, second naval lord at the Admiralty, was exasperated by the son of the secretary to the Navy Board canvassing or voting in opposition to a government candidate. In a letter of 2 February to the Admiralty Secretary, J. W. Croker, he maintained that Nelson had to be informed 'that allowing his son to go to Callington, after being informed that it is *offensive to the Government*, will be considered as an equivalent to a declaration from him of his desire to retire from his high and confidential situation at the Navy Office'. Nelson had been a clerk in the Navy Office since 1779, and secretary to the board since 1796. He died in post in September 1820, eight months after this declaration. University of Michigan, W. L. Clements Library, Croker Papers, f. 229.

37. Morriss, *The Royal Dockyards*, p. 107.
38. PRO ADM 106/2979, Description book of artificers, Plymouth yard.
39. W. Shrubsole, *A Plea in Favour of the Shipwrights belonging to the Royal Dock Yards* (Rochester, 1770).
40. NMM ADM BP/3, 15 Oct. 1782.
41. Acts of Parliament existed against artificers going abroad. These were those of 5 Geo. I, c. 27 (1718) and 23 Geo. II, c. 13 (1750). See D. Bonner Smith (ed.), *The Letters of Lord St Vincent, 1801–4* (Navy Records Society, 2 vols, 1921, 1926), vol. II, p. 175.
42. PRO ADM 106/3244, 12 June 1801.
43. NMM Middleton Papers, MID/8/6/3, paper watermarked 1794.
44. I. R. Christie, *Stress and Stability in Late-eighteenth Century Britain* (Oxford, Oxford University Press, 1984), pp. 144–5.
45. I am grateful to Dr R. J. B. Knight for this information.
46. NMM ADM BP/10, 16 June 1790.
47. See the Commissioner's report, PRO ADM 106/1844, 13 April 1801.
48. See the essays by Tony Barrow, N. A. M. Rodger and Norman McCord in T. Barrow (ed.), *Pressgangs and Privateers* (Whitely Bay, Tyne and Wear, Bewick Press, 1993).
49. PRO ADM 174/117, 19 Apr. 1782.
50. PRO ADM 106/5126, 20 Jan. 1800.
51. NMM ADM BP/47C, 20 July 1827.
52. For the fate of an informant see PRO ADM 106/3575, 6 Mar. to 30 Nov. 1792.
53. For resistance to attempts to abolish chips see NMM, ADM B/153, 18 June 1756; and B/155, 29, 30 April, 1 May 1757. For maintenance of the practice of horsing see PRO ADM 106/2513, 20 May 1801.
54. Sir J. Knox Laughton (ed.), *The Letters and Papers of Charles, Lord Barham, 1758–1813* (3 vols, NRS, 1907–11), vol. II, p. 219.
55. PRO ADM 1/5122/3, evidence of 9 Dec. 1802.
56. See L. Colley, *Britons: Forging the Nation, 1707–1837* (New Haven, Connecticut, Yale University Press, 1992), p. 188.
57. J. C. D. Clark, *English Society 1688–1832* (Cambridge, Cambridge University Press, 1985), p. 115.
58. NMM MID/8/6–11.
59. Rodger, *The Wooden World*, p. 314; R. J. B. Knight, 'Sandwich, Middleton and dockyard appointments', *Mariner's Mirror*, **57** (1971), 175–192; N. A. M. Rodger, *The Insatiable Earl: A Life of John Montagu, 4th Earl of Sandwich* (London, Collins, 1996), p. 166.
60. J. M. Haas, 'The introduction of task work in the Royal naval dockyards, 1775', *Historical Journal*, **13** (1970), 191–215. See also R. Morriss, 'Industrial relations at Plymouth Dockyard, 1770–1820', in M. Duffy, S. Fisher, B. Greenhill, D. J. Starkey and J. Youings (eds), *The New Maritime History of Devon* (2 vols, 1992, 1994), vol. I, pp. 216–23.

61. *6th Report of the Commissioners appointed to inquire into Irregularities, Frauds and Abuses practised in the Naval Departments*, 1803–4 (83), vol. III, pp. 20–36.
62. Ibid., pp. 65–114.
63. R. A. Morriss, 'Labour relations in the Royal Dockyards, 1801–1805', *Mariner's Mirror*, **6** (1976), 337–46.
64. *Memoir of the Life of William Marsden* (London, J. L. Cox, 1838), pp. 102–3.
65. See R. J. B. Knight, 'Pilfering and theft from the dockyards at the time of the American War of Independence', *Mariner's Mirror*, **61** (1975), 215–25.
66. PRO ADM 106/2516, 27 Aug. 1805; Adm. 106/2237, 19 Sep. 1805.
67. NMM ADM BP/33A, 25 Mar. 1813.
68. For the process by which this new rate was arrived at see R. A. Morriss, *The Royal Dockyards during the Revolutionary and Napoleonic Wars* (Leicester, Leicester University Press, 1983), p. 102.
69. NMM, *Orders in Council and some of the Acts of Parliament for the Regulation of the Naval Service* (London, Eyre and Spottiswood, 1856, p. 608).
70. J. Torrance, 'Social class and bureaucratic innovation: the commissioners for examining the public accounts, 1780–87', *Past and Present*, **78** (1978), 56–81.
71. NMM ADM BP/33C, 21 July 1813; see enclosure relating to an Act passed two sessions previously for granting superannuation to civil servants.
72. See R. A. Morriss, 'Labour relations in the Royal Dockyards, 1801–1805', *Mariner's Mirror*, **62** (1976), 343.
73. For example, shipwrights, smiths and sailmakers at Plymouth in 1804 were all concerned about the length of their hours or stint.
74. Parliamentary Papers 1805 (193), VIII, 509.
75. NMM ADM B/214, 7 Apr. 1804.
76. See, for example, the Admiralty response to the victualling yards' biscuit bakers, NMM ADM DP/34A, 3 Jan. 1814.
77. See, for example, the Comptroller's arguments in 1821 against reducing the number of shipwrights and reducing Saturday work instead: NMM ADM BP/41A, 22 Jan. 1821; and 41B, 18 Oct. 1821.
78. See the thanks of the Plymouth artificers for their continued employment, ADM BP/36A, 14 Mar. 1816.
79. NMM ADM BP/41B, 18 Oct. 1821.
80. NMM ADM DP/36B, 12 Dec. 1816; ADM BP/44B, 10 Dec. 1824; ADM BP/30E, 18 Dec. 1830.
81. For the case of the poor house in East Stonehouse, Devon, see PRO ADM 1/5121/8, 27 Aug. 1802; and for that at Sheerness, see NMM ADM BP/39B, 15 Nov. 1819; ADM BP/42B, 2 Sep. 1822; ADM BP/51C, 8 June 1831.
82. NMM ADM DP/13, 7 Oct. 1793.
83. The Act was that of 8 & 9 W.III, ch. 3, sect. 5. NMM ADM BP/37A, 11 Oct. 1817; ADM BP/37B, 9 Dec. 1817.
84. NMM ADM BP/37B, 22 Nov. 1817.

85. See the memorial of the overseers and churchwardens of the parish of Portsea, PRO ADM 106/3576, 20 Aug. 1818.
86. NMM ADM BP/38B, 19 Oct., 3 Dec. 1818.
87. Commissioner Shield to Lord Melville, 24 Aug. 1819–22, June 1820, Exeter Record Office, GD51/2/987–92.
88. See A. D. Lambert, *The Last Sailing Battlefleet: Maintaining Naval Mastery 1815–1850* (London, Conway Maritime Press, 1991), p. 168; also his 'Preparing for the long peace: the reconstruction of the Royal Navy 1815–1830', *Mariner's Mirror,* **82** (1996), 41–54.
89. I. Prothero, *Artisans and Politics in Early Nineteenth Century London: John Gast and His Times* (London, Methuen, 1979), p. 170; Sir Thomas Byam Martin to Lord Melville, 5–9 Oct. 1825, Scottish Record Office, GD51/2/1012/1–5.
90. Prothero, *Artisans and Politics*, pp. 232, 333; J. Rule, *The Labouring Classes in Early Industrial England, 1750–1850* (Harlow, Essex, Longman, 1986), pp. 288–307.
91. J. M. Haas, *A Management Odyssey: The Royal Dockyards, 1714–1914* (Lanham, Maryland, University Press of America, 1994), p. 73.

3

THE CHANGING NATURE OF THE DOCKYARD DISPUTE, 1790–1840

Philip MacDougall

During the period 1790 to 1840 the nature of industrial disputes within the Royal Dockyards underwent fundamental change. Whereas the eighteenth century had witnessed the increasing use of strikes, this trend had become completely blunted by about the first decade of the new century. Instead, those who found employment within the yards turned their full attention to an alternative method of achieving their objectives, that of the petition. In general terms, this would appear to be a surprising development for two distinct reasons. First and foremost, the use of the strike weapon, while by no means frequently used, had become associated with a number of clear successes. Secondly, repudiation of the strike weapon went completely against developments then taking place outside of the yards. During the 1820s and early 1830s, whereas dockyard workers frequently submitted petitions and gave no thought to the organization of strikes, numerous other groups of workers increasingly resorted to them.[1] This chapter, in examining the reasons why dockyard workers rejected the use of the strike during this period, also provides an account of the use of the petition during the same period. In particular, it shows how this tool of the industrial dispute developed from that of an inert and passive means of signalling discontent into that of a more forceful weapon that could bring pressure to bear upon the Admiralty.

Contributing to the introduction of these changes within the dockyards during this period was the complex level of organization that existed among those who made up the workforce. At a very basic level, this carefully created organizational structure provided effective links between those who shared the same trade and who were employed within the same yard. In addition, these links crossed the boundaries of the dockyard wall, allowing the different trade groups in one yard to contact and work with each other. Finally, and most importantly, these ties crossed the boundaries of status, bringing together the 30 or more occupational groups employed within each of the yards. If need be, the high status shipwright in one yard could, and did, make contact with the more lowly positioned labourer working in another yard. Such links, however, had taken a good many decades to create, honed to perfection during the final years of the eighteenth century.

Although it is impossible to accurately indicate from where and when such a structure originated, it can certainly be seen in a nascent stage at Chatham during the summer of 1675 when those employed in the ropery stood out against the introduction of new work methods.[2] Evidence exists that attempts were made to draw the ropeyard workers of Woolwich into the dispute. In July 1675 it was recorded that a certain William Rand had been desired by 'the whole company of Ropemakers in His Majesty's service at Chatham to enquire if His Majesty's Ropeyard at Woolwich performed ye tasks wch was here required'.[3] However, by the time William Rand returned, the strike was over and the Chatham ropemakers had gone back to work, having been repeatedly threatened with the likelihood of dismissal. Given that the dispute at Chatham extended over a period of eight weeks, it seems clear that the Woolwich ropemakers might more usefully have been involved at a much earlier stage. That they were not suggests that intra-trade activities of this nature were yet to become part of the overall strategy used in such situations. This was something to emerge in later years: those employed within the Royal Dockyards gradually realizing the advantage of keeping their fellow workers fully informed of their feelings and attitudes towards their employer, the Navy Board and the Admiralty.

Failure to achieve more than a basic level of inter-trade solidarity was a feature of a series of dockyard disputes which occurred between 1739 and 1745.[4] In a wartime period, the greater demands consequently placed upon artisans inevitably created a situation in which grievances were more likely to be resolved in favour of the workforce. It was a situation with which all those employed in the yards would have been aware.[5] As a result, a number of strikes, and threatened strikes, occurred within a relatively short time-span. The first of these occurred at Chatham in August 1739, only two months after the declaration of war. At that time, fines were imposed upon five shipwrights, the Master Shipwright having concluded that insufficient work had been performed upon the 64-gun *Nassau*, then undergoing a rebuild.[6] On 29 August over 600 shipwrights refused to enter the yard, resulting in the Navy Board taking immediate steps to attend to this particular grievance. While the early morning bell tolled on

31 August, a delegation from the Board presented itself outside the yard's main gate, informing the men that the fines were to be rescinded. The result was an immediate return to work.[7] Throughout the rest of that morning, so it can be surmised, the shipwrights at Chatham were engaged in a series of informal meetings during which it was decided that the time was right to present a few additional demands. These included fairer distribution of overtime, the automatic employment of apprentices once they had completed their apprenticeships and payment for time lost during the recent strike. That afternoon, following the break for lunch, 'they made a full stop at the gate of the yard, and not a man of them would come to work until they had been further redressed'.[8] Given the urgency with which ships were required to be at sea, the delegation from the Navy Board once again proved compliant. All of these demands were acceded to, other than payment for time lost during the strike.[9]

As with the earlier dispute in the Chatham ropeyard, a single trade group had shown considerable solidarity in an effort to obtain redress of irritating grievances. Given that the Chatham shipwrights' strike had so quickly erupted and was then settled in less than three days, it is impossible to examine sympathies at an inter-yard level. As for other trade groups employed at Chatham, they chose to give no support whatsoever. Apparently, if the words of Thomas Matthews, the resident Commissioner at Chatham, are to be believed, it appears that the shipwrights directly approached at least one other group, the ropemakers, but they 'would not be stopped by them and are at their duty'.[10] Other groups, following picketing of the main gate, refused to be persuaded that they should support the shipwrights, and entered the yard as normal.[11]

Despite their efforts to elicit support from other trade groups, the shipwrights were reluctant to extend their support to these same groups. During the latter part of 1739 both the caulkers and joiners at Chatham expressed grievances of a similar nature to those which had concerned the shipwrights. On neither occasion does it appear that these groups received an offer of support. Certainly there is no evidence of jointly supported activities.[12] Similarly, in 1745, when the Chatham ropemakers struck, they received no support from the shipwrights. Finally, the shipwrights at Chatham even refused to extend any support to their co-workers at Woolwich when asked to support a strike at that yard in September 1739.[13] The failure of the work force at Chatham to co-operate over the issue of fines was in marked contrast to events that occurred less than four years later at Portsmouth. On that occasion it was the shipwrights who were the main organizers of a strike that also involved opposition to employer-imposed fines.[14] This time the 'mulcts' were not merely restricted to one class of worker, but were levied against any artisan or labourer absenting himself from a day's work. Absenteeism appears to have been a particular problem at Portsmouth, a large proportion of workers having been recently recruited and yet to be disciplined into the desired work ethic.[15] At its height, the strike was supported by approximately two-thirds of the yard workforce, these drawn from all skills and trades. Despite this level of support, the strike did not meet with success, the majority of workers having returned to the yard within a period of two weeks.

That many of the strikes during this period were organized by shipwrights and ropemakers is a direct reflection of the numerical superiority of these two trades. Without doubt, the shipwrights were the single largest trade group, representing about 40 per cent of the total employed in each of the yards. Other groups fell far behind this figure. Indeed, the ropemakers, the second largest group, though only employed in the ropeyards attached to Chatham, Plymouth, Portsmouth and Woolwich dockyards, represented less than 10 per cent of the workforce in each of these yards. Occasionally other groups, such as the caulkers (5 per cent of the total dockyard workforce), joiners (4 per cent) and house-carpenters (3 per cent) might also threaten a strike. That they worked from such an inferior numerical basis meant they could never hope to emulate the success of the two largest trade groups. For this reason, it was substantially more important that they should seek to form links with other artisan groups. This they eventually achieved towards the end of the eighteenth century.

Evidence that shipwrights, for their part, could co-operate on an inter-yard basis comes with an extensive series of strikes that coincided with the outbreak of the American Revolutionary War.[16] The urgent mobilization of warships, which greatly strengthened their negotiating hand, led the shipwrights at Portsmouth Dockyard to strike over the issue of payment by piece rates, known in the Royal Dockyards as task work. Unable to persuade the Board to allow a return to payment by the day, the Portsmouth shipwrights chose to strike on 14 June 1775. At that time, they declared they would not return to work until 'task work was abolished'. Whether the shipwright of the various yards had discussed the possibility of a strike cannot be verified. However, a number of messengers were sent out from Portsmouth, with the majority of shipwrights at

Plymouth, Woolwich and Chatham also coming out on strike. Although the Navy Board retaliated, dismissing a small number of those they considered to be leaders, the strike held firm for a number of weeks, before achieving the desired concession.[17]

In tracing the development of inter-trade and inter-yard links, it has already been indicated that events played out towards the end of the eighteenth century were of some significance. Indeed, it was during the 1790s in particular, that those employed in the dockyards showed a willingness to break down the barrier of status, the main obstacle which still held them apart. That this should occur in the 1790s would appear to be related to two quite independent factors acting in unison. First and foremost were those issues of importance to the dockyard worker. Most of the disputes which had taken place during the seventeenth and earlier part of the eighteenth century were concerns that primarily affected one trade. Only when a dispute was clearly recognized as affecting all groups within the yards would the barriers that separated the workforce begin to tumble. Certainly, this had happened at Portsmouth in 1743, the shipwrights working comfortably with a high proportion of all other artisans. However, this particular show of unity failed to serve as a model for future disputes taking place over the next few decades. At Portsmouth, and other yards, the workforce returned to single-group issues and either failed to gain wider support or considered such support to be unnecessary. Only as a result of a unique blend of pressures, which came to fruition during the 1790s, did the dockyard worker finally destroy the barriers which prevented full inter-trade and inter-yard co-operation on a more permanent basis.

The epicentre of the blend of issues which helped to create the highest degree of unison was that of wages. Although frequently an issue that might excite the interest of employees, it was not something which normally brought differing trade groups together. With wage levels most frequently negotiated independently, one group of workers rarely saw it as an advantage to support the claims of another. Within the yards this was not the case. Instead, wages were carefully fixed on the basis of a formula that took into account the status and value of each trade. Any change in the remuneration received by one group stood the risk of upsetting the relevant position of each and every worker. Those within the various dockyard trade groups, aware of this situation, came to realize that, of necessity, a campaign for the improvement of wages would have to involve every group making their demands in a unified fashion and at the same time.

Following the general establishment of dockyard wage levels in the late seventeenth century, the desire for an upward improvement in wages only took place during periods of extreme crisis. Throughout much of the eighteenth century, general price levels were relatively static, only witnessing a series of dramatic short-term increases during periods of war. For the dockyard worker, such a situation rarely led to panic demands. Instead, any loss in purchasing power was strictly cushioned by a simultaneous increase in overtime payments and brought about as a result of that same war. However, an unprecedented and massive increase in food prices that took place during the final decade of the eighteenth century completely altered this state of affairs. According to estimates made by Rufus S. Tucker, the rise in food prices increased by some 90 per cent between the beginning and end of the decade.[18] Although the yard worker, as in most wartime emergencies, was in receipt of plentiful overtime, as well as wages further enhanced by a general acceptance of piece-rate earnings, the amount actually received was still insufficient for meeting this sudden increase in the cost of living. To alleviate this situation, it was necessary for each trade group to place the necessity of a higher workplace remuneration at the top of any individual set agenda. Furthermore, given that any settlement would be structured and differentiated, it made no sense for one trade group to work independently of another.

A second factor serving to coalesce the various trade groups within the six naval dockyards was external to the workplace. Evidence exists that many yard workers were becoming increasingly politicized, influenced by the radical ideas associated both with the French Revolution and home grown working-class organizations. Most certainly, the last decade of the eighteenth century saw branches of the radical London Corresponding Society formed in areas which housed a large number of naval dockyard workers.[19] Even at its best however, political activism among those employed within the dockyards would have been restricted to a small minority. The relatively small membership of the London Corresponding Society in these areas, even if they were composed only of yard workers, suggests no alternative conclusion.

In addition to those who had joined radical societies was the much larger number of workers who showed themselves, at least in Chatham, to be opposed to increasingly repressive government legislation. This legislation, which had its origins in ruling-class fears that events then occurring in France might transfer across the Channel, included both the Seditious Meetings Act and the Treasonable Practices Act. Both passed by

Parliament in 1795, these Acts forbade public meetings of 50 or more persons (unless a magistrates' licence had been granted) and extended the laws of treason to include both the written and spoken word. Known as the 'Two Acts', they were also seen as attempts at undermining the freedom of industrial employees to assemble and express a point of view contrary to that of their employers. In addition, however, this same decade of the eighteenth century saw the suspension of *habeas corpus* (1794), extension of magistrates' powers against newspapers deemed to be either blasphemous or seditious (1796–7) and reaffirmation of earlier legislation against combinations of workers (1799 and 1800).

It was opposition to the 'Two Acts' that first galvanized the workers of Chatham Dockyard into acting as a single unified group irrespective of their individual skills, status and wage level. These acts were apparently of greater concern to the dockyard worker than any of the earlier Combination Acts. In part, this was because the Combination Acts had long been in force and had, up to that point, never been used in any form to blunt the activities of those employed in the dockyards. The 'Two Acts' were seemingly very different. According to one hand-bill posted close to the dockyard, the new legislation was said to,

> completely deprive the People of the Liberty of speech, of writing, printing, preaching, or assembly in any respect whatever to obtain redress of Grievances however arbitrary or oppressive without the presence of a magistrate.[20]

Furthermore, it may be that yard workers saw behind the Treasonable Practices Act something far more sinister. While they had never been threatened by the Combination Acts, it was possible that the new law might be used against their own workplace activists when either speaking or issuing notices that threatened the possibility of strike. In wartime, a strike within a naval dockyard could be deemed as treasonable, as could organizing it. Opposition at Chatham to new restrictive legislation, namely the 'Two Acts', resulted in all trade groups working together in an issue of joint concern. According to John Gale Jones of the London Corresponding Society, who visited Chatham during this period, the Commissioner of the dockyard mustered the entire workforce

> and desired them to sign their names to an address to his Majesty, congratulating him on his late happy escape, and praying him to pass the Bills. By a singular circumstance, however, the men unanimously declared

> they would not sign away their liberties, and, rushing out of the yard in a body, went to the place where a petition against the Convention Bills laid, and everyone instantly subscribed his name.[21]

Jones was, in fact, wrong in one particular point. The yard workers did not immediately rush 'out of the yard'. On that first day they did nothing but return to work. On the following day, however, instead of attending to their respective work stations, all proceeded peacefully to the ropeyard where they 'took possession of the lower spinning house'.[22] Here, so the Commissioner at Chatham later reported,

> The respective officers used their endeavours before and after Breakfast, to indulge them, in vain, to go to their respective works. As the weather was exceedingly bad, I desired Deputies might be sent to me, which they positively refused and therefore I went to them and made another speech.[23]

The Commissioner then went on to make the following comments:

> They heard me with apparent quietness, when their spokesman said, that they all had determined not to sign either part of the address; and should proceed quietly out of the yard at 12 o'clock and go immediately to sign the petition.[24]

It was at the precise time indicated by this spokesman that the mass of yard workers left the yard, walking in an orderly fashion to the Guildhall in Rochester where they duly signed the petition. None of them were to return to the dockyard that day, but having made their protest no further action was devised. On 19 November the Commissioner was able to report,

> Of the artificers, workmen &tc who went out yesterday in the afternoon, to sign the Rochester petition, there have been only sixteen of them absent without leave, which is not uncommon at other times.[25]

The opposition to the 'Two Acts' as witnessed at Chatham serves as the first real example of extensive inter-trade co-operation occurring within the naval dockyards. Having been forewarned that Proby was to assemble the workers for the purpose of signing a petition of loyalty, workplace activists had been given several days to organize the eventual show of opposition. At the very least, considerable discussion must have preceded the final decision to assemble in the rope yard and then march to Rochester in unison. Yet, in general, the barriers of status and geography still existed. Despite the problems caused by inflation during the first three years of the war, other issues were still to the fore. For the shipwrights, a demarcation dispute over work to be performed by dockyard house-carpenters resulted in a stoppage of work at all six dockyards during the summer of 1795.[26] Surprisingly, given the fact that the nation was at war and the yards themselves were overstretched, the shipwrights were not successful in achieving their wishes. In essence, they had failed to co-ordinate their campaign, the strike at each of the yards not occurring simultaneously. As a result, the Navy Board felt less threatened and able to ensure that important war work was always being undertaken at the majority of yards. Only if all six yards had ceased functioning, with the Navy unable to get any further ships to sea, would the Navy Board have felt forced to concede the issue.

The pressing needs of the combined workforce to receive an upward adjustment in their respective wage levels was the factor that finally prompted full inter-yard, inter-trade co-operation. Proving itself to be a watershed in dockyard labour relations, the wage dispute of 1801 was to have a long-lasting effect upon workforce attitudes and behaviour that was to remain until the end of the following century. Prompted by the dramatic rise in food prices, the demand for a wage increase by the end of the decade overshadowed all other single trade demands. To help ensure that these demands would meet with success, those in the yards entered into a period of unprecedented organizational activity. Apart from forming a central committee, each of the yards also possessed their own separate committees from which delegates to the central committee were elected. These local committees, composed of representatives from each trade group, demonstrate that a high degree of solidarity had emerged. The events at Chatham yard, when the entire workforce marched in opposition to the 'Two Acts', may well have been a factor in this final honing of the workforce organizational structure.

In a meeting with the commissioners of the Navy Board in London on 1 April 1801, delegates of the central committee were offered temporary additional payments for those members of the workforce who had families. Although accepted by the delegates, it appears to have been rejected by the great mass of yard workers. Although not known with certainty, it seems likely that each of the yards organized some form of ballot, with Plymouth and the four eastern yards favouring strike action. In mid-April, delegates once again met with members of the Navy Board, but time was running out. A number of factors were beginning to operate in favour of the Navy Board. First and foremost, the dockyards were operating under considerably less pressure. A fleet under preparation for the Baltic had sailed in March and much of the remaining work was routine. Furthermore, the Navy Board was being persuaded to take a much tougher line by the Earl of St Vincent who, since February 1801, had held office as First Lord. He was an inveterate opponent of wage increases and had little or no respect for those employed in the dockyards.[27] The outcome was that the Navy Board chose to make no further offer other than a promise to review wages. The delegates, therefore, returned empty-handed. Following this, St Vincent came to the fore, demanding of the Navy Board that they form a committee to tour the dockyards, dismissing all workers who had engaged in the recent dispute. The first of the yards to be visited was Plymouth, this yard, throughout, proving the most militant. Here the combined workforce had extended its interests well beyond the dockyard wall, uniting with the local populace in their efforts to control rocketing food prices. According to Wells, the Devonport/Plymouth area was 'on the verge of starvation', with market stallholders capitalizing upon the distress of others.[28] Members of the elected central committee were certainly involved in the negotiating of fixed prices, reaching agreement with a number of local bakers. However, this had only limited effect, with the aggrieved local populace resorting to more direct methods during the late spring of 1801. A series of arrests followed, with the yard workers on two separate occasions choosing to march out of the yard and forcing magistrates to release these prisoners. The subsequent dismissal of 103 artisans and labourers (representing 3.6 per cent of the entire dockyard workforce) by the visiting committee of the Navy Board destroyed the carefully nurtured organization. Furthermore, it had an influence upon the local township, with Devonport butchers soon openly declaring 'that they shall do what they like now that the Dockyard men are silenced'.[29]

Prior to these dismissals, thought had been given to using the newly passed Combination Acts as a form of additional punishment. At any other time, this would have been a most unusual move, for the Admiralty already had a range of controlling mechanisms that were more than equal to anything which use of the Acts might have produced. Akin to using a sledgehammer to crack a nut, it would have been the decision of St Vincent to make use of these Acts. He was, perhaps, the most confrontational of all those who held the post of First Lord believing most of his successors, as well as those at the Navy Board, to have been far too moderate when dealing with those employed in the yards.[30] However, in contacting the Attorney General and Solicitor General, the Admiralty was informed that as the only act so far detected, that of petitioning the Navy Office, was not a crime, then it could not be a crime 'for their delegates to present their petition'.[31] Instead, the Admiralty had to rest content upon the full use of that means by which it had controlled the workforce in the past, dismissal, with a total of 340 artisans and labourers, duly receiving notice.[32] Compared with all previous disputes, this was an extremely high number, representing 3.08 per cent of the entire workforce. Unlike the earlier disputes, when some of those dismissed were allowed to return to yard service upon appeal, none of these individuals was permitted such an indulgence. Although, if treated only superficially, this might appear to have been of less consequence than a full recourse to the might of the law, it is unlikely that those within the yards viewed it in such a way. Dismissal would have had no small impact, as it brought with it loss of a guaranteed livelihood together with forfeiture of the comparatively generous right to free medical care, superannuation upon retirement and the strong possibility of any male offspring being permitted to enter the yards as apprentices. Few, if any of these, could be found outside of the dockyards and the connected naval establishments. For their part, use of the Combination Acts by the Admiralty might have reinforced such threats, but would hardly have added anything to the fears that yard workers already had when facing the possibility of dismissal.

Having successfully reached a point where those employed in the Royal Dockyards had broken down the several barriers that separated them, the outcome was quite disastrous. Despite a worthwhile addition to workplace remuneration for those with families, they had lost virtually the entire leadership of the yard. It was a disaster that was bound to have a considerable influence upon the direction of any future dispute. Certainly, those who have given thought to the post-1801 period have recognized that a change had come about. Among them is Roger Morriss. In a valuable contribution to the history of the dockyards during the period of the French Revolutionary and Napoleonic Wards, Morriss writes:

> Reports of discontent, demands for changes in working conditions and strikes occur less frequently [after 1801]. This may be related to the expansion in the size of the work force during the Napoleonic Wars, the improvement in the frequency and the calculation of payments, and the continuity of work procedure resulting from the sustained and seemingly interminable demands placed on the dockyards ... From the artificers'

point of view, in terms of their pay and conditions, the dock-yards were more satisfactory places of employment by the end of the Napoleonic Wars than they had been 20 years earlier.[33]

However, he also adds one contradiction, stating, when referring to the period 1801 to 1815, that 'the artificers' repeated use of their bargaining power ensured that conditions of work in the yards did not on the whole deteriorate'.[34] This, most surely, conflicts (given that he offers no measurable yardstick) with his earlier statement that 'demands for changes in working conditions occur less frequently'. From such a viewpoint, an assumption has also arisen that much of the rest of the nineteenth century was also characterized by reduced workforce demands. Such continued lack of outward concern for any possible deterioration in general work conditions and wage levels is explained by the lengthy period of peace that followed upon conclusion of the Napoleonic Wars. Waters is one of those who would take us in this direction when she says of the dockyard worker, 'it is not surprising that the long period of peace 1815–1852 brought quiescence'.[35] However, in fairness to her, she does pursue an alternative viewpoint for the post-Crimean period, explaining this continued 'quiescence' as the result of a special pact, created between shipwright and Admiralty and established during the 1860s while the ironclad battleship *Achilles* was under construction at Chatham.[36]

As it happens, neither viewpoint is strictly correct, although Morriss's 'repeated use of their bargaining power' statement has considerable validity. Throughout the post-1801 period, the yard workers were just as concerned about their working conditions as they had been prior to 1801. The only difference was that they now had an understandable reluctance to strike. This reluctance might well have been overcome if it had not been for the existence of an alternative, albeit less forceful, mediating tool: the petition. Used throughout the eighteenth century, it not only lacked the impact of the strike, but relied entirely upon the goodwill of those who governed the yards. Its use however, was not without occasional success, although the time-scale from first submission of such a document, or series of documents, to any achieved success, was much greater than that where strike action was employed. On the other hand, those involved in organizing and submitting a petition, providing no threatening or abusive language was used, knew that there was little chance of dismissal. Members of both the Admiralty and Navy Boards even went so far as to encourage its use.[37] Not only did they see it as less disruptive, but it also kept power firmly in their hands. To this end therefore, the petition had to be suitably worded and presented in a deferential manner. Thus, Commissioner Hughes at Portsmouth, in October 1739, had no hesitation in giving his full support to a petition presented by the caulkers of that yard, believing that such support was deserved because they had applied for help without being 'riotous, tumultuous or mutinous'.[38] This was in sharp contrast to a petition submitted by the caulkers only a week earlier and rejected because it was accompanied by threats of leaving the yard service and which Hughes described as being 'very impertinent' and containing the height of insolence. Writing to the Navy Board on the matter, Hughes stated that 'if there appear'd any cause for complaint, and they had made proper application' then he would have given it consideration.[39] Whereas the strike, or threat of some similar form of action, was nothing less than a demand, the submissively presented petition was a formalized request couched in highly deferential language. This maintained the accepted relationship between employer and employee while giving time for a more considered answer.

A notable success in the use of the petition occurred at Chatham in 1775 over conditions under which shipwrights were employed by task. On the second Saturday, the several task work gangs failed to assemble for work in the afternoon. The gang members felt that as they had finished a complete task, the rest of the day should belong to them, to do with 'as they pleased'.[40] The Commissioners of the Navy Board were less than happy with what they considered to be absenteeism, and wished to seek out the ringleaders for dismissal.[41] They relented upon being subsequently informed that the men had absented themselves not in a spirit of 'mutiny' but in 'a mistaken notion that, as they had wrought hard throughout the week, they might be allowed to dispose of that half day'.[42] To this the Navy Board replied that those men so employed should, upon completion of any single task item, remain in the yard and continue as if paid by the day.[43] Late in April the shipwrights submitted a petition in which they requested the right to leave the yard early if a particular task had been completed. It was because the shipwrights had resorted to what the Navy Board considered to be the correct method of approach that members of the Board adopted a more sympathetic attitude. While choosing to further chastise the shipwrights for their previous misdemeanor they agreed to the basic request.[44]

Aware of this, and other petitioning successes, those employed in the yards during the post-1801 period must have given thought, reluctantly, to the single all-important advantage of using the petition in situations where strikes might previously have appeared more appropriate. Certainly a large number of petitions were presented during the remaining years of the wars with France. These were sometimes on matters of considerable urgency. Among such grievances, and ones that might well have led to strike action during earlier wartime periods, was the continued rise in the cost of living, which greatly undermined the value of the unaltered dockyard wage.[45] In addition, both Wilson and Morriss note a range of further issues, with the latter highlighting the abolition of an apprenticeship system that, prior to this change, had added £70 to the wages of certain deserving artisans (December 1802). Furthermore, Morriss notes the removal of lodging allowance (1812).[46]

However, before concentrating upon the use of petitions, reference should be made to the millwrights. Employed only at Portsmouth, they struck over the issue of working hours in September 1806. Traditionally, millwrights tended to work shorter hours and felt aggrieved at the additional hours they were expected to work while in dockyard service. That they were able to resort to strike action at a time when other groups appear to have abandoned this tactic was directly the result of their recent arrival in the yard. They would have been less concerned with future pension rights, and job security was of little significance. The millwrights, who were members of a trade group in short supply, would have had little difficulty in finding alternative employment in the event of dismissal. An additional factor was the existence of their own trade society outside the dockyard at Portsmouth, making them less susceptible to the general thinking which now dominated an increasingly insular dockyard population.[47] Indeed, the unique position held by the millwrights was one that clearly affected managerial thought. Consider, for instance, the comments of F. L. Maitland, Admiral Superintendent of Portsmouth Dockyard. Writing to his superiors at Somerset House on 9 November 1832 he indicated that a proposed plan to reduce the workforce should not apply to millwrights. If it did so, he pointed out that it would lead to the 'remainder quitting their employment.'[48] Once in receipt of these comments, the Board of Admiralty in London chose to reverse earlier dismissal instructions, indicating that the millwrights who were to have been dismissed should now be employed on alternative works. At the same time, the concern not to upset the millwrights failed to be applied to other groups, and large numbers of shipwrights, caulkers and other traditional dockyard trades were savagely reduced in order to meet the needs of the dockyard economy.

As indicated by the activities of the millwrights, the continued use of the strike weapon within the dockyards was more closely connected with those groups recently recruited into yard service. It is not surprising to learn that, in July 1862, the ironsmiths, specifically recruited into Chatham Dockyard for the purpose of constructing *Achilles*, the first iron-clad battleship to be built in a Royal Dockyard, attempted the first major strike for 60 years. As Waters ably demonstrates, this strike was crushed by the Admiralty, the ironsmiths locked out of Chatham Dockyard and their work taken over by previously redundant shipwrights.[49] In going one stage further, Waters indicates a belief that the failure of this strike was the turning-point in dockyard labour history. However, as already demonstrated, the trade groups with long-held dockyard connections had already gained adequate proof of how the Admiralty dealt with those who chose to strike.

Despite having determined that the petition was the only means by which future grievances should be brought to the attention of their employers, there was by no means an abandonment of the organizational structure that had become associated with the strike. This was because the extremely high level of organizational sophistication achieved during the eighteenth century was not entirely dependent on the strike. Whereas activities which *were* associated with this form of confrontation were organized on an ad hoc basis, there being no permanently organized combination or union, other structures were more permanent. Within the dockyards, as elsewhere in society, members of trades were brought together in a variety of ways. Most common, though least organized, was the public meeting-place provided by local alehouses. Although frequently to the fore in newspaper reports of events associated with major strikes, it would seem likely that hostelries served as central meeting-places for the construction of petitions or airing of grievances.[50]

A more permanent form of organization was that of the friendly society. Organized around 'the box', containing money collected from each member and reserved for times of hardship, these societies abounded in the dockyard towns. Normally they were restricted to serving the interests of a small group of artisans drawn from one trade.

The artisans and labourers of the dockyard also boasted one further organizational structure that ensured continuity of workplace collaboration. This was the food co-operative. The shipwrights of Deptford, Woolwich and Chatham combined together during the 1750s to form a retail society open to all those employed within these yards. It appears that a mill and bakery were opened at Chatham, a corn mill at Woolwich and a butcher's shop in Church Street, Deptford.[51]

The years immediately following the conclusion of hostilities with Napoleonic France witnessed a great upsurge in the number of petitions presented to the Navy Board. While a large number were rejected out of hand, a small number met with success. Of the petitions, the majority concentrated upon redressing grievances associated with the lurch towards retrenchment that the onset of peace now permitted. Most of them were from individuals, many having suffered dismissal, and requesting that they be allowed either pensions or an early re-entry into dockyard service. Despite the total workforce being pruned by 30 per cent, considerable thought was given to ensuring that this number was as small as possible. In particular, Sir Byam Martin, Comptroller of the Navy Board, wished to ensure that there be 'the least possible diminution of the several classes of Artificers, not only from a feeling of charity towards the men' but as a means of ensuring a sufficient reserve in the event of war.[52]

To offset government and Admiralty demands for an even greater number of dismissals, Martin contrived a series of economies that would drastically reduce expenditure. At the heart of this was a 20 per cent reduction in the wage received by all retained artisans and labourers. In addition, the number of hours permitted to be worked would be reduced, with the yards working five days a week rather than six. Finally, to ensure as many shipwrights as possible were retained, some 500 were re-designated house-carpenters and joiners, with a similar number of house-carpenters and joiners reduced either to the rank of labourer or dismissed from the yards. In an effort to achieve full co-operation, the commissioner of each yard was commanded to inform the men that these unprecedented changes were the only means to prevent further dismissals.[53]

For their part, shipwrights and other artisans were far from convinced as to the advantages of these seemingly draconian measures. Before long, the Navy Board was in receipt of a range of petitions from shipwrights and other artisans seeking restoration of the recent wage cuts and the extension of the working week to include Saturday, the day upon which the yards had formerly been open prior to the reduction to a five-day working week.[54]

The Commissioners of the Navy Board were undoubtedly aggrieved that plans which they considered to be in the best interests of the workforce were so decisively rejected. Of course, this was not the only issue, for the Navy Board itself considered that the scheme had the advantage of retaining a large number of skilled workers at a minimal wage level. For this reason, they might well have chosen to reject these petitions, aware that the workforce was not in possession of an alternative negotiating tool. The strike was now seen as worthless, for if it had failed at the turn of the century, it was certainly not likely to prove profitable during this time of peace, when a cessation of work in the yards would do nothing but provide employers with the economies that were actually sought. Yet, having been made aware of the desires of those they employed, the Navy Board did choose to listen. Recognizing a general unity of feeling within the yards, the Commissioners agreed to comply with workforce demands. In December 1823, as a result of one further petition, it was agreed that not only should the 20 per cent pay cut be restored, but that the yards should be opened for work on Saturdays. Yet this was no graceful capitulation. Without warning, and looking suspiciously like punishment, a number of artificers and labourers were immediately dismissed. In one respect, this could not have been a surprise. The Navy Board had made clear that the original reason for the economies had been to prevent such a measure, yet the immediacy of its implementation prevented any further discussion or the chance to negotiate a workable alternative. This seeming annoyance on the part of the Navy Board extended to the end of the following year when it responded in a similar vein to a series of further petitions. These emanated from those shipwrights demoted to the class of house-carpenter and joiner and who now sought restitution to their proper trade. Instead of rejecting the petition, the Navy Board used it as an opportunity of demonstrating their power, informing the resident commissioners at Plymouth, Chatham, Woolwich and Deptford that this class of worker, some 370 in number, were to be dismissed and a similar number of labourers employed in order to make up the numbers. It was further stated that 'their Lordships have excluded Portsmouth yard from this arrangement as no complaining petition has been submitted from that yard'.[55]

The timing and wording of these petitions show clearly that the dockyard workforce of the 1820s was as solid in cross-boundary support as it had been at the turn of the century. The only difference was that of continued resistance to the strike by those employed within the yards and their giving a lower profile to those at the forefront of the industrial campaign. Other facets of dockyard life also witnessed this continued drift towards unrestricted solidarity. In particular, new co-operative ventures had been recently initiated by the respective workers at Sheerness, Portsmouth and Plymouth.[56]

The comparatively rapid capitulation of the Navy Board and Admiralty over the all-important issue of reduced wages generally strengthened the belief in the value of petitioning. Conversely, however, although it had united large elements of the workforce, this relatively easily-won success had resulted in a campaign that had failed to move beyond the passive strategy of simply submitting a document and awaiting a managerial response. The problem of an important and urgent demand being continually met by a negative response had yet to be confronted. Merely to submit the same basic request, reworded, was no real answer. Instead, a method of petitioning with greater impact would need to be developed.

The emergence of a more dynamic means of petitioning resulted from the bitter workforce opposition to a new method of organization that was first put into operation in 1833. It emerged from a desire, on the part of James Graham, the newly appointed Whig First Lord, to bring about greater efficiency within the yards. A particular target was that of the continuing use of piece rates, encouraging workers to rush their work rather than concentrate on quality. However, simply to return to the earlier method of paying a day wage was no solution, for here there was no guarantee, without close supervision, of any work being undertaken. The solution adopted by Graham was that each worker employed within the yard should be placed in one of three different classes, these influencing the levels of wage payment. Entry into the highest, or first, class was only allowed to those artisans who had a proven record of enthusiasm and efficiency, while the third class was seen as a punishment class and designed for the lethargic. The majority of workers were allocated to the second class with the promise that they might, through efficiency, gain entry into the first class with its higher levels of remuneration.

It was on 1 August 1833 that the workmen of the yards were organized into classes. Despite high hopes for it, the scheme was not well received, and signs of discontent were first brought to the attention of the Admiralty in September of that same year. This was on the occasion of the Board's annual visit of inspection to Devonport. A petition, signed by most classes of artisans and labourers, was presented to the First Lord. Mustering the workmen and showing annoyance at their temerity in taking this course of action, he proceeded to lecture them on the merits of classification.[57]

A more concerted campaign did not begin until the spring of 1835. At that time a series of petitions was submitted by the mass of artisans and labourers employed at Portsmouth, Sheerness, Devonport and Woolwich. The petitions were fairly general, all of them listing a range of grievances that included both the general depression of wages (brought about by the loss of piece rates) and classification. As regards the latter, reference was made to its inherent unfairness, it being stated that those appointed to the second and third classes carried out identical work within the same period of time, but received a pay difference of approximately 12 per cent.[58] Both the timing of these petitions and the similarity of their content show that they were the result of considerable organization. Contact, either of a direct nature or through written communication, must have been made. Possibly, indeed, some sort of ad hoc committee might have been formed.

To comply with the procedure as laid down, the petitions produced at this time were submitted to the Board of Admiralty through the Captain-Superintendent of each yard. Members of the workforce, unless requested, were banned from making a direct approach to the Board. Thus, safely cushioned from the dockyards, members of the Board of Admiralty would be unable to gain any real impression of the feelings of those they employed. Despite this isolation, members of the Board did appear to show sympathy, requesting the Captain-Superintendent of Woolwich, through their secretary John Barrow, to inform the petitioners that their memorial had been laid before the Board and that 'My Lords are by no means insensible to the complaints that have been made by the artificers not only in Woolwich but in other dockyards'.[59]

Over the next few years, petitions from the yards continued to be rejected, resulting in thought being given to a more dynamic approach. In 1836, important allies were recruited into the campaign. These were the local communities that thrived within the shadows of the various dockyard walls. Following considerable inter-yard communication, public meetings were held in Chatham, Woolwich, Portsmouth and Devonport. Each was well attended, resulting in lengthy petitions being signed, either at the meeting or during the following week, by many thousands of local inhabitants. These petitions called upon the Admiralty to both abolish classification and enhance the amount paid in wages.

During the public meeting held at Chatham, one of those present chose to question the value of petitioning. He felt that little would be gained in continuing such an approach as it would only result in the Admiralty saying that classification 'should not be done away with, and no further notice would be taken of it'. However, most of those present do not appear to have been in agreement with this view, the *Rochester Gazette* reporting that this particular speaker was widely 'hissed'.[60]

The meeting at Portsmouth was held on 7 December. It was chaired by Dr William Cooper, Mayor of Portsmouth and the son of a former dockyard worker. He not only intimated his full support for the current campaign, but also read out a letter from the Borough MP, John Bonham-Carter, who stated that he 'should be devoted most cordially towards obtaining a full and fair enquiry into the system complained of, with a view to a correction of its evils.[61] Of the yard artisans called upon to explain the background to their grievances, Richard Hobbs is of particular interest. Cooper stated that he was 'one of the favoured first class', while the newspaper carrying this report indicated him to be 'somewhat advanced in years'. On both counts he appears to have been an unlikely supporter of the campaign. As one who gained from classification he might have been expected to have supported the scheme, while his proximity to superannuation might have led him to remain in the background, so preventing any possibility of his losing that future pension. However, given that Hobbs did support the campaign, then it can be taken as possible evidence that opposition to classification was fairly widespread among the workforce and not restricted only to those placed in the third class.

Despite the apparent optimism of many of those attending the public meetings, the petitions appear to have had little influence upon members of the Board of Admiralty. There was neither a resultant abolition of classification nor an increase in wages offered. But this failure did not undermine the faith of dockyard artisans and labourers in the value of the petition. Over the next three years petitions continued to be submitted to the Admiralty on a regular basis, some of them from artisan groups, while others carried signatures drawn from the wider community. In addition, increased involvement of local Members of Parliament is also discernible. Often in attendance at these meetings, they also accompanied delegations of workmen who had been given permission to express their views to the Board in their London offices.

That the campaign to abolish classification was to meet with eventual success was only partly due to the ongoing petitioning campaign. More important was increasing Admiralty awareness of the difficulties involved in both retaining and recruiting skilled artisans into the yards. The Admiralty, concerned to reverse this trend, took a more careful interest in the actual demands put forward by those employed. Having a great deal of faith in the value of classification, Lord Minto, First Lord since 1835, attempted to placate the workforce by abolishing the hated third class.

Those currently in this class would, upon its abolition in January 1841, be raised to the second class.

While it was not a complete victory for the workforce, it was a move in the right direction. In May 1840 a delegation that consisted of two shipwrights from each yard together with thirteen Members of Parliament, all of them drawn from dockyard towns, visited the Admiralty. Although a wide range of matters was discussed, including that of low wages, the system of classification was very much at the heart of the meeting. According to the *Rochester Gazette* the deputation strongly protested 'against its continuance'.[62] Undoubtedly the matter that must have concerned members of the Board was a statement made by one of the deputation from Portsmouth. He strongly urged the necessity of a definite answer,

> as he represented a body of six hundred excellent workmen as could be found; and added that he did not wish to hold out anything in the shape of a threat, but he would tell his Lordship that 70 of them, and he was amongst the number, had resolved – unless something satisfactory was done – to quit the service, and they could at once obtain employment in a foreign country at double the rate of wages they were now receiving.[63]

While they were given no definite promises, the delegation 'left the Admiralty with full expectation that something will be done for them.'[64]

It was at the beginning of September 1840 that the Admiralty finally announced an end to classification. For the men at Chatham, the news was given to a deputation of artisans who had waited upon visiting members of the Admiralty during the annual inspection of the yard:

> The deputation was most courteously received, and their Lordships stated, that with respect to classification, they should accede to the wishes of the workmen. As vacancies occurred in what is now the first class they would not be filled up, but those now receiving the pay would continue to do so.[65]

Although a limited victory, as it still left the dockyard worker without a pay increase, it did ensure that the petition would remain the chief weapon in any further dispute with the Admiralty. Once again, those employed within the dockyards had seen its careful application gain an apparent victory. Some might have been aware that it was the willingness of others to leave the service that had been the final factor in ensuring victory, but most would have been unaware of the importance of this single factor.

For the future therefore, strike action continued to be repudiated. Even during the period of mobilization brought about the Crimean War, when more militant activity to improve low wage levels would have carried fewer threats to long-term employment within the yards, the petition continued as the only means by which the vast majority of workers brought their grievances to the attention of the Board of Admiralty. This, if nothing else, shows how fundamental were the changes wrought during the period 1790 to 1840. Such a major period of mobilization, as seen at the time of the Crimean War, would certainly have resulted in strikes were it to have taken place during the previous century. Instead, the traditional dockyard trade craft workers and labourers were convinced that any strike action would prove futile, choosing to pursue their demands through the continuing use of petitions. At the centre of such a decision were the ruthless discharges of 1801 and the apparent success of the 'classification' campaign. The workforce was seemingly convinced that the petition, as carefully honed during that earlier campaign, was the most appropriate means of achieving success. That requests appearing in numerous petitions continued to be rejected was of little overall importance. The evidence was there: petitions could be successful. As for the alternative, that of strikes, there were few dockyard workers in the mid-nineteenth century who were prepared to risk their future livelihood by organizing such action. The simple oral tradition of the yards continued to remind those who might be tempted of how the Admiralty treated those it deemed to be leaders in a campaign involving strikes.

Notes

1. The collected petitions submitted to the Admiralty during the period 1820–35 are located in the Public Record Office. See ADM 1/5132–6. An overview of the increasing number of strikes during this period may be found in J. Rule, *British Trade Unionism, 1750–1850* (London, Longman, 1988), esp. pp. 15–19.
2. A full discussion of this dispute and its cause may be found in P. MacDougall, 'Refusing to do the stint: an early industrial dispute at Chatham Dockyard', *Bygone Kent*, **16**(1) (1995), 45–53.
3. PRO ADM 106/309, f. 177.
4. A good account of the disputes in this period, particularly of this which occurred in 1739, is to be found in McL. B. Raft, 'Labour relations in the Royal Dockyards in 1739', *Mariner's Mirror*, **47**(3) (1961), 281–91.
5. This appreciation of the need to select the right amount for a strike has also been noted by Rule when he states of the Royal Dockyard shipwrights that

they were more likely to strike when fleets were being fitted out (J. Rule, 'The formative years of British trade unions', in *British Trade Unionism 1750–1850*, p. 5).
6. Rule, *British Trade Unionism*. See also P. MacDougall, 'A Social History of Chatham Dockyard, 1770–1801' (M.Phil. thesis, Open University, 1983).
7. PRO ADM 106/2553, 31 Aug. 1739.
8. PRO ADM 106/2553, 31 Aug. 1739.
9. PRO ADM 106/2553, 31 Aug. 1739.
10. PRO ADM 106/907, 30 Aug. 1739.
11. PRO ADM 106/907, 30 Aug. 1739.
12. Raft, 'Labour relations'.
13. *Ibid*.
14. A. Coats, 'Government community and the determination of labour disputes at Portsmouth Dockyard in the 1740s', unpublished paper given at New Researchers Conference, National Maritime Museum, 1995.
15. According to Coats, support for this strike also came from 'fifty country fellows' who joined a demonstration at the main gate. She takes this as possible evidence that the workers most affected by the fines were artisans and labourers recently recruited from nearby rural areas. See also PRO ADM 106/975, 2 Jan. 1743.
16. These strikes are more fully discussed by Dr R. J. Knight in the preceding chapter. In addition see R. J. B. Knight, 'The Royal Dockyards in England at the Time of the American Revolutionary War' (PhD thesis, University of London, 1972); J. M. Haas, 'The introduction of task work in the Royal Dockyards 1775', *Journal of British Studies*, 8(2) (1969), 60; and MacDougall, 'A Social History', pp. 370–83.
17. During the period of the strike, the shipwrights, despite picketing of the yards, failed to elicit support from other trade groups. In part, this was because inter-trade links had still not been developed. Indeed, most at this time still saw a close working together as undesirable. In addition, other trade groups were actively in favour of piece rates, some having requested that the Navy Board place them on a scheme similar to that rejected by the shipwrights.
18. R. S. Tucker, 'Real wages of artisans in London, 1729–1935', in A. J. P. Taylor (ed.), *The Standard of Living in Britain in the Industrial Revolution* (London, Methuen, 1975), pp. 21–35.
19. P. MacDougall, 'The English Reign of Terror', in John Gale Jones, *Sketch of the Political Tour through Rochester, Chatham, Maidstone, Gravesend &tc.* (London, 1796; reprinted Rochester, Baggins Bookshop, 1997), pp. 4–7.
20. NMM CHA/L/32, 18 Nov. 1795.
21. Jones, *Sketch of the Political Tour through Rochester*, p. 81.
22. NMM CHA/L/32, 18 Nov. 1795.
23. NMM CHA/L/32, 18 Nov. 1795.
24. NMM CHA/L/32, 18 Nov. 1795.
25. NMM CHA/L/32, 19 Nov. 1795.

26. NMM CHA/E/48, Feb.–Mar. 1795; NMM BP/16a, Jan.–Apr. 1795; *Kentish Chronicle*, Mar.–Apr. 1795. See also MacDougall, 'A Social History', pp. 410–16.
27. D. Bonner Smith, *Letters of Admiral of the Fleet The Earl of St Vincent*, II (London, Navy Records Society, 1927). Smith provides considerable evidence of St Vincent's attitude towards those employed in the yards and his overwhelming desire to utilize the same methods of authority adopted by the navy in disciplining the lower deck.
28. R. Wells, 'The revolt of the south-west, 1800–1801: a study in English popular protest', *Social History*, **6** (1977), 713–44.
29. PRO HO 42/62, 7 May 1801. Re-quoted from Wells, 'The revolt', p. 735.
30. Wells, 'The revolt', pp. 170–4.
31. PRO HO 48/10, 4 April 1801.
32. NMM ADM BP 21a, May 1801.
33. R. A. Morriss, *The Royal Dockyards during the French Revolutionary and Napoleonic Wars* (Leicester, Leicester University Press, 1983), pp. 125–6.
34. *Ibid.*, p. 126.
35. M. Waters, 'Changes in the Chatham Dockyard workforce, 1860–90', *Mariner's Mirror*, **69**(1) (1983), 55.
36. *Ibid.*, 55–63, 165–73.
37. PRO ADM 106/910, 18 Oct. 1839. Here, Richard Hughes, resident commissioner of Portsmouth Dockyard, indicates the petition to be the means of 'proper application' when faced with a request for improved conditions for dockyard workers employed in the ordinary.
38. PRO ADM 106/910. Quoted in Coats, 'Government community', p. 4.
39. PRO ADM 106/910.
40. NMM CHA E/31, 9 Apr. 1775.
41. NMM CHA E/31, 9 Apr. 1775.
42. NMM CHA E/31, 11 Apr. 1775.
43. NMM CHA E/31, 4 Apr. 1775.
44. NMM CHA E/31, 5 May 1775.
45. E. W. Gilboy. 'The cost of living and real wages in eighteenth century England', in A. J. P. Taylor, *Standard of Living*, pp. 1–20.
46. Morriss, *The Royal Dockyards*, p. 105.
47. PRO ADM 106/1870, 8 Sep. 1806. See also the Goodrich journals held in the Science Museum.
48. NMM ADM 1/3386, 9, 10 Nov. 1832.
49. M. Waters, 'Social History of the Chatham Dockyard Workforce 1860–1906' (PhD thesis, University of Essex, 1979).
50. Among those associated with dockyard strikes were the Star Inn, Chatham (which came to the fore in 1795, *Kentish Chronicle*, 3 Apr. 1795, f. 4) and the Ship and Castle, Portsmouth (where strikers met in 1743 (see Coats, 'Government community', p. 17)).
51. C. R. Dobson, *Masters and Journeymen* (London, Croom Helm, 1980), p. 98.

52. Scottish Record Office GD 51/2/984/1, Feb. 1816. Proposals submitted by Sir T. Byam Martin to the First Lord of the Admiralty, the 2nd Lord Melville. Also PRO ADM 106/2272, 16 Jan. 1817.
53. PRO ADM 1/3462, 20 June 1822.
54. PRO ADM 1/3462, 20 June 1822. It is interesting to note that thought was given to closing the yards either on a Wednesday or Thursday, it being believed that as the men were paid at the end of the week, then they would be more profligate with their money if Saturday were a non-working day.
55. PRO ADM 3/206, 18 Dec. 1824.
56. PRO ADM 1/3375, 20 Mar. 1816; ADM 1/3379, 28, 31 Mar. 1830. A Co-operative flour mill was formed by the workers at Portsmouth in 1814 while at Plymouth the Union Dock Mill Society was created in 1817.
57. *United Services Gazette*, 28 Sep. 1833. See also P. MacDougall, 'A demand fulfilled', *Southern History*, **19** (1997), 118. This paper provides a detailed analysis of the 1833–41 dispute.
58. PRO ADM 1/5136, 1 Feb. 1835 onwards.
59. PRO ADM 1/5136, 1 Feb. 1835 (appended note).
60. *Rochester Gazette*, 13 Dec. 1836.
61. *Devonport Independent & Plymouth Gazette*, 17 Dec. 1836.
62. *Rochester Gazette*, 28 Apr. 1840.
63. *Rochester Gazette*, 28 Apr. 1840.
64. *Rochester Gazette*, 28 Apr. 1840.
65. *Rochester Gazette*, 15 Sep. 1840.

4 Class Rule: The Hegemonic Role of the Royal Dockyard Schools, 1840–1914

Neil Casey

The idea that a formal education system might be valuable in forging a hegemonic occupational culture amongst an industrial workforce did not gain wider currency in Britain until towards the end of the nineteenth century. Employers were not necessarily convinced of education's value in promoting economic growth and efficiency nor did they seem persuaded of its ability to establish their own moral and political legitimacy amongst workers. Education, such as it was, was confined to ostensibly practical matters until well into the second half of the nineteenth century, with the majority of employers showing a marked reluctance to risk temporal and financial investment in anything more than 'rule of thumb' instruction.[1]

The Dockyard Schools present an important exception to this pattern, not least because they acted as a precedent for some of the elements (such as the 11-plus and sandwich education) of what would gradually become Britain's state educational system. Introduced in the major Royal Naval Dockyards (Chatham, Sheerness, Portsmouth, Devonport and Pembroke) in the 1840s, the schools admitted dockyard apprentices on their entry to the yards and taught them for up to seven years. They also made their facilities available to both labourers and qualified craftsmen keen to improve their position. Their historical interest resides not simply in their provision of a technical and academic education but also because boys were being educated in the very institution to which, as qualified artisans, they would devote much if not all of their employable lives. Upon leaving school there was every chance that a young man could be taken into the dockyard establishment and thus guaranteed a job for life. In effect, a direct cultural and structural link was being forged between school and work.

This chapter will evaluate the role of the dockyard educational system within the wider dockyard network during the period from the schools' formation to 1914. In particular it will consider the thesis that the schools were one part of an Admiralty strategy which, by encouraging employees to culturally invest in the dockyards, aimed to secure social and industrial relations. Political divisions within the Admiralty ensured that this was not a universal goal but it will be seen that, over decades, an 'enlightened' group were persuaded of the managerial worth of the schools. Accordingly it was intended that the schools should supply fundamental work skills, reproduce class structures, and generate attitudes and values conducive to institutional peace. The chapter will discuss factors such as workforce attitudes to authority, the everyday organization and definition of work, and meanings attached to the nature of personal satisfaction, to see if they can be traced from their production in the schools to their cultural reproduction at work. By way of a conclusion it is the intention to briefly consider the intriguing question as to why this precocious attempt at control should have been promoted by such a circumspect body as the Admiralty in, what was for state agencies, the politically hostile climate of nineteenth-century *laissez-faire* Britain.

There had been a lobby within the Admiralty to improve the education of dockyard apprentices since at least the beginning of the nineteenth century when the 1805 Barham Commission advised that the 'standards' of apprentices were to be improved as a matter of necessity. For many years the authorities at Chatham Dockyard had autonomously organized evening instruction in the '3 Rs', whilst in 1811 the School of Naval Architecture at Portsmouth had been opened in order to groom an élite, effective group of officers (the term for managerial staff within the dockyard service was 'officer'; an indication of the naval influence exerted by the industrial dockyards' environment).[2] The School of Naval Architecture was shut down in 1832 by Sir James Graham's Admiralty Board on the grounds that education of apprentices was both unnecessary and profligate, but the issue did not lie dormant. In fact, the proponents of 'education for work' were to be successful in the 1840s when the Dockyard Schools were established throughout the dockyard network.

The initial motives of the schools' founders would appear to have been mixed. What is apparent and unsurprising is that each motive was ultimately rooted in the Admiralty's organizational goals. There certainly was a concern that skills should be improved and that educating apprentices would be instrumental in achieving this. Similarly, it was felt that by improving the education of all future officers it would raise the standards of the men upon whom 'the safety of the empire depends'.[3] A further stimulus was the gradual shift, under pressure, away from promotion by patronage towards a promotion system based on the fair measurement of individual ability. Such a move demanded that participants attained a prior level of academic competence.[4] Influential advocates in the Admiralty were aware too of the moral advantages of education. There was a belief in the need 'to secure to [the apprentices] the benefits both of a religious and a professional education',[5] and, as some other commentators have shown, underlying the bestowal of religious knowledge in the nineteenth century was the intention 'to produce a God-fearing, law-abiding and industrious workforce; sober, honest, literate citizens imbued with a sense of duty'.[6]

It was this combination of aims, then, which prompted the Admiralty's innovatory introduction of free, compulsory education for apprentices. From the beginning, education was on a sandwich basis with the time in school being divided between vocational subjects such as drawing and algebra, and more academic lessons like history and religious knowledge. Teachers were appointed from among the dockyard officers with obvious implications for the overlap between authority in school and work. Initially, only one teacher per school was employed so that the sheer weight of numbers (Devonport School had 230 pupils) decreed that teaching should be monitorial.[7] There were to be annual examinations, success in which allowed apprentices to ascend to the next class with 'superior' pupils eventually being 'creamed off' perhaps as draughtsmen or even with promotion to the ranks of the higher officers.

To pretend that the Dockyard Schools immediately operated as finely tuned instruments of ideological control would be far from the truth. Unsurprisingly they were beset by problems. The annual reports of the Schools' Inspector, the Revd H. Mosely, observed the Schools' unpopularity both with the apprentices and the teachers, who were often reluctant volunteers prone to becoming more reluctant once they had experienced the anarchy inherent in supervising over two hundred caged youths.[8] As a response to their unpopularity and inefficiency the Admiralty introduced a series of 'rational' reforms over the next fifteen years which, by 1860, would see the evolution of the essential system administered up until 1914.

The number of teachers per school was to be increased and their status was to be improved. Results here were clearly uneven, as in 1863 it was noted with some reproach that Mr Robert Rae, the Devonport schoolmaster, had only the rank of foreman (a middle-management post in the dockyard service) despite turning out 'very many clever and intelligent young men'.[9]

Discipline was tightened with the inception of a common scheme of rewards and punishments. Academic content was to be standardized and entrance requirements raised with the aid of an annual Civil Service examination which included spelling, grammar, composition, geography, mathematics and English.[10] This, as will become evident later, had a number of ramifications for the character of education within all of the dockyard towns.

The policy of selective advancement was streamlined. Apprentices spent their first three years receiving an elementary education before some were 'creamed off' for a technically more complicated curriculum designed to breed individuals for the 'inferior' officer positions. From this upper echelon a further minority would be skimmed off, destined eventually for the 'superior' managerial posts. From 1848 to 1853 this élite was trained in naval architecture at the Central Mathematical School at Portsmouth where they were also blessed with a 'spiritual and moral' education from the yard chaplain.[11] In 1853 the CMS was closed down, reflecting some division and uncertainty within the Admiralty about the value of state-sponsored schooling. However, the lacuna was filled in 1864 with the opening of the Royal School of Naval Architecture at Kensington (soon to move to Greenwich) which reaffirmed the Admiralty's desire for two tiers of schooling. The entire system was then put under the central control of the Admiralty who organized surveillance with a team of inspectors, a move which of course mirrored the growth of a state inspectorate in various other fields.

Before describing their potential value to the Admiralty, the limitations of the Dockyard Schools in this context should be made clear. For many years, as depicted in parliamentary reports at the time, there was conflict within the Dockyard Service, at the level both of artisan and manager, between, on the one hand, the traditional 'rule of thumb' men lacking a formal education and, on the other, the products of the new schools. This problem would only be overcome in time.[12] Also, the number of entrants, and hence the number of youths coming under the schools' cultural influence, was prone to fluctuations in the demand for skilled labour. In the tranquil year of 1876, for instance, Chatham School had fewer than 40 apprentices in attendance.[13] Moreover, the full benefits of the schools were, until 1878, confined to shipwright apprentices, the historically dominant dockyard trade. Changes in shipbuilding technology and especially naval shipbuilding saw some extension of access but even then only to the growing band of engine fitters' apprentices. The rest of the apprentices in 'the minor trades' such as joiners, caulkers and smiths received considerably less formal education. From 1878 they were eligible for entry to a 'Lower School' but it was not until 1893 that they could enter the Dockyard Examination proper, and thence possibly ascend to the heights of the administrative, supervisory and managerial posts previously restricted to qualified shipwrights.[14]

These limitations indicate, therefore, that the influence of the immature dockyard schools on the workforce should not be exaggerated, but equally, that their potential should not be underrated. The schools were inaugurated to educate boys for a specific work life and as such had considerable hegemonic capabilities. Before examining their material and ideological utility in seeking to reproduce class relations, we will consider their ability to reproduce the requisite skills for the dockyard network's socio-technical division of labour.

Whilst sections of the Admiralty were almost certainly aware of the schools' potential as 'ideological disseminators', there was also a motive to provide and improve relevant work skills. The required design of technically and competitively superior ships prompted their Lordships to nurture educated ingenuity in the field of naval architecture.[15] Similarly, in ship construction the Admiralty demanded a degree of craftsmanship rare to nineteenth-century British industry. It was acknowledged that the Dockyard Schools helped attain those necessary standards. An order of 1849 declared:

> [My Lords] find a perfect unanimity of opinion as to the advantages of filling all vacancies in the yards by young men brought up in them, not only because of the habits of subordination which they acquire there, but also on account of the excellent education that they are now receiving.[16]

In fact, during a period when the state-owned dockyards were subject to frequent liberal attacks, one of the most persuasive arguments used in their favour was the quality of their production. This point was allowed by such unsympathetic witnesses as the predominantly liberal 1859 Admiralty Committee on Dockyard Economy.[17] This emphasis on quality could be pursued because of the dockyards' economic basis within the public sector and because of the Admiralty's desire for vessels of a high standard. However, it was the dockyard education system, with the schools at its core, which actually achieved and provided for the high standards.[18] An official pamphlet later explained how:

> When at work in the Yard each apprentice is placed under the charge of a workman of good character. Their complete training is thus an example of the 'sandwich' system in which the theoretical and practical parts alternate with a frequency approaching the practicable maximum. This arrangement combined with the fact that the school is conducted within the works makes it possible to secure a close connection between the two parts of the training.[19]

Hence a primary motive was an apparently genuine desire for the improvement of skills so as to maintain the effectiveness of production. But even the provision of practical education was broadly class-differentiated. Those boys destined to become officers received an advanced technical education and, more importantly, were coached in managerial skills. The Report of the 1859 Committee approved the fact that trainees could 'become acquainted with the habits and feelings of the workmen whom he will hereafter have to supervise'.[20]

The original organization of the schools reflects this aim of class reproduction with its splitting of individuals into 'the man who will be a hewer of wood and a drawer of water all his days' and those destined to become 'captains of industry'.[21] As we have seen, education was a two-tier system, the upper tier of which was inhabited by 'superior' apprentices (often of gentlemanly stock) ordained to become officers in the dockyard service. They were designated to be the representatives of a ruling-class fulfilling a patriotic obligation founded on

> the effectual discharge of so responsible a duty, as the training of the generation who are to follow us, and on whom it will depend, to a very material extent, whether the reputation and power of England as a naval nation, shall wax stronger or shall wane.[22]

Entrants to the lower tier were precisely defined by the Admiralty. They were to be of a background sufficiently respectable to have encouraged development of literacy and numeracy, 'the parents being in the receipt of such wages as makes the neglect of such instruction inexcusable', but, once entered, the scope of instruction was to be restrained, otherwise 'there is the danger of giving to the apprentice an Officer's rather than a Workman's education'.[23] Thus, the schools were designed to admit boys of a given social class and prepare them for work positions appropriate to that class. This effectively would have helped consolidate and reproduce class divisions within the dockyard.

Intrinsic to the yards, however, was a contradictory force which could have threatened this perpetuation of structural inequality. Previous decades had seen the development of an increasingly 'rationalized' labyrinth of promotion routes which progressive elements within the Admiralty had hoped would foster a competitive ethic within the workforce (see below). Officers boasted of the extensive opportunities to breach the gentlemanly officer ranks for even the most 'humble' of apprentices.[24] Setting aside for one moment the issues of how realistic or influential this organizational mobility actually was, it clearly perturbed liberal factions of the Admiralty who showed an inclination to direct artisan apprentices towards only the 'inferior' administrative positions. This conflict was writ large in the 1859 Report on Dockyard Economy. The Committee included private entrepreneurs who stood behind the standard of *laissez-faire* and were opposed to what they saw as the unnecessary expense of education. They were complemented by an anti-education bloc within the Admiralty itself, the periodic figurehead of which was Sir James Graham. The grounds for their disapproval did not conform with those of the industrialists but together these groups represented a considerable range of opponents to the education of the working classes. To quote from the report:

> It is not good to take young men of a lower position in society, such as the sons of working men, and by an examination in which they have been put into competition with none but their own compeers, raise them at once to a position superior to that of their own father, and families, which would necessarily be the case if any of the present class of shipwright apprentices were to be selected at an early age, and specially trained for the position of superior officers. We consider the selection from an inferior class, placing the person to be selected in a position superior to all his connection around him ... has a bad effect upon the individual to a greater degree.

Instead, the majority of higher officers should be 'young men of superior standing and education', trained 'in the same manner as young commissioned officers of the army and navy are trained for their position'.[25]

The continuing disagreement within the Admiralty was instanced in the frequent closure and reopening of the various 'superior' schools with their perceived capability for disturbing the dockyard's 'natural' order through the education of particularly able pupils of any background. However, as Waters has shown, even when the Central Mathematical School at Portsmouth was closed down, for instance, there was still an operative system of promotion, prizes and bursaries for ordinary apprentices.[26] This was quite possibly because, despite its corporate qualms, there were those within the Admiralty who realized that effective management was not jeopardized by competitive education. Rather, as will be seen, the Dockyard Schools contributed to industrial stability. The claim that 'knowledge unfits for labour, and should therefore be confined to the higher classes; or at least that its acquisition by the working-classes is rather worse than useless, and should be discouraged' was, hence, not only wrong but counter-productive given the schools' hegemonic value.[27]

The dockyard educational system did not confine itself, however, to the attempted preparation of working-class youths for artisan roles and 'gentleman' youths for officer roles. It also helped mould the important status differentials visible throughout the Royal Dockyards. Historically, the most influential group of craftsmen, as in private yards, were the shipwrights. On criteria of skill, danger and sheer numbers, they had attained an often resented eminence among the dockyardmen and had secured various benefits and privileges from the employer, the most consequential of which was the principle that only shipwrights could be promoted to technical, supervisory and managerial posts. The predictable unpopularity which this fanned amongst the rest of the trades provides but one example of how divisive the Admiralty policy was for the dockyardmen as a political force. Prior to 1840 this preferential treatment had been an unwritten tradition but by opening the Dockyard Schools solely to shipwright apprentices (who then became the only men qualified to fill the higher posts) the Admiralty formally enshrined labour segregation. As noted earlier, the prestige of the shipwrights was diminished to some degree over the course of the century as shipbuilding technology and naval requirements changed – engine fitters and electrical engineers acquired equivalent official status and all other apprentices became eligible for the full range of educational opportunities. However, their status and its accompanying privileges, with their fragmentary consequences, were to survive, albeit in a diluted form, up to 1914.[28] On top of this, the emergence from the schools of a group of élite ex-apprentices created a further schism among the shipwrights themselves, between what the Chatham men called 'gentleman' shipwrights (the ex-apprentices) and the supposedly more ignorant 'sledgehammer' shipwrights who had served their time elsewhere.[29]

The Dockyard Schools, then, could participate in the reproduction of broad social divisions within the workplace, and could forge additional disunifying scissions among the workforce. But this only explains their role in a structural sense, that is, their function as institutions with a capability of securing the conditions for class reproduction. What remains as yet unclear is how that capability was effected or, more specifically, how the schools tried to prepare individuals for given positions within the production system. The issue of the schools' wider cultural and ideological impact will occupy the following section.

The hegemonic role of the schools falls, for our purposes, into two categories; first, that socialization common to schooling in nineteenth-century capitalist society, and secondly, that which made the Dockyard Schools historically unique. The first category refers to the way in which schools attempt to discipline their charges not only to nurture submission within their current institution but also to prepare them for a future work life which, for working-class children, necessitates such character traits as 'good behaviour', industriousness, obedience and honesty. By way of illustration, in the Dockyard Schools, those pupils not 'creamed off' to the higher class were to receive an extra year's tuition simply 'for the sake of forming in them regular and industrious-ness habits'. The schoolmaster was 'strictly to enforce orderly behaviour as well as diligence and attention on the part of the Apprentices'.[30]

The correct work deportment was an element of the curriculum as well. There was an early emphasis on religious education – a prime example of what Althusser describes as pure ideology – with the resident dockyard chaplain being called upon to 'exercise a general supervision on ... this most important part of their education.'[31] A spiritual obligation, then, matched a social obligation to accept one's lot. It would seem likely, too, that these were complemented by illumination of the apprentices' duty to play their part in upholding the British Empire, a process common in the dockyards over the centuries.

The extent to which schooling was basically regulatory was illustrated by the consternation shown in 1857 at reports of pupils devoting too much attention to schoolwork. In his annual report the Inspector, Dr Woolley, warned:

[The schoolwork] is a great and an important work, but, so far as the Public Service is concerned, only valuable in so far as it tends to render the apprentices intelligent and conscientious workmen.[32]

From the copious evidence of the various Public Committees constituted in the 1860s to investigate dockyard affairs (which contain abundant, glowing reports of the dockyard artisan's moral virtue) and from the dockyardmen's 'moderate' reputation, it would seem therefore that the Schools contributed towards a comparative industrial peace.[33]

The schools, then, crystallized and concentrated class relationships in preparation for work but in certain key respects they went considerably further by virtue of their social location within an industrial organization. This positioning allowed that various aspects of everyday life in school coincided, to a considerable extent, with work life. Most blatantly, schoolteachers had the status of Dockyard Officers. In fact, in early years they had been plucked directly from the officer ranks. In the 1870s the School Commissioners urged that school staff should be ex-dockyard apprentices, being the most suitably qualified candidates. This would have added to the overlap between education and occupation.[34] So teachers were not merely figures of authority within the school, nor could they be classified simply as representatives of an objective managerial class; they were schoolmasters who were also members of the dockyard managerial staff unto whose authority the apprentices would soon be subjected.

A number of other school structures and the meanings attached to them acted to prepare the apprentices for their future working lives in the dockyard. The school disciplinary code, for instance, dovetailed with that of the dockyard service. On being reported to the Admiral Superintendent (the naval chief of the dockyard), mulcting (docking) of pay and subtractions from the annual raise of pay were among those punishments with which the apprentices would have become acquainted long before experiencing them as qualified craftsmen.[35] More mundane facets of school structure such as time-keeping, breaks, modes of address, and so on, were similarly replicated. All contributed to a process whereby youths in school would experience aspects of their ultimate work culture and structure. Admittedly, artisans were prey to a variety of other cultural influences and the imposed culture would have been mediated by the workmen in accordance with their own strong cultural traditions, but the schools helped propagate the dominant culture experienced within the dockyards.[36]

Probably the most crucial role played by the schools, and the one most apposite to the specific organization of the Royal Dockyards, was their generation of a competitive spirit suited for participation in the Admiralty's promotion labyrinth. As was noted before, one of the stimuli to the opening of the Dockyard Schools had been the rationalization of the promotion system. This required that the artisans should have the academic ability to partake in the extensive programme of open examinations upon which the majority of promotions depended. The ubiquity within the dockyard service of competitive examinations for promotion and their disciplinary relevance made the schools' introduction of competitive structures and values significant.

The emphasis on promotion according to formal academic criteria (with, it should be recorded, some reference also to practical demonstrations and written assessments by superiors of ability and experience) was officially phased in during the early 1860s. But the ambition to replace informal procedures, perpetually criticized for being corrupt and founded on political patronage, with a rational scheme had been an Admiralty goal since 1840. By 1860 virtually all promotions for shipwrights were subject to examination results, not merely in obviously practical subjects such as technical drawing, but also in more theoretical disciplines such as algebra, English and, in some instances, French. The severity and number of the exams increased proportionately at each level of the hierarchy. There were comparable, exam-based promotion ladders for other trades, for clerical workers and for labourers who, perhaps having originally entered as oakum or ropery house-boys, could rise 'on merit' to intermediary ranks such as sawyers or storehousemen, and eventually reach positions which supplied remuneration, if not status, equal to that of craftsmen.[37]

The Dockyard Schools sought to prepare boys for this kind of work environment. This was preparation both in terms of academic ability and orthodoxy, and with respect to what Waters calls the whole 'competitive ethos'.[38] The would-be apprentice first encountered examinations and the competitive ethos on taking the annual, open, public examination for dockyard entry. Because of the lack of skilled employment alternatives in many of the dockyard towns (this was particularly true of Devonport, Portsmouth and Pembroke), and because of the potential security of a dockyard post, apprenticeships were highly valued, exciting much interest in the press and throughout the community. An official pamphlet crowed:

> The achievements of apprentices in one generation have fired the imagination of those in the next, and at a very early age boys in these towns have come under the influence of a competition to which, as regards keenness and active interest of parents, there probably exists no parallel in any other part of the country.[39]

Similarly, entry itself had a competitive edge as those successful candidates with the highest marks could choose the most prestigious apprenticeships. From then on, the years of apprenticeship were guided by annual examinations and selective advancement to classes grooming individuals for technical and managerial positions.[40] Artisans grew up, then, amid the frantic activity and discipline required for the constant absorption of knowledge and its regurgitation in regular examinations.

For the Admiralty as an employer, the importance of this system, with the schools at its cornerstone, cannot be underestimated. It allowed the possibility that a range of beliefs and values could become integral to the dockyard work culture and in the process reinforce the workforce's wider social influence. First, and most crucially, the programme of meritocratic promotion actually generated the competitive ethos. One observer remarked that 'Competition was of the essence of the whole system – unlimited and fierce.'[41] It seems likely that competition had a fragmentary and divisive effect on the workforce with energies being channelled into personal achievement and conflict, rather than united, class-grounded political action. While individuals accepted that they could resolve their occupational circumstances by their own efforts they were less likely to resort to collective responses. This would provide one strand of the explanation for late unionization in the dockyards.[42]

Underpinning the competitive ethic was the belief that opportunities for 'deserved' ascendancy through the hierarchy were virtually limitless, a point frequently reiterated by dockyard service authorities. Officers would propound this meritocratic spirit because their own education was designed, as one naval official put it, so 'that these young gentlemen should feel, when they have taken their first position in the dockyard, that it is solely by their own established and demonstrated merits, that they can hope to rise'.[43] For apprentices the ascent to Master Shipwright (in effect the highest civilian position) was, according to their Lordships of the Admiralty, 'open upon fixed and intelligible conditions to every man of superior ability who cultivates his natural gifts and does his duty to the Crown as an Officer'.[44]

In fact, meteoric rises within the hierarchy are hard to find. Long climbs were known – William Edye had become Master Shipwright at Devonport Dockyard having originally been an ordinary apprentice – but, in the main, 'careers', and this was an increasing tendency following the 1859 rationalization, were plentiful but limited as regards distance. For instance, John Flexman of Devonport had attained, by 1859, the post of measurer of work, having started as an apprentice in 1834 and moved up via working at his craft for five years, then becoming a modeller, a draughtsman, an inspector and eventually a measurer. In twenty-five years he had achieved a position of some responsibility and status but essentially he was little more than an intermediate supervisor.[45]

Advancement in the Dockyard Schools was of a similar character, as borne out by one successful pupil:

> There was an open competition for entry as apprentice with probably ten times as many candidates as there were appointments; then from amongst each year's successful candidates – perhaps 30 or 40 in number – three only could reach the Naval College after 5 or 6 years work and frequent examinations. Supposing the College course successfully passed, and the student launched on his professional career as a fully certified naval architect, he then only began a fresh series of competitive examinations on the result of which depended his future promotion.[46]

Thus, controlled success was available to most – indeed a certificate of schooling was required for acceptance to the 'establishment' on completion of apprenticeship – but the more weighty fruits of the system, as advertised by the Admiralty and its acolytes, and as incorporated into dockyard culture, were denied to all but a small minority. In this way the promotion system gained popular legitimacy without, of course, threatening the stability of dockyard social relations.

To attain promotion, though, dockyardmen had to remain within the orbit of a value system which aimed to perpetuate the employer's dominance. Central to this system were characteristics – veiled but encapsulated in the Admiralty's previously quoted phrase, 'duty to the Crown' – such as diligence, sobriety and good behaviour. The successful candidate would be 'an industrious, intelligent, well conducted man'.[47] In other words, the chance of success required conformity. To *capitalize* on that chance required the additional attribute of personal sacrifice, a factor the Admiralty constantly stressed as important to its considerations. Thus, not only were a proportion of regular classes for apprentices held outside work hours (with, it should be said, not unflagging popularity) but also school facilities were made available for voluntary pupils (non-apprenticed boys and ambitious artisans) in the evenings.[48] In turn, this accommodation to the employer's preferred conduct could forge a homologous relationship with the labour aristocracy's (or in Crossick's phrase, the artisan élite's) esteemed traits of industry, discipline, respectability and, most importantly, its belief that the foregoing would be rewarded.[49] The dockyard town's political economy with their structural dependence on employment in the yards only served to concentrate investment in meritocracy.

Involvement with these structures, values and rules signified an engagement with the Admiralty's system itself, a structural involvement, it can be noted, which outweighed the workforce's apparent cultural independence.[50] The real possibility of personal advancement committed the dockyard workforce prior even to individual entry, to a willing commitment in an entangling hierarchical process.

Thus far we have dwelt predominantly on the potential of the dockyard educational system within the yards but, as has been hinted in the previous section, its influence on the wider communities of the dockyard towns should also be considered. In particular, attention should be focused upon the way that the schools shaped first, local education, and second, the artisans' non-work culture. It will be argued that these processes were instrumental in reproducing a specific pattern of class relations within the dockyards' urban communities.

The unusual security attached to dockyard employment in conjunction with the economic dependence that characterized the local labour markets of the dockyard towns (the town of Devonport for instance had originally grown up around the dockyard rather than vice versa) meant that dockyard apprenticeships were highly desired. As was seen earlier, the annual entrance examinations were significant community events. Because of this demand and because of the requirements of the schools upon entry, the developing educational systems of the dockyard towns were accordingly adapted. A more recent Devonport graduate outlined the essential relationship between his school and the local economy:

> You see in my early life it was the Dockyard and Dockyard only, that's all we had drilled into us ... I went to school, it was their intention to get boys into the Dockyard, and if a boy was to say to the headmaster 'I want to go

into the army, Sir', he would – his answer would be well you're in the wrong school. [At] our school, the curriculum is for the dockyard or naval apprentices.[51]

From the early years, schools aimed at attaining dockyard posts for their pupils mushroomed.[52] In Devonport, from 1850, a Mr Treglohan, the headmaster of St James' Church School, commenced evening classes for those wishing to take the dockyard entrance examination.[53] By 1860 the Plymouth newspapers were full of advertisements for private schools attentive to the requirements of Devonport Dockyard. Mr Burt of the Plymouth Classical and Mathematical School drew 'the attention of his Friends to his success in passing Young Gentlemen through most severe examinations into Government Situations'. Whilst the Central House Establishment School boasted of its prowess in gaining dockyard entrants thus:

> From this ESTABLISHMENT several gentlemen have during the past years been successfully prepared and obtained important Government Situations, viz: in SOMERSET HOUSE, CLERKSHIPS IN THE ROYAL DOCKYARDS ...[54]

Increasingly, and this was true of all the towns under discussion, schoolteachers were drawn from the ranks of ex-apprentices – the instigator of the Ragged Schools Movement, John Pounds, was both a teacher in a Dockyard School (Portsmouth) and an ex-apprentice.[55] Curricula, too, came under dockyard sway; when in 1860 the Admiralty gave mathematics a greater emphasis local schools immediately re-jigged their syllabuses.[56] This structural fit between local education and the Dockyard was, if anything, tightened with the evolution of state schools which in towns like Plymouth and Portsmouth had formal 'dockyard' classes.

Thus, in the wider community, acquaintance with the structures and values of dockyard work culture began long before dockyard entry. The schools had considerable post-apprenticeship influence as well. Probably the most durable effect was their key contribution to the cultural creation of the local artisan ethic. They encouraged self-improvement, stability, 'intelligence', and, most of all, respectability – traits the dockyardmen carried back into the community. Paul Robertson describes this process:

> In all, technical education for skilled workmen was deemed beneficial because it discouraged vandalism, promoted moral strength and broadened

a man's outlook, as well as giving him a better grasp of his job. It was important ... because it helped to inculcate habits of good conduct.[57]

Sir William White, always closely involved with dockyard education, lauded its uses pointing to the transference of this socialization beyond the workplace:

> There have been hundreds of young men ... who have been helped to fight evil habits, whose minds and bodies have been wholesomely occupied, who have been saved from becoming hooligans, and made better men.[58]

The Dockyard Schools provided the archetype for this goal of moral containment. In 1852 a Government Inspector remarked upon the apparent improvement in the behaviour of dockyard apprentices towards their colleagues and neighbours, attributing this to the character of their education. As evidence, he pointed to their patronization of both Mechanics' Institutes and savings banks.[59] It is interesting that in the Three Towns (of which Devonport, along with Plymouth and Stonehouse, was one) Mechanics' Institutes continued to thrive long after their national decline, exhibitions of naval architecture and the like being a regular attraction.[60]

The Dockyard Schools then, allowed the possibility of social and industrial hegemony with their influence spanning school, the workplace and the community. What needs to be addressed, though, is the issue of exactly why the Admiralty should have taken the radical and, with *laissez-faire* liberals, politically unpopular step of promoting a relatively expensive educational system. The answer lies in the individual characteristics of the dockyards' organization which, in turn, created the need for both new methods of long-term, social and industrial regulation and alternative inducements to attract employees.[61] The dockyards during most of their lifetimes have been geared not to a 'current' demand but to a potential demand – in this case, war – and that has necessitated the Admiralty employing a permanent workforce. But, in addition, because of the highly skilled nature of the work and the aforementioned stress placed on quality by the Admiralty, this workforce has been predominantly skilled. In the Victorian period these circumstances resulted in a distinct reluctance to dismiss artisans, a disciplinary laxity complemented by 'flaws' in other traditional modes of control such as systems of payment, technology and supervision.[62] Accordingly, the Admiralty had been pushed into searching for different ways of securing social and industrial relations. The Dockyard Schools as sites of ideological influence provided their Lordships with one such alternative tool.

The dockyards as productive units were, of course, necessarily funded by an imperialist state but in *laissez-faire* Britain they nonetheless attracted a constant barrage of criticism from liberals opposed to state monopoly in whatever form. Almost inevitably, where heed was paid to these criticisms efforts to cut costs were passed on to wages with the consequence that dockyard wages invariably rested below the market rate paid in private yards. This would incessantly be a source of resentment, but the Admiralty, rather than accede to wage claims, had provided an extensive range of alternative inducements such as guaranteed employment on the establishment, a pension, and benefits such as holidays and medical treatment. Central to these inducements was the opportunity to improve oneself, and central to that were the Schools.

The Admiralty, then, was constrained to address fundamental political questions of industrial control at a comparatively early stage in the development of industrial capitalism. Arguably, the essential driving force behind the creation of a system of technical education was the need for a highly trained workforce, capable of creating and maintaining a powerful naval presence on the world stage. However, given the political implications of such a desire, it also created a source of moral regulation, one which would provide a loyal and dependable workforce – an increasingly important requirement as the nineteenth century unfolded. A hint of meritocracy and the promise of job security encouraged dockyardmen to invest in a set of structures, ideals and practices by which they might also be said to have assented to their own subordination. In this way, the dockyard system could have acted as an impressive model for the central hegemonic role played by educational systems in modern capitalist societies. It certainly provided an effective framework within the Royal Dockyards for the establishment of a flexible and responsive workforce which was best suited to the particular needs of an expanding imperial power reliant upon its control of the seas and its ability to maintain naval supremacy over other industrializing nations.

Notes

1. P. Robertson, 'Technical education in the British shipbuilding and marine engineering industries, 1863–1914', *Economic History Review*, **27** (1974), 223–4.
2. D. R. Jack, 'A history of the Royal Dockyard schools with particular reference to the Portsmouth school' (MA thesis, University of London, 1969), pp. 5–9.
3. Sir William Snow Harris, *Our Dockyards: Past and Present State of Naval Construction in the Government Service: Its Future Prospects* (Plymouth, White Stevens, 1863).
4. M. Waters, 'A social history of dockyard workers at Chatham, Kent, 1860–1914' (PhD thesis, University of Essex, 1979), p. 155.
5. Letter from Sidney Herbert, Secretary to the Admiralty to Captain Superintendents of the Dockyards, 28 November 1842, quoted in Jack, 'A history of the Royal Dockyard schools', p. 15.
6. G. W. Roderick and M. D. Stephens, *Education and Industry in the 19th Century* (London, Longman, 1978), p. 2.
7. Jack, 'A history of the Royal Dockyard schools', p. 22.
8. *Ibid.*, pp. 25–6.
9. Harris, *Our Dockyards*, p. 27.
10. Letters from Admiralty to Admiral Superintendents 27 June 1846 and 29 November 1847. Waters, 'A social history', p. 156.
11. Jack, 'A history of the Royal Dockyard schools', p. 24.
12. British Parliamentary Papers, 1859, vol. XVIII, Report of the Admiralty Committee on Dockyard Economy, evidence of William Edye (Master Shipwright at Devonport), Q 1156; 1861, vol. XXVI, Report of the Commissioners on the Control and Management of the Naval Yards, evidence of Rear Admiral Pasley (Admiral Superintendent of Devonport), Qs 2697–2700 and James Peake (Master Shipwright at Devonport), Q 2913. Harris, *Our Dockyards*, pp. 16–17.
13. Waters, 'A social history', p. 156.
14. *Ibid.*, p. 157.
15. See, for instance, J. Scott Russell, 'On the technical education of naval architects in England', *Transactions of the Institute of Naval Architects* (TINA), **8** (1867), 223–43.
16. General Order and Board Minutes Relating to the Revision of H. M. Dockyard, January 25, 1849.
17. S. Pollard, 'Laissez-faire and shipbuilding', *Economic History Review*, **5** (1953), 104–5; British Parliamentary Papers, 1859, Report on Dockyard Economy, para. 17.
18. N. Casey, 'An early organizational hegemony: methods of control in a Victorian naval dockyard', *Social Science Information (Information des Sciences Sociales*, **4/5**(23) (1984), 677–700.

19. G. A. Baxendall, *The Admiralty Method of Training Dockyard Apprentices* (Board of Education Pamphlet No. 32 (London, HMSO, 1916), p. 5.
20. British Parliamentary Papers, 1859, *Report of Admiralty Committee on Dockyard Economy*, para. 372.
21. A. Denny, *Transactions of the Institute of Naval Architects*, **45** (1903), 56, quoted in Robertson, 'Technical education', p. 226.
22. Russell, 'On the technical education', p. 223.
23. Sidney Herbert's letter of 28 November 1842, quoted in Jack, 'A history of the Royal Dockyard schools'.
24. British Parliamentary Papers, 1859, *Report of Admiralty Committee on Dockyard Economy*, Chatfield's dissent, p. 113.
25. *Ibid.*, para. 359–60.
26. Waters, 'A social history', p. 155.
27. British Parliamentary Papers, 1859, *Report of Admiralty Committee on Dockyard Economy*, para. 341. See also the spirited rejoinder of the Portsmouth Master Shipwright in BPP 1860, vol. XLII, Observations of the Superintendents and Officers of the Dockyards on the Report of the Committee on Dockyard Economy, p. 11.
28. *Demarcation of Work in H.M. Dockyards* (London, HMSO, 1895), Naval History Library, p. 644. See also N. Casey and D. Dunkerley, 'Technological work cultures', in K. Thompson (ed.), *Work, Employment and Unemployment: Perspectives on Work and Society* (Open University Press, Milton Keynes, 1984).
29. Waters, 'A social history', p. 161.
30. Sidney Herbert's letter, quoted in Jack, 'A history of the Royal Dockyard schools', p. 40.
31. *Ibid.*
32. *Ibid.*, p. 44.
33. See the evidence to the 1859 *Report of Admiralty Committee on Dockyard Economy*, the 1860 Observations, and the 1861 Report on Control and Management. In particular, note Chatfield's Dissent in the first-mentioned.
34. Jack, 'A history of the Royal Dockyard schools', p. 54.
35. Sidney Herbert's letter, quoted in Jack, 'A history of the Royal Dockyard schools'. In extreme cases boys would have been denied an 'establishment' job on completion of their apprenticeship – this was paralleled in work by the same punishment of artisans being removed from the 'establishment' (that is, losing their permanent posts which were accompanied by a range of perquisites and pension rights).
36. The influence of the dockyardmen's own culture, while not the major focus here, cannot be ignored. Waters, 'A social history'; J. Field, 'Bourgeois Portsmouth: social relations in a Victorian dockyard town, 1815–75' (PhD thesis, University of Warwick, 1979); and G. Crossick, *An Artisan Elite in Victorian Society* (London, Croom Helm, 1978) have all indicated the strength and persistence of their cultural responses and resistance, and it would be

legitimate to assume that the same processes were evident to some extent in the Dockyard Schools as well. However, increasingly, the culture of the artisan elite – independence, respectability and self-improvement – merged with many aspects of school culture.

37. For examples of promotional ladders and the examination arrangements see the 1859 *Report of Admiralty Committee on Dockyard Economy*, paras. 282–303, 309–33, 349, 403, and 717–27. The basis of its recommendations and in some cases the details were implemented soon after. On the question of the advancement of labourers, see M. Waters, 'A picture of Chatham Dockyard in 1861', *Archaeologica Cantana*, **97** (1981), 24; Field, 'Bourgeois Portsmouth', p. 393; and N. Buck, 'An Admiralty dockyard in the mid-19th century: aspects of the social and economic history of Sheerness' (Urban and Regional Studies Unit, University of Kent), pp. 46–7.
38. M. Waters, 'Craft consciousness in a government enterprise – Medway dockyardmen, 1860–1906', *Oral History*, **5**(1), Spring 1977, 51–62.
39. Baxendall, *The Admiralty Method*, p. 10.
40. For examples of early curricula and assessment see Jack, 'A history of the Royal Dockyard schools', pp. 20, 35, and Waters, 'A social history', p. 154. Baxendall, *The Admiralty Method*, pp. 7–9, gives details of the refined curriculum and examination arrangements operated by 1914.
41. W. H. White, 'The Royal corps of naval constructors', *Nature*, **8**(5) (1994), 33–4 (also quoted in Waters, 'A social history', p. 152). On the effects of competition see also Casey, 'An early organizational hegemony'.
42. For a lengthier discussion of this issue see N. Casey and D. Dunkerley, 'Trade unions in naval dockyards in the late nineteenth century', *Maritime South West*, **2** (1986).
43. Comments by E. J. Reed on paper by Russell, 'On the technical education', p. 242.
44. Letter from Admiralty to Admiral Superintendents, 29 November 1847.
45. British Parliamentary Papers, 1859, *Report of Admiralty Committee on Dockyard Economy*, Qs 1102, 1139, 1187 and p. 88.
46. White, 'The Royal corps', p. 84.
47. British Parliamentary Papers, 1859, *Report of Admiralty Committee on Dockyard Economy*, paras. 312–23.
48. *Ibid.*, paras. 708–11; see also Jack, 'A history of the Royal Dockyard schools', pp. 30, 39; he notes (p. 52) that a total of 599 yard boys were attending the schools in 1859.
49. Crossick, *An Artisan Elite*, pp. 71–2.
50. Casey, 'An early organizational hegemony'. Clearly, mere participation in the education system did not guarantee a lifetime of docility – immediately one can point to the fact that many fully educated apprentices seized on the completion of their apprenticeship to leave the dockyard service, notwithstanding promotional opportunities, for the more highly paying but far less secure private yards on the Thames – but there is no doubting that the

selective, competitive advancement practised in the schools prepared those wanting a career in the Yard (and the many family clans meant artisans were often keen to stay put) for a particular kind of enmeshing work culture.

51. Interview with retired dockyard workers.
52. Field, 'Bourgeois Portsmouth', p. 360; Jack, 'A history of the Royal Dockyard schools', p. 88.
53. A. Kennerley (ed.), *Post School Education in the 'Three Towns', 1825–1975* (Plymouth Polytechnic, 1976), p. 28.
54. *Western Morning News*, 3 January 1860.
55. British Parliamentary Papers *Report of Admiralty Committee on Dockyard Economy*, evidence of Robert Rae (Headmaster at Devonport), para, 1485; Jack, 'A history of the Royal Dockyard schools', pp. 88–9.
56. Jack, 'A history of the Royal Dockyard schools', pp. 88–9.
57. Robertson, 'Technical education', p. 227.
58. *Ibid.*, quoting from *Transactions of N.E. Coast Institutions of Engineers and Shipbuilders*, **20** (1903–4), 82.
59. Revd H. Mosely's 1852 report, quoted in Jack, 'A history of the Royal Dockyard schools', p. 39.
60. C. L. Bowers, 'The development of Mechanics' Institutes in the south west of England during the first half of the nineteenth century' (MA thesis, University of London, 1971).
61. For a fuller explanation of this see Casey, 'An early organizational hegemony'.
62. *Ibid.*

5

THE DOCKYARDMEN SPEAK OUT: PETITION AND TRADITION IN CHATHAM DOCKYARD, 1860–1906

Mavis Waters

In the late nineteenth century the labour force in the Royal Dockyards was characterized by several peculiarities which distinguished it from the private sector of the industry. Most striking was the fact that in government yards the shipwrights, workers in wood, retained their position as the premier artisans, with responsibility for the material creation of the whole product – the battleship – although in private yards they were, by and large, ousted by ironworkers.[1]

In fact, dockyardmen had constituted a very early industrial workforce and therefore many of their workplace practices retained the style of medieval craft traditions (i.e. control through the officers, of their own craft) and of the early parliamentary method of protest through petition. These practices they managed to retain and adapt, carrying their craft-based culture into the modern period and relating it to the new conditions of the nineteenth century. Their ways of protecting themselves differed from those of other workers; nevertheless, by the end of the century we can see them using a blend of methods which, while including use of trade union strength, may have helped to develop particular forms and precedents for the state-as-employer to deal with its increasing numbers of employees.[2]

In earlier times historians have found the dockyardmen, led by the shipwrights, to be 'a turbulent lot',[3] very ready to strike and demonstrate, as ably portrayed by Knight and Morriss in their two essays in this volume. The purpose of this chapter is to focus on dockyardmen as independent and self-confident workers, whose engagement with labour relations did not necessarily translate into the negativity of subservience and deference. The transition from more militant action, based on the strike, to petitioning, as outlined by Philip MacDougall in a previous chapter, need not reflect a diminution of their sense of independence. It should be seen in a more positive light as forging a new form of labour relations between employees and the state, one which culminated in the creation of the Whitley system at the end of the First World War. In this, the argument espoused by G. D. H. Cole, in his book *Self-Government in Industry*, that 'it is the privilege of workers who are State employees to show the way to better conditions and a more dignified life-style'[4] is taken as the theme of this chapter. Although Cole was referring to postal workers, the notion may equally apply to the example of the dockyardmen.

In this context, it could be argued that the education and training programmes developed from the mid-nineteenth century provided solid evidence of the initiation of good practice on the part of the British state in opening up opportunities for advancement for working men. Casey has argued, earlier in this volume, that education should be seen essentially as a form of social control. It is possible, however, to see the system of technical education instituted by the Admiralty from 1859 onwards as empowering its workforce. Boys admitted by examination as 'apprentices of the dockyard' were provided with a high level of technical schooling in mathematics and naval architecture during their training years. From this they emerged as workmen-technicians with both the knowledge and the opportunities to progress, after a few years 'at their tools', to posts of a clerical, supervisory or managerial level, or to absorption into the technical planning departments of Admiralty management. It was a way for able and industrious lads to rise from the labouring level to middle-class status, have better lives and feel the superiority of their own style of knowledge.[5]

This was a genuine ladder of advancement. One shipwright foreman told in 1975 how his father had come to the dockyard from farm labouring and had worked as a labourer on construction there, side-by-side with convict labour. Another, a foreman of the yard, spoke of his pride in the knowledge that gave him control over work:

> I liked the work... because I was up there on deck with the officers, telling *them* what to do. Some of them liked it, some of them didn't; but they had to listen because I was the one who knew what had to be done.[6]

Many more of those who rose in the dockyard and the Admiralty service were the children of craftsmen who came to work in the dockyards from less rigorous apprenticeships in little wood-building yards around the coasts and riversides of Britain, partly drawn by the hope of advancement for their sons, partly driven by the decline of wooden shipbuilding.

The key to all this was the dockyard examination, an institution of enormous importance in all the dockyard towns. It was the Civil Service examination taken by boys at the age of fifteen for entrance to apprenticeship in the dockyard, and though theoretically a national public examination, it was, in practice, generally only taken by lads resident in the dockyard towns, where it was held every year. The results were watched with eagerness by the population, who quickly identified the elementary schools with the highest score of successes and sought to send their own children to those schools. An electrical engineer in the 1975 collection of interviews produced the list of successful candidates for his year (on which his own name stood fifth) and could tell, after 50 years, which school each boy came from and what trade he chose.[7]

Predictably, all this gave an impetus to the general level of elementary (primary and junior) schooling in the towns. In Gillingham, one of the Medway towns, where the population was overwhelmingly dockyard employed, a dockyard storehouseman, William Lewington, led a movement between 1890 and 1906 to provide for, build and staff a new generation of elementary schools, to raise the standard of primary education and thus equalize the opportunities for passing the dockyard examination. The examination was all-important because only those admitted to the dockyards in this way were eligible to proceed through the hurdles of subsequent internal schooling and examinations to the higher positions.[8]

It could be argued that the experience gained by the state in constructing such a system of technical education provided the basis for extending provision in the twentieth century along similar lines. Sir Alfred Ewing, the Director of Naval Education in 1903, claimed that the Admiralty were model employers with regard to technical education.[9] Although the provision of technical education for apprentices was largely ignored by private shipbuilders until the early years of the twentieth century, the initial recommendations for the education of shipbuilding apprentices in local technical colleges emanated from the experiences and aims of dockyard education.[10]

There is another area, moreover, in which governments were able to profit from previous experience with dockyard hands, and that comes to light in the study of the consideration, control and relief of grievances, first, through Parliament and, secondly, through the revived use of that long-standing method of negotiation, the petition.[11] In the later part of the nineteenth century, dockyard workers had made a good deal of use of the method of direct representation to Parliament, through their MPs, for relief of their grievances, particularly on the issue of low pay. What made this possible was that dockyard matters regularly came up for discussion once a year in the Commons as part of the annual debate on the Navy Estimates. When this happened the Members of Parliament for the dockyard areas could sometimes be persuaded to speak on behalf of their constituents, bringing up issues of low wages, unpopular policies and dangerous conditions. Progressive widening of the franchise after 1867 meant that the MPs stood to gain votes if they would do this and lose them if they would not. In the Medway area in the early 1870s, the Liberal MPs Arthur Otway and Philip Wykeham-Martin put up strong parliamentary arguments for improving the wages of dockyard labourers, and for protecting the position of dockyard writers (the technical clerks).[12] A Gladstonian Liberal, Sir Andrew Clarke, ran a five-year campaign as candidate for Chatham that was based on his avowed intention to look after the dockyardmen.[13]

An interesting development of this method is that dockyardmen who found the representative of their own area too Conservative to back them could sometimes enlist the help of a more liberal MP who sat for another dockyard constituency. For instance, in 1876 Wykeham-Martin acted again for the labourers to secure recognition of the category of 'skilled labourer' for establishment purposes, thus increasing the chances of establishment of those who did not fall in the clearly defined artisan categories. At this time Chatham (the predominantly dockyard constituency) had elected the Conservative Admiral Eliot who refused to act in the matter, so the labourers' leaders went to Wykeham Martin as the Liberal MP for Rochester, which housed a section of dockyard unskilled men. In 1887, when all the dockyards had reason to fear redundancies, they appealed through the Liberal member for Portsmouth. In 1890, when the Chatham dockyard labourers could find no parliamentary champion in the Medway area (Wykeham-Martin was dead by then), they went to Parliament through the Conservative MP for Woolwich, Colonel Hughes.[14]

By this time there were strong inter-yard organizations for each occupation. In particular, the labourers from 1889–99 were organized under William Lewington into the Federal Council of Government Employees.[15] The skilled workmen, more cautious, were experimenting with their inter-yard associations in the same period, but after the election of a Liberal government in 1892, there was an upsurge of trade union activity, bringing the shipwrights, with the help of the Associated Society of Shipwrights led by Alexander Wilkie, back to the centre of the stage.[16]

There was, of course, a traditional basis for this co-operation between the different dockyards. Employees moved frequently between them and, consequently, there was a strong sense of blood relationship and, in spite of the friendly rivalries, a unity of interests. In 1872, when James Kingsland, ordinary labourer, was organizing a Society of Dockyard Labourers to raise pay levels, he knew quite well what was the usual procedure to follow. You called a meeting, elected a committee, and invited delegates from the other dockyards to join in.[17] In 1890, the Dockyard Labourers' Association, under Lewington, raised through Parliament a request for improved conditions in all the yards, which assembled behind it a strong coterie of dockyard area MPs. This combination was strong enough to force a Departmental Enquiry in 1890, of which there is a very full record.[18]

At this point the Admiralty officials, who did not much relish these developments, sought to persuade their workmen that the right and customary method of protest was that of petition[19], through the officers of their craft, to the Admiralty. Wisely, the dockyard workers did not neglect the petition as a means of protest; they continued to use it in conjunction with continued resort to Parliament and growing interaction with the trade union movement. It had certain advantages attached to it. For one thing, it was a relatively safe and acceptable activity, and, in the earlier period, working with the system could be seen as more beneficial than direct challenges such as strike action. The process or organization for the petition, just described, would inevitably focus on grievances; it would have an effect of consciousness-raising and improve the solidarity and cohesion of the workshop or work gang. It created a channel of communication which would heighten awareness of grievance on both sides; educate workers and widen the support from the shop floor with regard to the matters being carried forward by the unions and at Westminster.[20]

The language of these turn-of-the-century petitions and the verbatim reports of the visitations made to the dockyards by the Admiralty Secretary, or his representative, show a form of consciousness which seems to contradict the image of a subservient workforce. Arthur Forwood's visitations in 1891 and 1906 were recorded and the reports highlight the style of the approaches made to him by individuals. They display little servility or timidity on the part of the workmen; their attitude is businesslike and self-confident. 'We don't think we've gone out of our way to ask for anything unreasonable in that petition', says one

Chargeman of Shipwrights, 'and I want to impress that upon you.' 'Two years ago you promised us that', say the boilermakers, 'but we haven't heard anything more about it.'[21] Forwood himself commented on the 'free, frank and friendly' nature of the expositions made to him. Perhaps best of all is the affronted retort of a riveter representative when the secretary remarked with some condescension that his memorial was surprisingly well drawn-up. 'Us men,' he says, 'is not odd men; we have been brought up to the work from boys'; and he adds with a gloriously Elizabethan turn of phrase, 'Ever since they started iron shipbuilding here I have been.'[22]

Broadly speaking, an analysis of the petitions shows up five levels of demand, advancing in organization and political awareness. At the first level there were the petitions from individuals with grievances, often presented in such a way as to feature custom and precedent. A. Cornelions, leading-man ropemaker, asked for extra pay since he also filled the duties of a layer, an office now abolished. C. Carter, a leading-man of labourers, thought he should get a pay rise because he was stuck at the top of his pay scale, believing that after 31 years' service he was worth more than 5s. 6d. a day. An acting leading-man of patternmakers prayed for confirmation like others of his kind, after holding the rank for twelve years.[23] The officials seemed to be most at their ease with this sort of petition; it was the sort of thing they were looking for. They did not always brush them aside or ignore them; indeed they were often regarded as pointers to something wrong in the system. It was as a result of such individual petitions that, in 1893, their Lordships inquired carefully into the identity and rank of those cutting sails for sailmakers and recommended an increase in their pay, further informing Portsmouth Yard that the man who heats the pitch is in future to be a skilled labourer. Similarly, when two ropemakers asked for an increase in pay, the Director of the Works Department recommended a rise for the whole class of ropemakers on the grounds that they were men apprenticed to a trade. However, not everyone was so lucky; in 1906 a foreman of sailmakers complained that he had had no reply to his personal petition of 1904, and a surgery attendant had been waiting since 1903.

Individual petitions were the first level of complaint. The second level of sophistication came from the circumstances of special detachments of men working outside their normal units and therefore able to compare themselves to other groups. For instance, the shipwright modellers working in the mould-loft above the drawing office were on drawing-office staff pay, but were not getting paid leave like that staff. The boilermakers, working with silicate cotton, wanted a nuisance allowance on the ground that outside firms gave it. One bureaucrat was inclined to grant this, but another reminds him, 'All dockyardmen working on ships are provided with over-all suits which are washed at the expense of the Crown. This is not the case in private firms.'[24] This reference to private yards indicated the long tradition of comparison with work outside the state sector. Knight has shown that such a perspective existed as far back as the eighteenth century and it has persisted through to the current day.[25]

The third level of petition, still basically pre-modern, was the most common – petitions from the various trades and occupations. In the minor trades, where there were usually fewer than 50 men in each trade, these were often compact united demands. However, the larger trades, for petition purposes, were often subdivided into hired and established men, and the apprentices might also send their separate requests, as the shipwright, smith and joiner apprentices did in 1906. This made three divisions for the workmen of each trade and, in addition, the officers of each rank might send their petitions. Each trade could thus readily produce five or six petitions, although they did not, in practice, multiply them more than they thought necessary. Some trades (the more unionized ones) progressed so far as to send identical petitions from each yard,[26] thus challenging the competitive and divisive hierarchies of dockyard employment.

These occupational petitions are almost always concerned with pay rates and special allowances or the status of the trade or occupation, but sometimes they touched on demarcation issues. For instance, in 1906 a complicated issue between shipwrights and engineers regarding the work of patternmakers reached the desk of a Director of Dockyards. He wrote across it the laconic comment 'Precipitate action is undesirable.'[27] Indeed, these inter-trade disputes allowed the Admiralty to avoid action and, by the first decade of the twentieth century, dockyardmen could see the advantage of combining different trade grievances and requests under a common banner. This represents the fourth, and most modern, level of petitioning. In 1906, a group of minor trades combined to show how many pence per day they were being paid below the 'outside' rate. The issue was really a more general one – government employees should be paid at the same rates as the workmen of private employers. The same year all the skilled labourers from various workshops were asking for an enquiry into the utility of pneumatic tools, since they were perceived as injurious to health – a still more general matter. Ex-apprentices of all trades came as a group to ask for security of employment for dockyard apprentices once they were out of their time – this was a cross-trades matter. When all the hired men of the yards of Portsmouth and Chatham came together to ask for pensions for hired hands, as they did from 1902 onwards, the government faced a demand for three-quarters of the workforce at the two largest and most important yards. Finally, in 1905, the Admiralty answered a petition from 'various classes' that widows should be allowed to inherit pension rights. 'Various classes' meant everyone.[28]

Behind this growing unanimity lay the increasing power and influence of the trade union movement. As Galliver's following chapter shows, membership of trade unions was not officially disallowed in the dockyards. However, trade union recognition for bargaining purposes was not formally implemented until just prior to the First World War. By 1906, certain trades made their representations almost as a trade union branch and were assisted in the presentation of their grievances or requests by full-time trade union officials, although the Admiralty would only negotiate directly with yard employees. For example, the shipwrights were advised by Alexander Wilkie of the ASS, a union increasingly supported by dockyard shipwrights.[29] (Wilkie had been elected as a Labour MP for Dundee in 1906.) The engine fitters and the ship fitters were also accompanied by delegates from the Amalgamated Society of Engineers, including George Barnes, another Labour MP.[30] It is obvious that when the men from the shop floor came to discuss their petition with the backing of a trade unionist who was also an MP, this began to undermine the existing process of negotiation established by the Admiralty, which they now perceived as based on a paternalistic style of management.

The whole process began to make an impression outside the dockyards, particularly within the Navy, where naval technicians, or artificers, often trained within the dockyards, were active on lower-deck benefit committees, and sailors carefully monitored the progress of the civilian workforce. Englander and Osborne, in a 1978 article on the Navy in the *Historical Journal*, quote an appeal of 1909 from a joint committee of lower-deck benefit societies:

> That lower-deck representatives selected by the men shall have an official opportunity of direct representation to the Admiralty, at stated periods, in a similar manner to the concession enjoyed by the men of H.M. Dockyards.[31]

At the same time, within the dockyards there was a growing impatience with the antiquated machinery of the petition system, which matched the growing strength of trade unionists among employees, and their appearance at the annual sessions. By 1912 there was a Dockyard Advisory Committee within the Shipbuilding and Engineering Federation of Trade Unions, and also, in Parliament, there was a Committee of MPs for the dockyard towns to carry the issues on that front. At the same time, in 1912, we hear of a Dockyard Committee in Chatham Dockyard which begins an attempt to alter the form of workplace representation while still keeping its original base and nature. It seems that the three strands of protest – trade unionist, parliamentary and petitioning – were twining together in pursuit of reform.[32]

The Chatham Dockyard Committee appears to have been a final unification of the workshop committees which had operated for petition purposes for centuries; it was obviously recognized by Admiral-Superintendent Anson. In late 1912, Percy Terry, for the Dockyard Committee, wrote to the Admiral to complain on three counts: that the roof of the smiths' shop was admitting the rain and was in need of repair, that the horse-drawn trams at the dockyard gate were so badly regulated as to cause great confusion in the mornings, and that workmen assigned to the floating dock needed better conveyance, to and fro. Anson wrote back after an interval stating that the smiths' shop had been repaired and that he would do his best about the horses, but on the third point he referred the men to the traditional method of petition, with a warning that this new method of approach must not be taken as a precedent. Terry's response was to suggest that it might be better for all concerned if the questions concerning dockyard employees generally (which obviously meant the 'various classes' type of complaint) were to be presented through his Committee. Admiral Anson, unwilling to be responsible for ditching the traditional methods, referred him to the Admiralty Secretary.[33]

The very fact of the preservation of this correspondence in the Admiralty records indicates its significance in what followed. The Secretary, who was also under pressure from the engineering unions, who were mounting a campaign to boycott overtime unless they got a rise in pay,[34] responded by promulgating a memorandum suggesting a new method of organizing and rationalizing the employee representations. Individual petitions would now be separated from the general ones to be dealt with locally, but matters affecting a whole class of workmen were to be dealt with by a central meeting of delegates in London. In future, after the annual petitions had been sent in, each class, or group of classes, would elect two delegates (only one of whom need be a dockyard employee) to attend (with expenses paid) one central meeting in London for all the yards. Each representative would be nominated by four supporters, and elections would be unified over the five dockyards. (There were three classes of workmen: artisans; skilled labourers, who were semi-skilled workmen and had not served an apprenticeship; and ordinary labourers who did unskilled work such as cleaning, carrying, etc.) This indicated, therefore, a reduction of the traditional delegate representations to a simplified, centralized format in the shape of an early workshop committee. Also noteworthy is the opening that it afforded for trade union officials to be nominated as delegates, thus constituting a three-way mixed body: government, employee and union.[35]

The scheme was overtaken by the exigencies of war, but the proposal formed an unmistakeable transitional stage between the customary annual visitations and the Whitley Council scheme of 1919 which, however, gave much more specific representation and power to the unions. Under the Whitley scheme, as eventually applied in the dockyards, each shop (meaning each workshop, storehouse, ship or group of workmen) had its committee and so had each department of each yard. Members from the employee side, numbering about twelve in each case, were to be elected to represent the trade unions at each level (i.e. from each of the above categories) and were to confer with the appropriate officials at each work station on wages, conditions of work and all matters which had by now become familiar through the petition movement. Within the Whitley Council system, which still preserved the connection between the workshop floor and government policy, the paternalistic relationship between the Admiralty and the employee was, arguably, removed.

The experience which the dockyardmen obtained in handling issues at the workshop level was an important contribution to forms of political and industrial organization then being discussed in trade union circles. 'The true basis of Trade Unionism', wrote Cole in 1920, 'is in the workshop ... a natural unit which is a direct stimulus to self-assertion and control by the rank and file.'[36] The dockyard workers of this period, along with other groups of public sector workers, such as postmen and policemen, were hammering out a method of dealing with the state as an employer, including a readiness to use all the bureaucratic machinery which that state put into their hands or to which it gave them access. By their insistence on their traditional rights and privileges, they developed a habit of regular self-representation which soon led them to transcend the medieval origins of the procedure and tackle contemporary issues with all the self-confidence it gave them. The dockyards preserved, in a modern context, a concept of themselves as a political estate with the power to link, vocally, the political and economic aspects of the state.

Notes

1. For further details on the transition from wood to iron in shipbuilding practices, see M. Waters, 'Changes in the Chatham Dockyard, 1860–90. Part 1: From wood to iron: change and harmony, 1860–87', *Mariner's Mirror*, **69** (1983), 55–63.
2. See Galliver's chapter and Lunn and Day's chapter in this volume for fuller details on the development of state management.
3. Waters, 'Changes in the Chatham Dockyard', p. 55.
4. G. D. H. Cole, *Self-Government in Industry* (London, G. Bell and Co., 1920).
5. H. M. Baxendall, 'The Admiralty method of training dockyard apprentices', Board of Education Educational Pamphlets No. 32 (London, HMSO, 1916).
6. This and subsequent quotations are from a group of interviews with Chatham Dockyard workers who worked there as boys in the years immediately preceding the First World War. The tapes are deposited with the Essex Oral History Archive.
7. Essex Oral History Archive.
8. M. Waters, 'Craft consciousness in a government enterprise: Medway dockyardmen 1860–1906', *Oral History*, **5**(4) (1977).
9. J. M. Haas, 'The best investment ever made: the Royal Dockyard schools, technical education, and the British shipbuilding industry, 1800–1914', *Mariner's Mirror*, **76** (1990), 325–35.
10. P. L. Robertson, 'Technical education in the British shipbuilding and marine engineering industries, 1863–1914', *Economic History Review* (2nd Series), **27**(2) (1974), 222–35.
11. For the origins of the petition system see M. Pariss, *Staff Relations in the Civil Service* (London, Allen and Unwin, 1973).
12. *Hansard Parliamentary Debates*, 3rd series, vol. 211, cols. 731–2 and 734 (1872).
13. *Chatham Observer*, 30 July, 6 August, 27 August 1887 and 1 October 1888.
14. M. Waters, 'Dockyard and Parliament 1860–1900', *Southern History*, **6** (1984).
15. *Chatham News*, 8 March 1890; 2 September 1899.
16. Annual Report of the Associated Society of Shipwrights (1891, 1892).
17. *Chatham Observer*, 18 May 1872, and *Chatham News*, 4 May 1872.
18. Arthur Forwood, 'Report on memorials presented to the Lords Commis-

sioners of the Admiralty by the workmen employed in H.M. Dockyards and victualling yards at home', Naval History Library, Da053 (henceforth referred to as 'Forwood's Report').
19. Passfield Papers, Trade Union Collection, Section A, vol. 32, item 2.
20. There exists in the Public Record Office and the Naval History Library a mass of petition material from all the yards, accumulated, sorted, annotated and bundled by various officials.
21. Naval History Library, Da054; PRO ADM 116/875 (1892–3) and PRO ADM 116/1029 (1906). See also Forwood's Report and 'Admiralty response to petitions', *Associated Society of Shipwrights Quarterly Report*, **4** (1905).
22. PRO ADM 116/875 (1892–3).
23. Forwood's Report, pp. 102, 104, 149.
24. PRO ADM 116/875 (1892–3) and ADM 1029 (1906).
25. See Lunn's chapter on the post-war period in this volume.
26. *Chatham News*, 27 September 1902; *Associated Society of Shipwrights Quarterly Report*, **4** (1906).
27. PRO ADM 116/1029 (1906).
28. *Chatham News*, 27 September 1902; *Associated Society of Shipwrights Quarterly Report*, **4** (1906).
29. See Galliver in this volume and D. Dougan, *The Shipwrights* (Newcastle upon Tyne, Frank Graham, 1975).
30. PRO ADM 116/1029 (1906), 'List of delegates received'.
31. D. Englander and J. Osborne, 'Jack, Tommy and Harry Dubb: the armed forces and the working class', *Cambridge Historical Journal*, **21**(3) (1978).
32. *Chatham News*, 16 August 1913.
33. PRO ADM 116/1216, correspondence; Dockyard Committee and Admiral-Superintendent, Chatham (1912–13) and 'As to the making of representations by employees in respect of conditions of employment'.
34. For further details on this see Galliver's chapter in this volume.
35. PRO ADM 116/1216, correspondence.
36. G. D. H. Cole, *Workshop Organisation*, Appendix G, 'The Whitley Scheme in the Royal Dockyards' (Oxford, Clarendon Press, 1923).

6 TRADE UNIONISM IN PORTSMOUTH DOCKYARD, 1880–1914: CHANGE AND CONTINUITY

Peter Galliver

Introduction

Speaking to an audience of dockyardmen at Devonport in 1913, the Labour MP, George Barnes said that 'he was glad to see that Dockyardmen were in tune with the general labour movement. Previously they had held aloof because of their privileges ...'[1] This comment was reported in the Portsmouth press and the same point could be made with regard to Portsmouth dockyardmen. By 1913, trades unionism extended throughout the workforce; from the craftsmen, with substantial memberships in nationally organized unions, embracing private as well as Admiralty employment, to the semi-skilled and unskilled in the Government Labourers' Union. Moreover, the occasion for George Barnes addressing dockyardmen was an overtime ban, and threatened strike, showing that dockyardmen had been caught up in the mood of militancy apparent in the years just before the Great War. By looking in detail at the experience of workers in Portsmouth, it is possible to identify a model which, in its broad application, applies in all the British yards in this period. The common elements, which will be identified in this chapter, draw on the national experiences of the labour movement in the period up to the First World War.

Portsmouth Dockyard retained, as did the other yards, many of the characteristics which made it such a distinctive workplace. As will be indicated, there was some attempt by the Admiralty to introduce systems of management and accountability which reflected practices within the private sector, although these were relatively ineffective. In industrial relations, there was a growing dissatisfaction with the petitioning system and increasing demands for more formal recognition of trade unions. In 1914 the Admiralty proposed a national conference which tacitly recognized the TUC-affiliated trade unions as the representative organizations of the dockyard workers. This conference was overtaken by the outbreak of war, but it can be seen as foreshadowing the Whitley Committee of 1917 and the subsequent establishment of the Whitley Council, with its recognition of the trade unions as representative of the workforce, as the key element in dockyard industrial relations.[2]

Analysis of the way in which dockyardmen became more in tune with the general labour movement has to be set against the broad development of trade union history. Coming into the 1880s, whatever the pessimism about this period felt by the early historians of the labour movement, the national picture was one of some vitality for organization amongst skilled workers.[3] The view which emerges from more recent research is one of skilled workers creating and sustaining trade unions, friendly societies, consumer co-operatives and a wide variety of mutual self-help clubs. This organizational activity was identified as essentially defensive. While the skilled workers may have had substantial pay differentials, and considerable control over the production process, they operated in an atmosphere of insecurity. British industry, largely small-scale in its organization, and fearful of having costly capital investment standing idle, used labour wherever possible instead of machinery. In times of depression the swift response of employers was to shed labour. Hence the attempts of the skilled workers to control local labour markets through trade union activity, the sectionalism of the various trades and the investment in friendly society and related activity.[4]

From the later 1880s this picture began to change, albeit slowly and erratically. The tendency was for the scale of industrial organization to increase and the larger, more impersonal firms to adopt more bureaucratic forms of management which made inroads into the autonomy of skilled workers. In this period, localism became less of a feature of skilled trade unionism and so-called 'New Unionism' after 1889 saw the extension of organization to the unskilled. Trade union activity became increasingly politicized as appeals were made to the state to interfere in the labour market as arbiter, or, with the extension of municipal employment, as exemplar. Alongside these developments was the growth of the socialist societies, the creation of the Labour Party and the syndicalist activity of the years prior to the Great War.[5]

Dockyard trade unionism has to be seen in this context. In the 1880s dockyardmen worked for a large-scale, impersonal employer. Admiralty policy from this time, for the most part, was recognizing the employment practices of private industry. In the later 1880s dockyardmen became more managed and attempts were made by the Admiralty to create a more competitive working environment within the dockyards. In so far as the Admiralty did this, and removed some of the privileges referred to by Barnes, dockyardmen responded by adopting the forms of trade unionism developing within the wider industrial world.

Some dockyardmen regretted this, and blamed the unions, as can be seen in the 1894 comment of the Portsmouth shipwright, Alexander Anderson:

> By its interference the trade union had made conditions in the Dockyard very much worse in many respects ... all the concessions made to the trade union have been accompanied by a steady tightening of the conditions of work. Formerly the Government was the most lenient of employers. The men were allowed all sorts of little privileges, as, for instance, three minutes after bell-ringing in the morning and at meal times and if on dirty work to leave ten minutes earlier to get washed up etc. ... The conditions came every day more to resemble those prevailing in commercial yards.[6]

A larger number, however, saw the Admiralty as taking the initiative in the removal of their privileges and looked to the developing trade union and labour movement for the protection of their interests. The lack of positive response to petitions only highlighted the need for more effective forms of representation and negotiation.

This study will chart this process by looking at the features of dockyard employment which, coming into the 1880s, kept dockyardmen aloof from joining trade unions that included non-dockyardmen. It will then focus on the development of trade union organization among the shipwrights and the skilled labourers to illustrate how dockyardmen were integrated into the wider labour movement. These were the largest and most distinctive categories of dockyard workers. In 1891 the shipwrights accounted for 26.2 per cent of the workforce, in 1900 22.8 per cent. The skilled labourers made up 30.3 per cent of the employed in 1891 and 30.5 per cent in 1900.[7] It will conclude with a survey of trade unionism within Portsmouth Dockyard on the eve of the Great War, focusing on the engineering trades-led unrest of 1913.

1880s: Dockyardmen Aloof

At the start of the 1880s dockyard society was essentially inward-looking. Dockyardmen had long been involved in organizations, but these were specifically dockyard affairs, stressing the peculiarities of dockyard employment and tending to isolate dockyardmen from other workers. The main impetus to organization came from the dockyardmen's right to present petitions to 'Their Lordships' during the annual visitations made by the Admiralty to each of the dockyards. These petitions could be on behalf of individuals or groups, as MacDougall and Waters have shown. Examples of organization for the presentation of group petitions are provided by the existence in the 1880s of separate societies representing the hired and established shipwrights.[8] The dockyard also provided plenty of scope for friendly societies and a variety of clubs. In 1899, for example, the Dockyard Burial Fund Society, established in 1868 (popularly known as the 'Penny Death'), had 4661 adult and 1141 juvenile members.[9]

While strikes in the dockyard occurred in the eighteenth and early-nineteenth centuries, by the end of the French Wars such militancy was no longer rational in the dockyard context. What kept dockyardmen from creating the sort of unions common in private shipbuilding, with their bargaining power ultimately resting on the threat of strike action, and from wanting to co-operate with workers outside of Admiralty employment, was the security offered by dockyard employment. To emulate workers in the private trade and risk dismissal for taking strike action would be to jeopardize too much, as MacDougall has illustrated.

At the heart of the security afforded by Admiralty employment was the establishment system. Established workers, subject to 'behaving' themselves, were in guaranteed employment and entitled to pensions at the age of 60. Although some workers in private shipyards were given preferential treatment in the allocation of work, such as the 'royals' of the North East,[10] there was nothing in the private trade genuinely to compare with the institution of the Admiralty establishment list.

Establishment did little to create fertile ground for trade union development within the dockyard. It was remarked by a *Hampshire Telegraph* reporter that, as a rule in the 1880s, if men were trade union members when they came into the dockyard, they resigned on becoming established.[11] It is easy enough to see why this should be so. Once taken onto the establishment, there would be little incentive for a worker to look beyond the particular world of Admiralty employment and to become involved with organizations which might antagonize his employer and put his pension at risk.

Hired men were more likely to be trade unionists, but even among them, the establishment list exerted its influence and entered into their calculations on how to treat their employers. For the well-behaved hired man there was the possibility of establishment, and, even if a hired man never reached the establishment list, there was a bonus paid on leaving the dockyard calculated on length of service. In practice, hired men also had some degree of job security enjoyed by the established men. Apart from the major reductions of the dockyard workforce in 1887 and 1905–8,[12] dockyard employment was stable. Hired men might be laid off briefly to balance the books before the new Naval Estimates came into effect, but this was minor in comparison to the uncertainty in the private shipbuilding yards where men were laid off as jobs were completed. As E. H. Kelly, a social investigator, commented of Portsmouth, 'The effect of trade cycles, so keenly felt elsewhere, is here scarcely noticed.'[13]

By being associated with this level of job security, the Admiralty was not going to be challenged in the way private shipbuilding firms were. In the dockyards 'Their Lordships' were able to maintain a working environment characterized by relatively low wages, with established men being paid less than hired men, hired men earning less than those working in comparable jobs elsewhere, and a unique demarcation system.[14] Clear evidence of the impact of job security on the thinking of dockyardmen is provided by the absence of a serious challenge to the establishment system, in spite of all the complaints about the low wages, and the practice of Admiralty management stemming from it. It was often said that if the establishment, bonuses and pensions were swept away dockyardmen could strike for, and get, the wages of the private yards. Faced with this prospect, Admiralty employment practice would change for the better. Typical of this analysis was the 1893 comment of Portsmouth's Liberal MP, John Baker:

> Should bonuses and pensions be abolished the government would as employers keep themselves in the front rank with regard to the treatment of workmen and pay them as much as their labour would buy on the Clyde, the Mersey and other great private shipbuilding establishments.[15]

There is, however, little sign that the majority wanted to transfer such rhetoric into action. The shipwright trade unionist, Richard Gould, tried to persuade his union branch, one largely composed of hired men, to oppose establishment in 1891, but, as he admitted in his evidence to the Royal Commission on Labour, he received minimal support.[16] In 1899 ship joiners at their annual conference called on the Admiralty to increase the establishment among their numbers.[17] Most dockyardmen wanted the security and status afforded by establishment and were prepared, even if they grumbled about deferred wages, to accept the lower pay rates given to established men in return for secure employment and a pension.[18]

Given this, it seems surprising that the dockyard acquired any more than a handful of members of the TUC-affiliated trade unions. However, as has been shown, the nationally organized trade unions did become an important dockyard presence by 1914. An examination of the experience of the shipwrights provides an explanation of this.

The Shipwrights: The Beginning of Integration

The original mass organization of the dockyard shipwrights was the Ship Constructive Association (SCA), an exclusively dockyard body, formed in 1883 and embracing all shipwrights; hired and established, and those promoted to the supervisory grades. That such an organization should be formed is no great surprise. By the 1880s dockyard shipwrights were rather embattled and needed better organization. They were not popular with their fellow Admiralty employees, and, for much of the trade union movement, were objects of suspicion, sometimes attack.

The dockyard shipwrights were in this position because of the Admiralty's response to the advent of iron shipbuilding in the mid-nineteenth century. While private yards became dominated by iron-working trades, boilermakers, fitters, *et al.*, in the Royal Dockyards, the shipwrights – the builders of wooden ships – remained the core trade, taking on the basic tasks of iron shipbuilding and leaving only the most specialized tasks to other trades.

Shipwrights, moreover, occupied a key role in the evolving management structure of the dockyard.[19] For a handful, there was the chance of showing sufficient promise as an apprentice to be trained as a constructor. Sir William White and Sir Philip Watts, the Admiralty's principal naval architects of the period, were both ex-shipwright apprentices. For many, however, there was the more realistic prospect of promotion to a supervisory post within the manual workforce. Shipwrights were used to supervise not just fellow shipwrights but unskilled and skilled labourers, and could be used to supervise minor trades. In 1908, for example, one of the grievances of the sailmakers in Portsmouth was that their inspector was a shipwright.[20] The promotion prospects associated with the trade of shipwright help explain the popularity of shipwright as the trade choice of the boys successful in the dockyard entrance examination. While engineering trades earned the highest wages in the dockyard, the boys at the head of the pass list invariably opted to become shipwrights. In 1894, for example, of the 73 boys successful in the entrance examination and entered as apprentices, the majority of the top 35 chose to be shipwrights.[21]

In the process of remaining the core trade in the dockyards, shipwrights did not become popular with their fellow dockyard workers. It was frequently alleged that the presence of so many shipwrights within the dockyard's management hierarchy reinforced the Admiralty's predisposition to decide in the shipwright's favour when confronted with demarcation disputes. In their correspondence with Sidney and Beatrice Webb in the 1890s, the Portsmouth fitters complained that they should have had all of the jobs concerning valves, pumps, gunmountings and watertight doors. These jobs, however, were undertaken, 'by shipwrights, backed up by the officials, the majority, if not the whole, belong to the shipwright interest'.[22] The success of the shipwrights in matters of demarcation was further illustrated in 1899 when the Portsmouth Times reported:

> It having been rumoured that the Admiralty had under consideration the subject of making changes as between engineers and shipwrights in the Royal Dockyards by reason of the alleged over-lapping of trades, the latter class recently asked Their Lordships not to sanction any alteration of shipwrights' work in the construction of war vessels. Their reply made known on Saturday is that Their Lordships do not contemplate making any such change.[23]

Hostility by other trades towards shipwrights was still apparent in the 1920s when it was observed that

> The stranger to Dockyard routine is surprised that one single craft can continue to have demarcation disputes with plumbers, with fitters, with blacksmiths, with joiners, with boilermakers, with patternmakers and with electricians, 'It's not a trade,' I once heard a workman of another craft say, 'it's a disease.' And it must be confessed that the boundaries of the trade still wander from time to time.[24]

As part of these demarcation disputes, dockyard shipwrights had to contend with the interference of TUC-affiliated unions concerned with the interests of their members in the dockyards, and with the example being set by Admiralty employment practice. It was in response to such trade union intervention that the SCA was formed. In 1883, the Lib-Lab MP, Henry Broadhurst, on behalf of the Amalgamated Society of Engineers (ASE), complained in Parliament about shipwrights being used to fit engines:

> He thought he had satisfactorily proved that it was next to impossible for shipwrights or workers in wood to engage in the fitting of delicate and complicated machinery, but the Admiralty had answered his motion by increasing the number of shipwrights employed in the various dockyards.[25]

Shortly after this the dockyard shipwrights organized. As W. B. Robinson, a constructor, said in 1883 at the formation of the Portsmouth branch of the SCA,

> their association was born of necessity, and the questions raised in Parliament when the late Navy Estimates were under consideration by Mr Broadhurst and also on former occasions by the same gentleman were sufficient reason, if any were needed, for the formation of their Association.[26]

For the founders of the SCA it was of vital importance that their organization was an association embracing all shipwrights, or ship constructors as they preferred. This further stressed the distinctiveness of Admiralty employment, and opened membership to those involved in management as well as those working on their tools in a way that an organization modelled on the trade unions would not.[27] The Portsmouth shipwright and National Secretary of the SCA, H. T. Earle, noted this at the Association's fourth annual conference:

> He alluded to the mistaken notion as to the Association being only a trade union, remarking that if this were so many who now gave the Association valued support would have withdrawn from it. The duty of the Association was to first of all break down old prejudices which even now held with some persons outside of the service, to afford mutual help, to provide professional intercourse and individual culture and to show all men that in the varied and important works they had to perform the shipwrights of the Royal Dockyards stood without parallel in any service.[28]

At its inception the SCA appears to have achieved near universal support among the dockyard shipwrights, claiming 4000 members. By 1893, however, the nationally organized, and TUC-affiliated, shipwrights' trade union, the Associated Shipwrights' Society (ASS) – founded on the Clyde in 1887 by Alexander Wilkie – had begun to recruit significant numbers in the dockyards. In 1900 the ASS had nearly double the membership of the SCA and in 1907 the remnant of the SCA was absorbed into the ASS, which now called itself the Shipconstructors' and Shipwrights' Association.[29] The failure of the SCA, although, in its origins, apparently so well suited to the needs of the dockyard shipwrights, and the success of the ASS, can be best explained by the shrewd response of the ASS to changing circumstances. The expanding dockyards were increasingly open to national influences working in favour of the trade union movement. This enabled the ASS to present itself as better suited to the requirements of Admiralty-employed shipwrights than the dockyard-founded SCA. The ASS was a trade union founded and based in the world of private commerce, yet interested in the peculiar world of Admiralty workers. Dockyard craftsmen were frequently looked at with suspicion by outsiders; they were accused of working under the rate for the job and of allowing themselves to be given labourers' work. Their credentials as craftsmen could be challenged. It was alleged that Admiralty officials, when entering men into the dockyard, were more interested in practical demonstrations of ability than with proof of indentured apprenticeship. This attitude was illustrated in 1898 when the Dockyard sailmakers tried unsuccessfully to gain admission to the Federation of Sailmakers. The dockyardmen's cause was advanced within the Federation by the Grimsby branch. The Secretary of the Hull branch responded:

> Our members do not look upon this movement with any great favour. There is a feeling that the object is not to benefit sailmakers who have served an apprenticeship of seven years so much as it is to assist men who have picked up the trade.[30]

In spite of this, however, the dockyardmen could not be ignored by the trade union movement. They were a too numerous and a significant section of the country's workforce.

This was especially true of the ASS. The shipwrights were under pressure in the private sector where iron shipbuilding was coming to dominate the industry. Tending to lose their demarcation disputes to iron-working trades, especially the boilermakers, they were largely confined to working in wood. With over 20 per cent of shipwrights in Admiralty employment by the end of the nineteenth century and 28.2 per cent by 1911,[31] the ASS could ill-afford to neglect the dockyardmen. Moreover, what happened in the dockyards could be quoted in negotiations with private employers. This was admitted by a Navy minister, Lord Spencer, in 1895, in correspondence with Alexander Wilkie, when he said, 'The Admiralty was aware that any change would affect shipwrights in private yards as well as those in the dockyards.'[32] This was a point which mattered to all trade unionists. As the TUC increased its influence, and as trade union leaders began to appear in Parliament, there was an increasing stress by the labour movement on the extent to which the government should be a model employer. Two examples serve to illustrate this point. In 1906, Jenkins, the Labour MP for Chatham, argued in the House of Commons that the government, 'as a model employer', should not pay less than the rates recommended by trade unions in the locality of the dockyards.[33] In 1914 a TUC deputation to the Admiralty complained of the bad example which was being set to private employers by the denial of apprenticeships to yardboys who were being trained in metal-working skills accorded trade status in the private yards.[34]

It is easy enough, therefore, to see why the ASS was so determined to build its membership in the dockyards and to replace the SCA as the representative organization of Admiralty shipwrights. In the accomplishment of this, the ASS was served by activists in the dockyards, many of whom had come into Portsmouth Dockyard as hired men, apprenticed elsewhere, and already ASS members. An example of this is provided by the president of the Portsmouth branch in the 1890s, Richard Gould. Gould was a Portsmouth man but had been apprenticed and first worked as a journeymen shipwright in Falmouth, returning to Portsmouth in 1881 after a brief spell in Chatham.[35] Men such as Gould were uncompromising in their dealings with the SCA. By 1893 the ASS refused to continue the practice of sending in a joint petition when the SCA would not accept Alexander Wilkie as a representative of the shipwrights during the annual visitation. By 1894 the union policy was that men could not belong to the ASS and SCA.[36]

This discussion of the ASS's attitude and behaviour towards the SCA, however, leaves the question of how the aim of superseding the SCA was achieved. The answer to this lay in the ASS's ability to prove itself the more impressive campaigner on issues relating to conditions of work and the appeal of its friendly society provision to the security-conscious dockyardmen.

The ASS was as well-attuned to the realities of industrial relations in the dockyards as the SCA, as Richard Gould pointed out in his evidence to the Royal Commission on Labour. The dockyard's ASS men appreciated that they did not have recourse to the negotiating methods available in private industry. In reply to a question by the Duke of Devonshire, Gould said:

> You could not strike against the powerful arm of the Government. We do not wish to do that. We do it more by petition ... We would rather move public opinion and get the question brought on in the House of Commons, or some other place of responsibility, rather than have recourse to extreme measures with the Government.[37]

The ASS, with its links to the TUC and Lib-Lab MPs was well suited to this. The SCA might have some influence with dockyard MPs but the union had this and more. The value of this to dockyardmen can be seen in the dispute over classification.

Classification, introduced in 1891, was the Admiralty's attempt to exploit its special position as an employer to have a low-cost, flexible workforce, and at the same time introduce the competitive elements of commercial practice into the dockyards. In 1847, for example, an Admiralty Order relating to dockyard promotions referred to, 'ensuring the early introduction into the Government Yards of the best modes of working in private establishments'.[38] Trying to compensate for the awareness on the part of its workers that a dockyard could not go out of business and to undermine the sense of security engendered by the establishment system, the Admiralty decided to introduce a competitive element into the workforce by classifying shipwrights on one of five grades with weekly wages ranging from 30s to 34s.

The background to the introduction of classification was the setting up of a committee under Admiral Graham in 1885 to investigate work practices in the dockyards and the means of making these more cost-effective for the taxpayer. In this search for greater efficiency the Admiralty was not alone. Several of the large-scale employers in the late-nineteenth century, notably in the engineering industry and the railway companies, sought to maintain profits by the tightening of the management of their workforce and introducing forms of piecework to increase the productivity of labour.[39] In the Admiralty's case, the main burden of its

Committee's findings was that dockyardmen were not given sufficient incentive to work hard and that they were inadequately supervised. These views were encapsulated in the evidence of H. D. Grant, the Admiralty Superintendent of Devonport, and Commodore R. O. B. Fitzroy. Grant was

> not satisfied that there is a proper amount of work obtained from the men. This could only be checked by an independent measurement of the work, as if they were on task and job, and necessitate a disciplinary treatment of the men which does obtain in private yards.[40]

Fitzroy was critical of management control:

> My general opinion as to the supervision of labour in our dockyards is that it is very indifferent, a want of trustworthy leading hands and a dread of making themselves unpopular with the men on the part of many officials of the yard.[41]

In light of these views, Admiral Graham's Committee reported positively on the value of classification:

> We are of the opinion that classification, carrying with it different rates of pay, could be carried out with considerable advantage to the Service; it would, without a doubt, create a spirit of emulation, especially if the men are made to distinctly understand that their retention in a higher class will depend upon their continued exertions and good conduct.[42]

The response of the men to the implementation of this recommendation was that classification was inappropriate to their work and would lead to management by favouritism. The former view was expressed to the Royal Commission on Labour by the Pembroke shipwright, C. S. Caird. Replying to a question about whether the best men were placed in the first class, he said:

> The men think not. In fact, shipwrights generally recognise an equality in the efficiency of workmen. One may be a little better than his fellow at one particular class of work, but the other might excel at something else, and so on, so that taken as a whole, the men are, roundly speaking, equal.[43]

The latter view was put by the Portsmouth ASS man, T. Kersey, to a protest meeting at Portsmouth in 1893, 'The officers would have their favourites and if there was any difference in the qualifications of the workmen it would not be the best man who would obtain the highest figure under the pernicious system.'[44]

This was the issue which played a major role in enabling the ASS, with its access to the lobbying power of the TUC, and Lib-Lab MPs, to begin the process of eclipsing the SCA. The ASS started out as a junior partner in joint protests but by the end of 1893 the ASS was in a position to put serious pressure on the SCA, resulting in a partial success for the men with a major modification of the system.[45]

At anti-classification meetings in Portsmouth, the ASS exploited the opportunity by bringing to town the Lib-Lab MP, George Howell, and its nationally known leader, Alexander Wilkie, to support local activists such as Gould and Kersey. These mass meetings also helped the committed trade union men to spread the union message with the support of the influential local figures of the Revd Robert Dolling of St Agatha's and the Baptist minister, Revd Charles Joseph of the Lake Road Chapel. Both of these men, Dolling especially, were active in working-class affairs, and keen to encourage dockyardmen to look to co-operation with their fellow workers beyond the dockyard gates. In October 1893, for example, the ASS held a Dockyard Branches Convention in Portsmouth. At the main meeting, in Fuller's Hall, and to a packed house, Dolling reminded the men that

> a better condition of things had gradually been brought about and he rejoiced to know that the day was coming when those who worked would be perfectly equal at any rate with those who employed them. This was entirely due to organisation.[46]

Alexander Wilkie picked up this theme:

> He urged Dockyard shipwrights to put their shoulders to the wheel and help forward the Society, pointing out that even from a Christian standpoint, it was the duty of every man, whether hired or established, to do what he could towards ameliorating the conditions of his less fortunate brother.[47]

The extent to which the campaign against classification worked to the ASS's advantage can be seen in the surge in its membership between 1891 and 1892. The ASS increased its membership in all dockyards from 640 to 917.[48]

Moreover, for those less inclined to be swayed by high moral arguments, the SCA failed to compete with the ASS as a provider of insurance benefits covering accidents, sickness and pensions. Speaking to the 1893 Dockyard Branches Convention of the ASS, Wilkie took the opportunity to impress upon his audience the soundness of the union's actuarial base with its £30,000 on deposit in the bank.[49] The best that the SCA in Portsmouth could offer was a short-lived 1d.-a-week sick club. The ASS could provide a sophisticated range of schemes, the most attractive to dockyardmen being the 9d.-a-week package which gave high benefits with regard to sickness and pensions, but which did not include unemployment and strike pay.[50] As an SCA man, Welsford, remarked in correspondence with the Webbs:

> He much regrets that no successful attempt was made to add friendly benefits to the SCA early in its career. Had such been the case it would now have been a powerful and wealthy organisation. As it is, however, it has but little hold on its members and the ASS with such friendly benefits attracts them away from the SCA.[51]

The final element in the demise of the SCA was the pattern of dockyard recruitment in the early twentieth century. The rundown of 1905, when the numbers employed in Portsmouth Dockyard fell from 11,070 to 10,494,[52] struck a blow at the sense of security which did so much to sustain the attitude that dockyardmen operated in different circumstances from other workers, and which was at the heart of the SCA. This rundown, moreover, coincided with a national depression. In these circumstances, the 'Lights on Labour' correspondent of the *Evening News* in Portsmouth could tell the cautionary take of the fitter, who

> had been a member of the A.S.E. but in an evil moment, thinking as many others had done that he was employed for life, he allowed his union subscription to lapse ... Then he is discharged and finds he has been utterly wasting his time, for he is now too old to rejoin the A.S.E. and likewise considered to be too old to be engaged in another government yard if a vacancy happened to fall his way.[53]

The collapse of SCA membership after 1905 was marked. In 1904 the SCA had 1459 members, the ASS 2384; in 1906, the SCA had 724, the ASS 2351.[54]

Given the above, it is not difficult to work out a rationalization of the demise of the SCA and the absorption of its remainder by the ASS. The ASS men who survived the 1905 rundown were unlikely to surrender their union membership, while SCA men were likely to have been less enamoured of belonging to an organization so closely identified with the distinctive character of Admiralty employment. When Portsmouth Dockyard expanded again, as it did from 1906, hired shipwrights coming into the dockyard, if already unionized, would have little reason to join the SCA. The ASS would not allow dual membership and threatened its members with the loss of their already-paid-for insurance benefits if they joined the SCA. If a shipwright were to belong to an organization it might as well be the trade union. Most of his workmates belonged to it, it provided insurance benefits which were of everyday importance, and, in the business of dealing with the Admiralty as an employer, the ASS had access to the growing political influence of the labour movement. After 1906, Alexander Wilkie was one of the 30 MPs in the Labour Party.

The Skilled Labourers: The Extension of Trade Unionism to the Dockyard Labourers

The skilled labourers, like the shipwrights, represent a category of worker distinctive to the dockyard. Men such as riveters and drillers, who in private yards might claim trade status, were, in the dockyard, paid as skilled labourers and switched to purely labouring work when it suited the management. This was an important element in giving the Admiralty its relatively flexible and low-cost workforce. From the perspective of potential for trade union development, these workers presented a complicated picture. There is some indication that a significant number were time-served tradesmen who could well have acquired union membership in private shipyards. In the evidence presented to Admiral Graham's Committee on Dockyard Management it was said by an official that 'a great number of labourers who came in are men who have learnt their trade but they cannot get into the Yard any other way and then afterwards they are employed as skilled labourers'.[55]

Working as semi-skilled workers in the dockyard, however, it is unlikely that the craft unions would have allowed men to continue in membership. The Boilermakers' Society did not admit ironcaulkers and riveters to membership until 1914, and did so then, according to the dockyard columnist of the *Hampshire Telegraph*, 'to induce the Admiralty to fall into line with large private firms in this respect and classify the men doing rivetting and caulking as mechanics instead of labourers and pay them a higher wage'.[56] An even greater depressant to the prospects of trade union organization among the labourers was the presence of ex-servicemen in receipt of government pensions. The pensioners were less likely to be as animated by the comparatively low dockyard wages and unlikely to risk their relatively secure employment by involvement with something suspect in the eyes of their Admiralty employers.[57]

In the 1890s, however, in the wake of the London Dock Strike of 1889, trade unionism was extended to these unskilled and semi-skilled workers of the dockyard. Clem Edwards led a London deputation from the Dock Labourers' Union to Portsmouth and a branch was formed in the town.[58] The Dock Labourers' Union proved vulnerable, however, to an employers' counter-attack on the Thames and it did not last long in Portsmouth. In 1894 the Portsmouth branch folded. Trade unionism among the skilled and unskilled, however, was not extinguished and a Government Labourers' Union was formed. Besides this, the riveters and hand-drillers had their own associations.[59]

The Admiralty, however, was not well-disposed towards such trades unionism. It was prepared to tolerate it among craftsmen; the official line was that men were free to belong to any organization they wished but that no trade union would be recognized as having negotiation rights. Even among the craftsmen there were complaints that trade union involvement hampered progress at work. Richard Gould made this point in his evidence to the Royal Commission on Labour; in 1894 Willis, an engineer, and Vine, a shipwright, cited this as their reason for resigning from the Trades and Labour Council and, in 1908, the Navy Minister, McKenna, had to deny in the House of Commons that trade unionists were singled out for discharge during reductions.[60]

When it came to trades unionism among the skilled labourers, the Admiralty was much more openly hostile. Just as there was an employers' backlash against the new unions in the late 1890s, when the economic climate had changed and the bargaining position of workers had weakened, so the Admiralty took action to curb the influence of trades unionism among its unskilled and semi-skilled workers. The crunch point came in Portsmouth in 1898. By this time, many unions involved in the post-1889 surge of activity associated with the 'New Unionism' had been eliminated, or all but destroyed by private employers. This, for example, had been the experience of workers on the Humber and the Thames.[61] In 1897, even the skilled men in the ASE had suffered defeat during a national dispute.

The Admiralty's action in Portsmouth was triggered by a meeting held outside the Unicorn Gate on a Saturday afternoon, outside of working hours, to discuss the grievances of the skilled labourers. These grievances were principally concerned with pay levels and the administration of piecework schemes. The theme of the meeting was summed up by A. G. Gourd, when he argued that 'they had to work hard all week under conditions so tyrannical that they would not be tolerated for twenty-four hours in a private firm'.[62]

This meeting resulted in its chairman, who was also president of the Portsmouth Trades and Labour Council (the shipwright Richard Gould), and three officers of the skilled labourers' unions – Sparshott, president of the Riveters' Association; Gourd, secretary of the Hand-drillers; and Knott, vice-president of the Boilermakers' Society – being dismissed, the reasons given for this by the Admiralty being 'conduct prejudicial to public service', by acting outside of the system of making grievances known through the petitioning during the annual visitations, and, in the case of the skilled labourers involved, irregularities in their piecework claims. It was denied by the Admiralty that the dismissals had anything to do with trades unionism. In reply to a letter from one of Portsmouth's Liberal MPs, Sir John Baker, W. Grahame Greene, the Private Secretary to the Navy minister, Goschen, was at pains to make this clear:

> You will perceive that the action of the Admiralty was not directed against the four men as trade union leaders but because they were men who headed an improper agitation against the legitimate functions of the Admiralty in the administration of Her Majesty's Dockyard.[63]

This argument was not accepted in Portsmouth or in the wider labour movement. The local press was full of letters denouncing the action as anti-trade union, and a resolution passed by the Portsmouth Trades and Labour Council and the Parliamentary Committee of the TUC had Sam Woods challenge the Admiralty on this issue in the House of Commons.[64] That the dismissals were seen as being directed against trade unionism, whatever might be said by the Admiralty, was further shown by the reaction of the men in the dockyard. The skilled labourers' unions' support fell dramatically in the wake of the dismissal of their leaders. The Hand-drillers, whose membership in 1897 had been 120, was reduced to 20 by 1899 when the society was dissolved.[65]

In Portsmouth Dockyard, however, as elsewhere, the labourers' trade unions, while severely damaged, did not entirely disappear. By 1914, A. G. Gourd, who had been allowed back into the yard in 1904,[66] headed the Government Labourer's Union, which, after struggling along with a membership of around 200 in the first decade of the century, had 1025 members out of nearly 5000 labourers in Portsmouth Dockyard.[67] As Waters has shown, there was similar growth in Chatham at this time. The sharp increase was achieved in the aftermath of the trade union-led agitation of 1913.

1913: No Longer Aloof

By 1913 trade unionism had progressed a long way within the dockyard since the 1880s. By then, all of the trades had substantial memberships of the nationally organized, TUC-affiliated shipbuilding trade unions; the shipwrights approaching 70 per cent, the engineering trades more.[68] In 1911 the Portsmouth Trades Council had formed a Dockyard Grievances Committee. Writing to the Admiral Superintendent of Portsmouth to inform him of this development, the president of the Trades Council, G. W. Porter, a dockyard sailmaker, was able to say, 'The Dockyard Grievances Committee is representative of the organised men in the dockyard. The Portsmouth Trades Council has thirty-nine branches affiliated to it, twenty-six of which have members who are employed in the Dockyard.'[69] Also, Portsmouth Dockyard, in common with the other yards, had become a more militant place. The engineering trades, led by the ASE, the Steam Engine Makers' Society (SEMS) and the Patternmakers' Society, spearheaded a campaign focused on the demand for a 6s. 6d.-per-week pay rise and an attack on the petitioning system.

That the engineering trades should take the lead in militancy was no great surprise. This stemmed from the Admiralty's structuring of its workforce. With the shipwrights providing the core of the skilled workforce, the engineering trades had only been allowed into the dockyards to perform those tasks which even the Admiralty had to accept were beyond the shipwrights. The Admiralty, while it did offer apprenticeships in engineering trades, tended to look for such workers from private industry where men were likely to be unionized. Fewer engineering tradesmen were kept on the establishment than shipwrights and the many grievances felt by engineering craftsmen further tended to promote trade union membership. As has been seen in the development of the SCA, the nationally organized trade unions gave the dockyard's engineering workers a chance to air their complaints against the Admiralty. In 1913, however, while the lead in the campaign for the

6s. 6d.-a-week pay rise and reform of the petitioning system was taken by the engineering trades, the shipwrights joined in. This culminated in an engineering trades' overtime ban in which the shipwrights threatened to participate. Such militancy had been unheard of for a century.

Fundamental to this development was the extent to which the dockyard had ceased to be different from private yards. In large part, this could be attributed to Admiralty policy. In 1899 the Admiralty adopted a measure which, in effect if not intent, was to blur the distinction between hired and established men. The Admiralty had always kept established and hired men in separate gangs. In future, gangs were to be a mix of one-third established, two-thirds hired. The *Portsmouth Times* offered an explanation of this decision:

> For the first time hired and established shipwrights are to be associated in the same working parties. Roughly speaking there are twenty-five gangs of established and fifty gangs of hired shipwrights at Portsmouth, and as the established men claim a certain degree of superiority, the officials have been able to work upon the jealousies of the two classes and to extract the best work from each.[70]

More significantly, from the point of view of the distinctiveness of the dockyards, in the first decade of the century, it sometimes seemed that the Admiralty was seeking to run down the establishment lists. Above all, this would affect shipwrights, of whom some 40 per cent were established, while only 2 per cent of engine fitters held that status.[71] In 1909, the *Hampshire Telegraph* noted that there seemed to be the intention of 'gradually allowing the established list to die out'.[72] This clearly provoked some reaction from dockyardmen, and, given the increasing pressure of naval expenditure at this time, it was deemed important to avoid conflict among the workforce. In 1910, the establishment lists were opened again. The *Hampshire Telegraph* reported:

> The growing unrest among the working classes, largely fostered by trade unions, is believed to have had a strong effect in persuading Their Lordships to restore a system in the Royal Dockyards which would make them independent of any possible labour dispute.[73]

By 1912, though, the ratio of established to hired had been allowed to slip again, and the *Telegraph* returned to the point, arguing that the cost of increasing the establishment would be 'money well spent if it gave additional assurance that the Dockyards would not be affected by strikes'.[74]

As was the case with the growth of trade unionism amongst the shipwrights, an important element in the changing of attitudes towards industrial relations was the character of those coming into the dockyard as hired men at times of expansion. These included able and experienced trade unionists and Labour politicians. The Scottish shipwright, J. M. MacTavish, elected in 1908 as Portsmouth's first Labour councillor and later prospective parliamentary candidate, is the obvious example, but important in the context of the trade union militancy of 1913 was David Naysmith. He had been president of the Barrow and District branch of the ASE until being blacklisted by Vickers in the wake of the engineering disputes of 1897–8.[75] By 1901, in the view of the *Evening News*, 'Since he [Naysmith] had come to Portsmouth the strength of the [ASE] Branch had been increased by 300 members and now numbered over 1000 and thus Portsmouth had been made one of the most important of the Society's districts.'[76]

Other external factors combined with Admiralty policy to create conditions likely to foster increased trade union membership and more militant attitudes inside the dockyards. The compensations for relatively low dockyard pay and the peculiarities of Admiralty employment were becoming less marked after 1910. The naval race with Germany created near full employment in shipbuilding. The shipbuilding trade unions reported only between 3 and 4 per cent of their members out of work between 1910 and 1914 and there were signs that the dockyard was finding it difficult to recruit labour. In the local press there were reports of shortages of shipwrights and the widespread working of overtime. Men were allowed to stay on beyond the retirement age of 60.[77] The social legislation of the twentieth century, starting with the Workman's Compensation Act, and the measures of the Liberal governments from 1905, old age pensions in 1908 and National Insurance in 1911, all added to a climate in which the security of employment in the dockyard, and its pensions and bonuses, did not seem so special. That dockyardmen were aware of this is shown by the Dockyard Ex-Apprentices Association during their 1910 annual conference, where a resolution was passed that the introduction of state pensions undermined the value of the established dockyardman's pension which was paid for by low wages.[78]

For the non-craftsmen of the dockyard, as for unskilled workers elsewhere, the National Insurance Act proved a considerable stimulus to trade union recruitment as trade unions were included among the institutions through which National Insurance contributions could be made. At the Annual General Meeting of the Portsmouth branch of the

Government Labourers' Union in 1913, the surge in membership from 426 to 1025 since 1911 was largely attributed to the National Insurance Act.[79]

Moreover, the period after 1910 was one of inflation, and low dockyard wages were made even more irksome. The Portsmouth MP, Lord Charles Beresford, made forceful representations on behalf of his constituents to the Navy Minister in 1913. 'They [the dockyardmen] have only received 2s. extra pay in the last twenty years in which time the cost of living has risen by 20 per cent.'[80] This may have been something of an exaggeration but figures published by the government in 1913 showed that between 1910 and 1913 retail prices had increased by 7 per cent in Portsmouth. There had also been a 7 per cent increase in a rent and retail prices index.[81]

It was these material considerations rather than any major shift in the ideological position of dockyardmen, brought about by the dissemination of socialist and syndicalist thought, which was at the root of the unrest of 1913. In this connection there was a revealing exchange between Tom Mann and the local Labour activist, J. M. MacTavish, during a mass meeting in Portsmouth at the height of the agitation. Mann addressed the dockyardmen on the importance of their combining to take control of the dockyard, saying that 'he did not mean control in the sense of being able to obtain an increase in pay, but that entire control of industries would make it unnecessary for anyone to be above them or even advise them.'[82] MacTavish would not support this line. While he was a socialist, his socialism consisted of political action to achieve social reform, and, in the industrial context, was much more immediately concerned with collective bargaining. Rather than worry about workers' control of industry, MacTavish was more taken by the idea that 'with organisation, at a time of boom in the shipbuilding trade, they could have prevented an extra twenty-four shipwrights being taken on without an increase in pay rates to outside levels'.[83]

Dockyard militancy and dockyard working conditions, however, had not been made so similar to the private yards that the dispute was pushed to the point of a strike. It did not take major concessions by the Admiralty to take the sting out of the agitation. Pay rises of around 2s. a week in all categories of the workforce were enough to make the continuation of action too radical for the majority. Once the pay rises were announced, opposition to the Admiralty gave way to the reappearance of the sectional rivalries which characterized the relationships between the trades. Shortly after the publication of the pay increase, the *Portsmouth Times* reported that '[T]he threatened strike of the engineers has practically fizzled out ... It is thought that at present no benefit could be obtained by continuing the agitation.'[84] The *Hampshire Telegraph* reported a dockyard fitter saying that '[T]he increases have all been given to the shipwrights and labourers and the engineering trades have got absolutely nothing out of it.'[85]

When things had calmed down, the Admiralty increased the ratio of established to hired men. The overall percentage of established men was increased from 17.2 per cent in 1913 to 22.9 per cent in 1914. While the shipwright establishment was increased by 24.6 per cent, the troublesome engine fitters saw an increase of 66.6 per cent.[86] The Admiralty's response, therefore, to increasing trade union consciousness and to the threat of industrial action, was to shrink from attempts to move closer to the conditions of the private sector and to re-emphasize the distinctiveness of the Royal Dockyards, thereby turning back the clock.

The clock, however, could not be turned all the way back to the 1880s. The impending demise of the petitioning system was the clearest sign of this. Trade unionists had always resented the system. Petitioning was seen as servile and denied official recognition to the unions, even if national trade union officials were allowed to participate as nominated representatives during the annual visitations. In private, the attitude of dockyard trade unionists to petitioning was succinctly expressed by the secretary of the Portsmouth Sailmakers' Society, A. W. Hawkins, to the Hull headquarters of the Federation of Sailmakers: 'Well we have just been before My Lords but what a farce. It is enough to make me ill.'[87] In public, the ASE official, A. G. Slaughter, was prepared to write to the *Evening News* at the height of the 1913 agitation stating that petitioning was unacceptable. 'The style of application is slavish in the extreme, the form of the petition requiring the workmen to acknowledge themselves as "the humble servants" of "My Lords". An emotion which they are far from feeling in these days of democratic control.'[88] As ever, the Admiralty was reluctant to abandon tradition entirely – the annual visitations were to be retained for private petitions and local matters – but the Admiralty had to accept that it was now operating in a different world of industrial relations. Just as the larger railway companies and the engineering employers had come to acknowledge the expediency of dealing with the trade unions as the representatives of their workers, so too did the Admiralty.[89] In 1914, recognition by the Admiralty that TUC-affiliated unions now represented the majority in the main categories of its workforce was given with the proposal that the principal vehicle for the exchange of views between it and the workers should be an annual London conference, for all dockyards, with up to half of the representatives being non-dockyardmen. The non-dockyardmen would be full-time trade union officials.[90]

On the eve of the Great War, Portsmouth Dockyard continued in many respects to be different from a commercial shipyard. The establishment system still offered the prospect of a job for life, underpinning the low-wage and relatively quiescent dockyard working environment. The Admiralty persisted with its own way of organizing its workforce; shipwrights, for example, continued to work in metal as well as wood and there was still the influence of a tradition created by centuries of civilians working for, and alongside, the Royal Navy. On balance, however, it is change rather than continuity which is the more striking in the history of the dockyard from the 1880s. In its pursuit of greater efficiency the Admiralty may not have consciously wanted to introduce changes in its employment practice which would foster the growth of trades unionism and the integration of dockyard workers within the wider labour movement, but, in the context of the increasing scale and political influence of organized labour from the later 1880s, this had been the effect of its policies.

Notes

1. *Hampshire Telegraph*, 2 May 1913.
2. R. Charles, *The Development of Industrial Relations in Britain, 1911–1939* (London, Hutchinson, 1973).
3. See J. Lovell, *British Trade Unions 1875–1933* (London, Macmillan, 1977), pp. 9–12, for a discussion of the work of H. A. Clegg, A. Fox and A. F. Thompson, *A History of British Trade Unions since 1889* (Oxford, Clarendon, 1964), in modifying the views put forward in G. D. H. Cole, *A Short History of the British Working Class* (London, 1948).
4. A critical summary of recent research in these areas is given in M. Savage and A. Miles, *The Remaking of the British Working Class* (London, Routledge, 1994). For a detailed discussion of the labour-intensive character of British industry see: A. Stinchcombe, 'Bureaucratic and craft administration of production: a comparative study', *Administrative Science Quarterly*, **4** (1959); R. Samuel, 'The workshop of the world: steam power and hand technology in mid-Victorian Britain', *History Workshop*, **3** (1977); A. E. Musson, *The Growth of British Industry* (London, Batsford, 1978). For the pay and conditions of skilled workers see the chapter on the Labour Aristocracy in

E. J. Hobsbawm, *Labouring Men* (London, Wiedenfeld and Nicolson, 1968). For the degree of workplace autonomy enjoyed by skilled workers, especially in shipbuilding, see K. McClelland and A. Reid, 'Wood, iron and steel: technology, labour and trade union organisation in the shipbuilding industry, 1840–1914', in R. Harrison and J. Zeitlin (eds), *Divisions of Labour* (Brighton, Harvester, 1985).

5. For a summary of these developments see Savage and Miles, *The Remaking of the British Working Class*, pp. 48–56. For detailed study of the changes in the organization of British industry see: L. Hannah, *The Rise of the Corporate Economy* (London, Methuen, 1976); A. D. Chandler, *Scale and Scope: The Dynamics of Industrial Capitalism* (Cambridge, MA, Harvard University Press, 1990). For changes in management and trade unionism from the 1890s see: J. Melling, 'Non-commissioned officers: British employers and their supervisory workers 1880s–1920', *Social History*, 5 (1980); W. J. Mommsen and H.-G. Husung (eds), *The Development of Trade Unionism in Britain and Germany, 1880s–1914* (London, George Allen and Unwin, 1985), especially K. Burgess, 'New unionism for old? The Amalgamated Society of Engineers in Britain', E. J. Hobsbawm, 'The new unionism reconsidered', R. Price, 'The new unionism and the labour process', and A. Reid, 'Politics and the division of labour, 1880s–1920'; R. Price, *Labour in British Society* (London, Croom Helm, 1986).

6. This quotation is taken from the correspondence of Sidney and Beatrice Webb kept in the British Library of Political and Economic Science, the London School of Economics. Webb Collection. A XXXIII. Correspondence with A. Anderson, 1894.

7. These figures are taken from a breakdown of the Portsmouth workforce given in a letter from the Admiral Superintendent of Portsmouth dated 5 April 1900. It is in the Public Record Office PRO ADM 116 Case 3002.

8. *Hampshire Telegraph*, 28 March 1885. The report of the annual meeting of the Portsmouth Established Shipwrights' Society mentions a similar organization for the hired men.

9. *Portsmouth Evening News*, 14 January 1899.

10. See H. Mess, *Industrial Tyneside* (London, 1928).

11. *Hampshire Telegraph*, 6 February 1886.

12. Numbers employed in Portsmouth Dockyard: 1880 – 5892; 1886 – 7727; 1887 – 7343; 1888 – 7390; 1889 – 7024; 1890 – 7615; 1891 – 7795; 1900 – 10,044; 1904 – 11,924; 1905 – 11,070; 1906 – 10,494; 1907 – 10,601; 1908 – 11,595; 1909 – 12,190; 1910 – 12,896; 1911 – 13,505; 1913 – 14,736; 1914 – 16,692.

    Source: 'Health of the Navy returns'. Parliamentary Papers (PP) 1908 LXV Cd. 296, Table 7, p. 319 for 1880s–1907. Thereafter, PP 1909 LIV Cd. 272, 1910 LXI Cd. 302, 1911 XLVIII Cd. 264, 1912–13 LIII Cd. 348, 1914 LIV Cd. 714, 1914–16 XL Cd. 421.

13. E. H. Kelly, 'Portsmouth', in H. Bosanquet (ed.), *The Social Conditions in English Towns* (London, 1912), p. 2.

14. For a detailed discussion of the structure of the dockyard workforce, pay differentials between hired and established men and a comparison of dockyard and private shipyard pay see P. W. Galliver, 'The Portsmouth Dockyard workforce, 1880s–1914' (unpublished M.Phil. dissertation, University of Southampton, 1986), pp. 1–31. Using shipwrights as an example, the gap between dockyard and commercial pay rates on the Tyne could be in the order of 6s to 7s.
15. *Hampshire Telegraph*, 2 February 1893.
16. Royal Commission on Labour, PP 1893–4 XXXII, Minutes of evidence Q. 21904.
17. *Hampshire Telegraph*, 9 September 1899.
18. Established men's pay rates could be between 1s. and 2s. a week lower than those given to hired men. In 1893, for example, the highest-paid established shipwrights were on 5s. 6d. per day, the comparable hired men on 5s. 8d. (*Hampshire Telegraph*, September 1893). This pay differential was justified by the Admiralty as enabling it to finance the established men's pensions, hence the talk of 'deferred pay'. The real value of the establishment was the guarantee of permanent employment. Pensions at least as good as those paid by the Admiralty could be provided for through friendly societies. See the evidence of Richard Gould to the Royal Commission on Labour on this issue, PP 1893–4 XXXII Question 21821. There is a discussion of this in Galliver, 'Portsmouth Dockyard workforce', pp. 10–18. An indication of the status of established men is provided by a comment in the *Portsmouth Times* in 1899 that established shipwrights regarded themselves as a 'superior class' of workmen (28 January 1899).
19. For a detailed discussion of the development of the dockyard management structure see Galliver, 'Portsmouth Dockyard workforce', pp. 31–47. For the process by which shipwright apprentices could become Naval Constructors see N. McLeod, 'The shipwright officers of the Royal Dockyards', *Mariner's Mirror*, **4** (October 1925).
20. The records of the Federation of Sailmakers are kept in the Library of the University of Warwick (Warwick Collection) MSS 87/3/5/16, letter of 27 March 1908, Hawkins to Hicks.
21. *Hampshire Telegraph*, 16 January 1894.
22. Webb Collection, B LXXXIV, Letter 4.
23. *Portsmouth Times*, 15 July 1899.
24. McLeod, 'The shipwright officers of the Royal Dockyards', p. 280.
25. Parliamentary Debates, 16 July 1883, cols 1528–1651.
26. *Hampshire Telegraph*, 28 July 1883.
27. The SCA extended its membership to the higher levels of the management, to the level of Constructor. The TUC-affiliated unions did not extend membership beyond the supervisors of gangs, the chargemen. Promotion to chargeman, however, did not preclude trade union activity. High-profile trade union activists and local political figures in Portsmouth such as

A. J. Willis and D. Naysmith of the ASE and J. McGuigan of the ASS were promoted to chargemen. The presence of lower-level managers as trade unionists reflects the situation in private industry before the Great War. This can be seen in Melling, 'Non-commissioned officers'.
28. *Hampshire Telegraph*, 17 September 1887.
29. SCA and ASS Membership, all dockyards:

	SCA	ASS
1900	1338	2238
1907	540	2510

Figures based on the ASS Annual Reports kept in the Goldsmiths' Library, University of London. See Galliver, 'Portsmouth Dockyard workforce', table on p. 73.
30. Warwick Collection, 87/3/2/30.
31. 1911 Census, Table 20.
32. Cited in D. Dougan, *The Shipwrights* (Newcastle, Frank Graham, 1975), p. 88.
33. *Hampshire Telegraph*, 3 March 1906.
34. *Ibid.*, 27 February 1914.
35. Gould gave biographical details in the course of his evidence to the Royal Commission on Labour, PP 1893–4 XXXII, Q. 21821 and 21884.
36. For a detailed discussion of the rift between the ASS and the SCA see Galliver, 'Portsmouth Dockyard workforce', pp. 92–5.
37. PP 1893–4 XXXII W. 21960.
38. The Admiralty Order of 27 February 1847 is included in the report produced in the wake of the scandal relating to dockyard appointments which affected the ministry of Lord Derby. PP 1852–3 LX.
39. For developments on the railways see: P. W. Kingsford, *Victorian Railwaymen* (London, Cassell, 1970); F. McKenna, *The Railway Worker* (London, Faber and Faber, 1980). For engineering see: K. Burgess, 'New unionism for old: the Amalgamated Society of Engineers in Britain', in H. J. Mommsen and H.-G. Husung (eds), *Development of Trade Unionism*; R. Price, 'The new unions and the labour process', in *ibid.*; R. Price, *Labour in British Society*.
40. PP 1886 XIII 139, p. 19.
41. PP 1886 XIII 139, p. 20.
42. PP 1886 XIII 139, p. 18.
43. PP 1893–4 XXXII, evidence of C. S. Caird.
44. *Hampshire Telegraph*, 9 September 1893.
45. The five-point scale was replaced with a standard rate for hired and established shipwrights, a year-long probationary rate for new entrants and allowances for special work such as gunmounting. The ASS still denounced this as classification but the issue appears to have moved down the shipwrights' list of grievances. Details of the changes are given in *Hampshire Telegraph*, 4 October 1893.

46. *Hampshire Telegraph*, 14 October 1893.
47. *Ibid.*
48. The Annual Reports of the ASS are kept in the Goldsmiths' Library, University of London.
49. *Hampshire Telegraph*, 14 October 1893.
50. The ASS Annual Report for 1904 gives a breakdown of categories of benefit and levels of subscription. Seventy-seven per cent of Portsmouth men paid in for category 3, high friendly society benefit but no unemployment insurance or strike pay.
51. Webb Collection, XXXII, Welsford correspondence.
52. PP 1908 LXV Cd. 296, Table 7, p. 319.
53. *Portsmouth Evening News*, 3 May 1905.
54. See Galliver, 'Portsmouth Dockyard workforce', table on p. 73.
55. PP 1886 XIII, Q. 1614.
56. *Hampshire Telegraph*, 3 July 1914.
57. There are comments on the influence of the pensioners in this respect in *Portsmouth Times*, 11 January 1890 and 23 April 1904.
58. *Portsmouth Times*, 11 January 1890.
59. PP 1900 LXXXIII Cd. 422, 6th Annual Abstract of Labour Statistics, p. 24.
60. PP 1893–4 XXIII Minutes of Evidence 756; *Hampshire Telegraph*, 16 June 1894; Parliamentary Debates, 15 October 1908, Col. 454.
61. See J. Lovell, *Stevedores and Dockers* (London, Macmillan, 1969); R. Brown, *Waterfront Organisation in Hull* (Hull, University of Hull, 1972).
62. *Hampshire Telegraph*, 29 January 1898.
63. *Ibid.*, 5 February 1898.
64. *Ibid.*, 12 February 1898.
65. PP 1900 LXXXIII Cd. 422, 6th Annual Abstract of Labour Statistics, p. 124.
66. *Portsmouth Evening News*, 4 December 1936.
67. Galliver, 'Portsmouth Dockyard workforce', table on pp. 182–3. Figures taken from PP 1900 LXXXIII Cd. 422, p. 124; PP 1912–13 XLVI Cd. 6109, p. 110. *Portsmouth Evening News*, 16 August 1912; *Hampshire Telegraph*, 14 February 1914.
68. Calculating the number of trade union members by occupational group for any given year is not easy. I have only been able to find breakdowns of the Portsmouth workforce by trade for 1891 and 1900. These are contained in PRO ADM 116 300A. Using these figures and the ASS Annual Reports, I reckon that in 1900 of 1637 Portsmouth shipwrights (750 established, 887 hired) 68.7 per cent were ASS members. For the engineering trades I have used figures which appear in the Portsmouth press. In 1900 according to the *Evening News* of 26 July 1900 there were 1000 ASE members in Portsmouth. This would give the ASE 79 per cent membership. Given the impression created by subsequent comments in the local press I cannot see these percentages declining in the twentieth century.
69. PRO ADM 116 1129A, letter of 30 August 1911.

70. *Portsmouth Times*, 28 January 1899.
71. Galliver, 'Portsmouth Dockyard workforce', p. 28.
72. *Hampshire Telegraph*, 20 March 1909.
73. *Ibid.*, 12 February 1910.
74. *Ibid.*, 26 February 1912.
75. *Portsmouth Evening News*, 31 October 1907.
76. *Ibid.*, 14 May 1901.
77. *Hampshire Telegraph*, 3 January 1913.
78. *Portsmouth Times*, 5 February 1910.
79. *Hampshire Telegraph*, 4 February 1913.
80. *Ibid.*, 3 January 1913.
81. PP 1913 LXVI Cd. 6955, 'Working-class rents and prices'. General Report, p.xvi.
82. *Hampshire Telegraph*, 14 February 1913.
83. *Ibid.*, 14 February 1913.
84. *Ibid.*, 9 May 1913.
85. *Ibid.*, 16 May 1913.
86. *Ibid.*, 20 March 1914.
87. Warwick Collection. MSS 87/3/3/26, letter of 24 June 1902.
88. *Portsmouth Evening News*, 26 February 1913.
89. For the development of collective bargaining in the railway industry, especially on the Great Western Railway, where something resembling the petitioning system existed with the practice of presenting memorials to the directors by the men, which was replaced by negotiations between management and unions, see P. Bagwell, *The Railwaymen* (London, George Allen and Unwin, 1963). For the engineering employers' acceptance of the utility of dealing with trade unions see J. Zeitlin, 'Industrial structure, employer strategy and the diffusion of job control in Britain, 1850–1920', in H. J. Mommsen and H.-G. Husung (eds), *Development of Trade Unionism*.
90. Details given in PRO ADM 116 1216, letters of 11 June and 20 June 1913. Also in *Hampshire Telegraph*, 3 October 1913.

7

CONTINUITY AND CHANGE: LABOUR RELATIONS IN THE ROYAL DOCKYARDS, 1914–50

Kenneth Lunn and Ann Day

As indicated in the previous chapters by Waters and Galliver, the essential basis of labour relations within the Royal Dockyards was undergoing significant change in the immediate pre-First World War years. Although clearly fighting a rearguard action against the forces of emerging trade unions as representative workers' organizations, the Admiralty was being pressurized into conceding ground to the principle. Despite the petition system remaining as the characteristic form of 'bargaining' by 1914, important and significant concessions towards formal union representation of workers' grievances had been made. The introduction of the Whitley system by the end of the war seemed to finalize this process of transition from petitioning to trade union bargaining and negotiation at all levels throughout the naval dockyard system, that is at local shop committee through to the Admiralty Industrial Council and the Shipbuilding Joint Trades Council. The structure of the Whitley system seemed to provide a far more conciliatory and power-sharing approach to industrial relations in the post-war era. Indeed, there is significant testimony to the effect that, under Whitleyism, new approaches to the overall management of labour were introduced and a more sympathetic approach towards conditions of work and pay were displayed by management at many levels.[1] However, there is also evidence of continuity of attitudes, of an underlying preservation of the old approach of command and control. The existing secondary literature on both the history of the Royal Dockyards and of industrial relations pays scant attention to any significant evaluation of the workings of the Whitley system, at least for the period under consideration,[2] and thus its study is long overdue.

Another major area deserving of consideration in any discussion of labour relations is the employment of women in what has generally been considered to be a bastion of masculine work. Not only is it an important dimension of the history of women, but the processes of negotiation around their employment offer considerable insights into the nature of dockyard work and of male attitudes towards that work. This was especially so during the two World Wars when women entered the Royal Dockyards in large numbers, and there are similarities between the two periods as far as negotiations between the Admiralty and trade unions were concerned. These centred around the acceptance of women as substitutes for male workers and the problems involved in 'de-skilling', or in the subsequent 'feminization' of the work process. However, the Second World War experience was particularly significant for the way it revealed the more far-reaching effects surrounding redefinitions of work and how these were to contribute in no small way to social and economic changes in the post-war period.[3]

Whilst it is clearly important to examine the workings of the Whitley system and the ways in which male trade unions were able to negotiate the employment of women workers, the history of labour relations in the Royal Dockyards in the first half of the twentieth century cannot be contained simply through the institutional workings of the elaborate committee system. However important that may have been for day-to-day bargaining and for its impact on the lives of the workforce, other sets of values and attitudes were also powerful in shaping and influencing the framework of labour relations. Despite the desire by some in government that the state should be seen as a model employer, hence the moves to ensure that Whitleyism was extended to Admiralty industrial employment,[4] there were entrenched attitudes on the part of many layers of dockyard management which could not simply be eradicated overnight. The centuries of direct control of the workforce left a legacy which continued to effect the forms of labour relations within the yards in the inter-war years. Alongside the apparent acceptance of Whitleyism must be considered the attempts by the Admiralty to subvert official union recognition within the negotiating process in the 1920s. In addition, labour activism was discredited through sabotage scares and allegations of a 'Red Menace', through the influence of communism, in the 1930s. Thus, it is important to see this period as one which reveals distinct elements of hostility and concerted opposition to a growing role for organized labour and the perceived intrusion of 'politics' into the time-honoured traditions of state service. Arguably, it was not until after the Second World War that trade union recognition was more firmly acknowledged within the managerial strands of the Admiralty.

Before looking in detail at some of the elements referred to above, the context of political and economic change needs to be established. For many dockyard workers, the onset of the First World War marked a considerable improvement in pay and conditions, given the exigencies of the conflict, and the agreement that future industrial relations would be dealt with through the progressive machinery of consultation and conciliation further strengthened the workers' position. However, such gains need to be set against other circumstances which undermined these advances. Not least of these were the economic crises of the 1920s and early 1930s, which had a drastic affect on the fragile structure of labour relations that had been put in place through the Whitley scheme. A retraction in dockyard production at the end of the war meant an inevitable reduction in workforce numbers. At the outbreak of war in 1914, the total workforce in all Royal Dockyards was 54,370 and this increased to an unprecedented total of 93,370 during the wartime period.[5] In March 1922, orders were received at Portsmouth and Devonport for the rate of discharges to be accelerated from 50–60 a week up to 90 in the former dockyard, and from 30–50 a week in the latter,[6] so that by 1923 the reductions in Portsmouth Dockyard were nearly 6000.[7] However, the programme of reductions was not particular to these two dockyards, but were taking place throughout all the Royal Dockyards during the early 1920s. The high level of discharges in such a short period engendered a hostile reaction from the trade unions, who were rapidly losing their position of power in a workplace where supply was overtaking demand.

The reasons for cutbacks in Admiralty programmes of work were twofold. A government initiative was put into action during the 1919–22 coalition government, not only in a bid to counteract the effects of wartime expenditure, but also in response to an anti-waste campaign being waged by the Conservatives at that time. This was to become known as the Geddes Axe, the committee heading the initiative being under the direction of Sir Eric Geddes (a former businessman and the Minister of Transport, as well as, for a brief spell, First Lord of the Admiralty in 1917), who had been appointed by Lloyd George.[8] National economic strictures had severe effects on the level of Naval Estimates, which even prior to the war had been increasingly annually at an alarming rate. These estimates were presented to the House of Commons by the First Lord of the Admiralty, via the Financial Secretary, and gave projected figures for expenditure in the forthcoming financial year, running from 1 April to 31 March. In the financial year 1921–22, Colonel Sir James Craig, parliamentary secretary to the Admiralty, referred to the necessity of closing at least two of the home dockyards in order to rationalize Admiralty expenditure. It was therefore decided to close Pembroke Dockyard and to hand back Haulbowline Dockyard to the Free Irish State in 1923, 'these being the yards least adequately equipped to meet modern naval requirements'.[9] Proposals were also being put forward by the Admiralty at this time to close Rosyth Dockyard and in 1926 both Rosyth and Pembroke Dockyards were put on a care-and-maintenance basis with many of their established workers and apprentices being sent to the other dockyards.[10] Despite the frequently defined universality of the dockyard experience, the dispersal of these workmen served to bring different patterns of work practice, of cultural and political attitudes, to the host communities, and thus altered somewhat the nature of the local workforce.

The other effect on dockyard employment in the early 1920s came at an international level in the signing of the Washington Treaty by the naval powers of the time: Britain, America, Japan, France and Italy. Under this treaty all plans for the construction of capital ships were to stop, together with the scrapping of some older ships, followed by a ten-year standstill in naval shipbuilding over a stipulated tonnage. As Paul Kennedy states, the effect on British naval dominance was devastating, the Royal Navy accepting uniformity with its competitors rather than superiority of naval strength and acceding to international agreement on its requirements instead of keeping in line with its own foreign policy.[11] The Admiralty, understandably, tried to resist such incursions into its control of naval policy, but in the face of defeat were forced to adhere to the conditions set down by the government. The huge decrease in their shipbuilding programme had significant ramifications for dockyard workforces and the resulting reductions in employment levels did little to accelerate the process of harmonious industrial relations.

Whilst therefore it is clear that the Admiralty were restricted and controlled to a large extent by general government policy, it is also evident that they had their own separate agenda and their long-term plans were often hidden under the more immediate concerns of dockyard closures, workforce reductions and pressure from private shipyards at a time of chronic unemployment throughout the country and widespread civilian dissatisfaction. A reading of naval policy in the immediate post-war period would seem to indicate that the economic strictures required for British dockyards were intertwined with an Admiralty decision to establish a large naval base in the Far East, namely Singapore Dockyard.

This proposal was based on strategic expediency, as it was considered by the British government that any future wars were likely to take place in the Pacific, with the emergence of Japan as a new world power.[12] Bernard Porter sees this alone as a sure indication of Britain's self-perception as a continuing world power, not just a player in the European arena,[13] and makes clear that Admiralty decisions on dockyard policy had far wider dimensions than the effects these may have had at local level. It can be no mere coincidence that proposals for the establishment of a dockyard in Singapore were being made in 1921 and funds voted in under a Conservative government in 1923, all this during the peak time of discharges in the home dockyards.[14]

Above all, perhaps, there is the need to consider the British state's attitudes towards the construction and maintenance of a major fleet. This requires an appreciation of the often competing elements within what might be said to constitute 'the state', the fact that policies and approaches, as has been illustrated, were determined by external forces and that they did not remain constant. Secondly, the changing technology within shipbuilding was beginning to make significant inroads into the traditional balance of power and status within the workforce. New crafts associated with the increasing importance of electrical equipment and riveting and welding were challenging the supremacy of the shipwright.[15] This balance was not completely overturned but, in part, through the agency of wider trade union influence, labour relations were beginning to shift.

Whatever the elements influencing Admiralty policy, the eventual effects of unemployment on such a huge and unprecedented scale had obvious repercussions in local dockyard communities, particularly in the case of Pembroke and Rosyth Dockyards where the existence of the local townspeople was decimated by their closure.[16] Underlying the hardships caused by the economic measures being taken was the constant menace of 'contracting out', that is the placing of orders for naval construction with private shipbuilding companies. This was taking place at a time when the British shipbuilding industry was in decline because of greater foreign competition,[17] and the result was a gradual redefinition in the primary role of the Royal Dockyards from that of naval construction to a more secondary function as repair and maintenance depots. In some senses, there had always been a confusion regarding the specific role of the dockyards. As Haas notes, in the eighteenth century one-third of the fleet had been built by private contract outside the yards. This division of work continued through the nineteenth and twentieth centuries — of the 42

Dreadnoughts built between 1905 and 1914, 25 were constructed in private yards.[18] However, when the dockyards appeared under threat in the inter-war period, the situation was highlighted. The Admiralty clearly felt the need to 'retain' private shipbuilding capacity, particularly if large-scale rearmament was to take place.[19] A general downturn in shipbuilding in these years had seemed to threaten this position and thus it does appear that the balance of construction was being given to private firms. Changing technology and increasing size encouraged this trend, reducing the need for direct investment costs on the part of the state. However, for dockyard communities based around a single industry and lacking any significant sources for alternative employment, this changing emphasis was particularly acute. Political lobbying became decidedly vociferous in these years and Labour Parliamentary candidates for those areas most affected frequently based their election manifestoes on a call for 'national ships for national yards'.[20] The First Lord of the Admiralty, Sir Eyres Monsell, was still attempting to justify Admiralty policy on 'contracting-out' when he stated in the House of Commons in 1934 that '[T]he principal function of the Royal Dockyards is the work of repairing and maintaining the Fleet ...' and that 'Even in normal times it would be impossible for the Royal Dockyards to build all the ships required.'[21]

Reductions in the dockyard workforces continued during the late 1920s and into the early 1930s, reaching the lowest total workforce number of 43,320 in 1933 and it was not until the government's rearmament programme in the mid-1930s that numbers began to rise, regaining their 1914 level by 1937.[22] However, because of the wide-scale dismissal of workmen during the previous eighteen years and the restrictions placed both on the establishment and the admittance of apprentices, the Admiralty experienced acute problems in finding the necessary skilled workers to meet the demands of increased production.[23] A trawl of available labour was undertaken nationally by the Admiralty Labour section, many workers from the declining private shipyards in the North East of England and Scotland being transferred to the southern dockyards.[24] It could be argued that, as in the 1890s when the dockyard workforce was expanded by the introduction of hired labour from the northern areas of England,[25] the introduction of a more trade union-conscious section of workmen added to the process of industrial negotiation.

Thus, the inception of the Whitley system, the foundation of a more open style of negotiation between trade union representatives and the

Admiralty, was added to by the changing nature of the Royal Dockyard workforce and a growing trade union consciousness. The origins of Whitleyism were related to the concerns raised by some of the industrial unrest that was encountered nationally during the First World War. A committee, under the leadership of J. H. Whitley, MP for Halifax, was formed in 1916 to examine ways of improving industrial relations. Its initial recommendations were for joint councils of employers' associations and trade unions, with committees operating right down to factory level. The early report dealt only with private industrial concerns but, under pressure from both Civil Service unions and those industrial workers specifically concerned with state employer agencies, a second report, published in October 1917, suggested that state and municipal authorities should form joint councils.[26] Sidney and Beatrice Webb suggest that, despite 'obstinate resistance by the heads of nearly all the departments', the government as a 'model employer' felt 'constrained' to implement the scheme throughout the public service.[27]

A. G. Gourd, secretary of the trade union side of the Admiralty Joint Industrial Council, wrote in 1924, 'I do not suppose any great number of workpeople would wish to go back to the old days of petitioning.'[28] In his introduction to a new journal designed to provide information about the working of the Whitley system, Gourd, also a prominent member of the Workers' Union, provided an evaluation of the scheme which, on balance, was quite positive. He noted the ways in which grievances and negotiation had been put on a much firmer footing. The debate about the introduction of Whitleyism revolved around questions about the extent to which the unions, as representatives of the workers, would be genuinely involved in any power-sharing or control over wages and conditions and, in parallel, whether the local communities would offer anything other than a talking shop for the simple airing of grievances. Although the question was rarely expressed in an open way, the point of discussion was whether trade unionism, having been only recently admitted to a representative role in dockyard bargaining, could ever make a significant impact on labour relations. Initially there was a good deal of optimism, and the responses to Whitleyism in the early 1920s amongst dockyardmen were generally positive. In the second issue of *The Dockyard Industrial Review*, published in 1925, H. Berry, secretary of the trade union side of the Shipbuilding Trades Joint Council, reiterated the general sentiment that the old system of petitioning was at last banished.

> The day has passed away, I hope for ever, when Petitions to 'My Lords' setting forth the burden of one's complaint and praying for redress thereof ... it is not my purpose to say whether the Whitley Council is the best machine for improving 'Rates and Conditions', but it has given the men, at least, a good opportunity of having their claims presented, listened to, and redressed in many cases.[29]

However, by the time of the next issue, the closure of Pembroke and Rosyth had been announced and this seems to have suggested a very raw and obvious sense in which dockyardmen's destinies were in the hands not of joint committees but the Treasury and the Admiralty.[30] In one display of real power relations, much of the goodwill which seemed to have been generated by the principles of Whitleyism and some of the early negotiations appeared to have been eclipsed.

Subsequent events in the inter-war period did little to alter this dichotomy between the stated mediation of interests offered by joint committees and the *realpolitik* of state agencies' control. Against this background, a study of the proceedings of the joint committees raises the question of whether Whitley really did offer a significant advance on petitioning. Scanning the minutes of the committees, the formality of the proceedings in many ways continued to reflect the old patterns of authority. The trade union side would raise issues, and the employers, including Ministry of Labour officials, would generally reject the proposals or requests, sometimes after long delays between one meeting to the next. The system allowed for formal arbitration: the trade union side could request that issues be sent to the Arbitration Court but decisions in their favour were few and far between. Ultimately, the language and bearing of the official side seemed to reflect the inheritance of petitioning; the refusal to negotiate around the table. Points were made, little discussion ensued, responses were delivered as set pieces at the next meeting and refusals to accept decisions sent for arbitration. Whatever the formal intentions of the JSTC and its wider framework of Whitleyism, it seems clear that old attitudes and entrenched positions were powerful factors in inter-war industrial relations.[31] At a local level, yard committees may well have been effective in producing improved conditions and offered a sense of participatory industrial democracy. Fundamentally, real decision-making was still very much in the control of the Admiralty and other state agencies.

Whilst, therefore, the existing literature, sparse as it may be, has tended to emphasize the relative harmony introduced by the installation of the

Whitley machinery, the reality of labour relations was often very different. Before considering in detail some of the underlying challenges to Whitleyism, it is valuable to examine the ways in which it could be said that the interests of male trade unionists may have prevailed over the demands of the state. The First World War period had seen a focus of trade union interest in an area not previously considered problematic in dockyard labour relations: the employment of women as industrial workers. By the very nature of the types of work carried out, the Royal Dockyards have been perceived as predominantly male environments with little scope for female employment. One small enclave was the presence of women in the Colour Loft, making flags, canvas overalls and tool bags. These women were traditionally the widows or orphans of serving naval personnel, and in the nineteenth century they had also worked in the roperies of the larger dockyards, mostly on the spinning and winding of ropes.[32] Both these types of work were largely mechanized and fitted into the ideal of 'women's work' at that time, so were not perceived as a threat to male employment in the dockyards.

It was only the exigencies of war and the huge loss of male lives during the First World War that forced the government to look for alternative ways of maintaining wartime production at a national level, and in this case the ability of the Royal Dockyards to build and repair the Navy's ships. With a decreasing skilled workforce, the first step was dilution. This was a process where unskilled or semi-skilled workers were used to take over the more minor aspects of skilled work, mainly through the mechanization of these tasks, and employers had attempted to implement such a strategy prior to 1914 but had met with a great deal of resistance from the craft unions. As pressure for wartime production increased, agreements were made between government and unions to relax restrictive practices and increase the use of dilutionary methods of work,[33] but it soon became clear that even these were insufficient and the 'hidden reserve' of female labour was unwrapped and presented to male workers as a *fait accompli*.

Not surprisingly, there was an immediate reaction from the trade unions, focusing on the disparity between 'men's work' and 'women's work' and on issues of equal pay for equal work. Perceptions of the former were founded on pre-war gender divisions of labour and the 'unsuitability' of heavy industrial work for women. Initially the Admiralty continued with their policy of employing widows of naval men, including war widows, but only introduced them into areas of employment where women had already claimed a toe-hold, that is as clerical workers.[34] The trade unions were not actively involved until the need for more industrial employees led to the infiltration of women into the Constructive, Engineering and Electrical departments of the dockyards. In July 1916, 45 women entered various workshops in the Manager Constructive Department in Portsmouth Dockyard and female employment in this department was expanded so that by the end of 1917, there were 406 women employed (in Portsmouth Dockyard, the total number of women workers in 1917 was 1750).[35]

For male trade unionists, the introduction of female labour into the engineering workshops was in direct contravention of the Amalgamated Society of Engineers' ruling on this matter. During the early years of the war, a national agreement was reached between the Engineering Employers' Federation and five of the largest engineering unions, including the ASE, whereby the unions would relax their rulings for the duration of the war only and the employers would maintain standard rates of pay and a return to pre-war conditions upon cessation of hostilities. However, because Admiralty establishments were not designated as 'controlled establishments' under the Munitions of War Act, 1915, they were not obliged to abide by any trade union agreements and, indeed, resisted any formal negotiations with trade union representatives until the formation of joint industrial councils from 1916.[36]

There was an obvious dichotomy for male trade unionists on the question of female employment and union membership (the ASE did not allow female membership until 1943).[37] On the one hand it was clearly deemed of paramount importance for skilled male workers to protect both their status in the hierarchy of the workforce and the higher wages that accompanied this. As such, it was not just an issue related to female employment, but in the wider context of the introduction of unskilled and semi-skilled workers into the sphere of skilled employment, a battle that had its roots in the early years of the industrial era. But, in retrospect, it is abundantly clear that the acceptance of the principle of equal pay for men and women carrying out the same work would negate the use of unskilled or female employment as a form of cheap labour. However, it has to be recognized that in the case of women workers it was an entrenched part of the contemporary social structure for the male role to be that of the 'breadwinner', and any work carried out by women to be merely supplementary and therefore worthy of a lesser rate of pay.[38] This was not only a male viewpoint, but accepted by a large number of women themselves, and expressed in terms of their predominant role as wife and mother and the mainstay of the domestic sphere.[39]

Despite these perceptions, once the use of female labour during the wartime period was firmly established and had become widespread throughout many industries, the unions recognized the need to raise women's level of wages to an acceptable standard as a way of maintaining their own interests. Initially, wages for women working in munitions were assessed at pre-war levels for female employment, resulting in enforced 'sweated' labour.[40] The unions pushed for the government to set up a Labour Supply Committee to deal with the problems of dilution and the use of female labour. The most important outcome of the Committee's decisions was the issue of Circular L2, whereby a standard wage of £1 per normal working week was established for women substituted in men's work. However, as the terms of this Circular were initially optional and not mandatory, many non-controlled employers, including the Admiralty, refused to abide by this minimum rate for women employees. Even in places of work where L2 proposals applied and later in 1916 when the terms became mandatory, employers often found ways of avoiding the payment of a minimum wage, such as maintaining that female employees needed supervision or were not carrying out the same job as men had previously and therefore were not entitled to the same wage.[41]

In the Royal Dockyards the most vociferous in demanding equal pay were the female clerical workers. Their perspective was however somewhat different from that of female industrial workers, whose jobs were almost exclusively for the duration of the war only, whereas women taken on as clerks during the wartime period were entering an area of employment with a previous tradition of female employment and they therefore had the opportunity for permanency. This gave women clerical workers something to fight for; a removal of the marriage bar and the institution of equal pay for men and women doing the same type of work. The advantage for female Civil Service workers is borne out by Barbara Drake's statistics which show that in November 1918, 225,000 women were employed, decreasing to 163,000 by October 1919, a drop of 27.6 per cent, whereas in the corresponding periods for women employed in government establishments (including dockyards, arsenals and national factories) the figures were 246,000, decreasing to 16,000, a drop of 93.5 per cent.[42]

It is perhaps understandable therefore that calls for equal pay during the inter-war period were at the forefront of action by such bodies as the Civil

Service Equal Pay Committee, formed in 1935, and the Women Power Committee. Because of increasing pressure from such organizations, the government eventually persuaded the Engineering and Allied Employers' National Federation and the trade unions to accept the principle of equal pay.[43] During the Second World War, the Admiralty did finally agree the maxim of equal pay for both non-industrial and industrial female workers, for the wartime period only,[44] but again often found ways of circumventing this in practice, in much the same ways as they had during the First World War.

Once again, the acceptance of women employees as a substitute for men in the Royal Dockyards during the Second World War was subject to agreement by the Shipbuilding Trades Joint Council at a meeting on 21 June 1940.[45] The terms proposed were again based on the protection of men's skilled work and the acceptance of women as substitutes for men on a temporary basis only. However, in some respects the trade unions appear to have shifted somewhat from the intransigence on female employment that they displayed at the time of their introduction into the workforce during the previous war. The minutes of an industrial court regarding bonus payments for women workers show that the wages of women were set as a ratio of men's and fluctuated accordingly, but that the level of bonus, as established under the Morris Award of 1924, did not apply to women, who had received a reduction in wages in 1922. The male trade unionists were therefore bringing a case in 1932 to challenge the official side of the Admiralty Joint Committee who wanted to reduce the adult bonus from 11s. per week to 9s. per week. The matter was still not satisfactorily resolved by 1938, apart from the official side agreeing to a 1s. increase in the basic rate of pay for women workers in the Colour Loft, roperies and upholstery section.[46] In 1940 an agreement was made between the Engineering and Allied Employers' National Federation, the Transport and General Workers Union and the National Union of General and Municipal Workers for a 3s. per week increase on the bonus for women over 18 years of age. The Admiralty offered 2s. per week increase, stating that this would bring their total pay up to that agreed by the trade union side and the engineering employers.[47] This was the first time the Admiralty had related wages of women to those employed in the outside engineering industry. It appeared to be a clear case of the unions supporting the cause of women workers. But whilst this could be read as a turnaround in male union attitudes to female workers, it could also be argued that by forcing the issue on women's wages and bonus, bearing in mind that these were always based on the level of pay for men in the Royal Dockyards, they were protecting their own wage and bonus levels. Whilst, therefore, under the agreements made most women had left dockyard employment by 1946, the negotiations between trade unions and Admiralty officials on their employment alongside male workers had helped to shape the negotiating process by highlighting the issues of 'skill' and status.

However, the strength provided by the Whitley system which allowed this to occur was not sufficient to deal with other challenges taking place during the inter-war period. By comparison with other industries, labour relations at this time were relatively non-confrontational. Nevertheless, there were moments when it seemed that the 'traditional' patterns of deference or subservience were reversed. More frequently, too, the Admiralty initiated moves against trade unionism or responded to perceived threats in both overt and covert ways. If there were doubts on the workers' side about the effectiveness of the Whitley system as representing a genuine advance towards democratic representation, there were also displays on the official side of deep scepticism about the value of incorporating trade unionism.

Deeply entrenched notions of resistance to unionism, as previously outlined in this collection of essays, could not be overcome simply by the introduction of a scheme of conciliation, imposed against the better judgement of many Admiralty officials. It was not long after the introduction of Whitleyism that the first responses emerged. In a strike of moulders, which mainly involved non-dockyard workers, the few members of the union in the yards were said to be on 'leave of absence' rather than on strike to avoid any possible repercussions.[48] Trade unionism was clearly associated with strikes and disputes and, in 1920, there was a national boilermakers' strike which, although mostly involving the private sector, received some support within the yards. Again, to escape immediate censure, those boilermakers in the yards concerned in the dispute were said to be on 'unofficial leave' rather than on strike. What followed was a serious question of the right of dockyard workers to strike. The trade union side of the Shipbuilders' Trade Joint Council, in an attempt to clarify the issue, elicited a rather duplicitous response. The official rejoinder was that there was nothing to prevent civil servants going on strike; no official ban existed, as it had not been found necessary in the past. Civil servants had, it was claimed, 'recognised the fact that they were servants of the state'. By this was meant that the specific conditions of employment for established workers, in particular a pension on retirement, required specific loyalties and obligations. However, the sting in the tail was that the pension was dependent on 'faithful and satisfactory service' and striking displayed a negation of these qualities.[49] By implication, any established man going on strike was likely to forfeit some of his pension and ran the risk of losing his established status and the right to continuity of employment.

Admiralty fears were again aroused by the General Strike in 1926. As far as can be detected, no dockyard workers were involved in the May stoppage but the apparent conviction that state employees did not go on strike was subverted by the experiences in and around London. As Altfield and Lee have shown, some 450 of the 600 employed in the naval victualling yard at Deptford came out on strike, a figure which included 37 established men, i.e. those with security of employment and pension rights. There were also strikers in the Army section of the victualling yard. In both cases, victimization of some of the strikers took place.[50] The Admiralty's response was to re-employ most of the hired men, as and when appropriate, but to deal rather more severely with the established workers.

The events at Deptford invoked the 1920 ruling that strikers were to forfeit some pension rights. In addition, the union leaders were forced to sign 'confessions' that those who went on strike were at fault. Samuel Topping, chair of the Yard Industrial Whitley Committee, had to acknowledge that those members of the Workers' Union who went on strike without notice 'thereby committed a wrongful act'.[51] All established men had to sign a declaration acknowledging that they had broken their contract of employment with the Admiralty and undertaking not to do so again. The Admiralty also took the opportunity to discharge one established man, Lubbock, a storehouseman, for 'definite acts of misconduct in improperly instigating the men to this breach of regulations'.[52] Lubbock, an activist in the Workers' Union, seems to have deliberately misled his fellow workers over claims that dockyardmen at Chatham and Sheerness had come out on strike. The Admiralty, alarmed at the involvement of established workers in this major industrial and political dispute, exacted a powerful revenge, no doubt as part of a strategy to discourage similar behaviour.

The Conservative government sought to confine trade union rights the following year with the Trade Disputes Act of 1927. One particular section prevented civil service 'unions' from associating with unions outside the service, and thus, as Clegg identified, forcing them to withdraw from affiliation to the TUC and the Labour Party.[53] He suggests that workers in government industrial establishments were exempt from this particular clause but other evidence suggests that the Admiralty sought to interpret the implications rather differently. It was determined that it would be a condition of establishment for those entering after 29 July 1927 'that they are not, and will not be, members of Trade Unions in the narrower sense'.[54] This meant, in effect, that established men were now to be prevented from being members of TUC-affiliated unions.

What followed, then, were attempts by both dockyard workers and Admiralty officials to undermine the working basis of the Whitley system, which meant the formal representation of the workforce through officially recognized trade unions. Following the Admiralty instruction, there was an upsurge in membership of associations not formally part of the labour movement and consistent lobbying for recognition of these associations by employers. It was used by some workers to circumvent trade union-imposed restrictions on types of payment. A very illustrative case study is that of the National Union of Government Ship Joiners, Furnishers and Allied Trades. Based at Devonport, this group of workers were all on piecework or PBR (Performance by Results), practices officially opposed by conventional trade unions as divisive and contrary to the principles of trade unionism. These workers, and their colleagues, the Portsmouth Royal Dockyard Ship Joiners Association, were therefore not part of any conventional union and thus debarred from Whitley representation.[55]

The Devonport men, in the summer of 1928, were looking for ways of breaking union monopoly within the Whitley system and the Admiralty's response was indicative, too, of its lack of commitment to the principles of Whitleyism. At the end of June, discussion with the Ministry of Labour was seeking to identify the case for non-TUC unions in the Whitley system: 'There will probably be trouble with the rest, but within the constitution it seems difficult to refuse them representation, even if we wish to do so.'[56] The Ministry of Labour was slightly more circumspect. Sir Horace Wilson, a leading civil servant in the Ministry, argued that recognition by the staff side was essentially a matter for them alone. All that could be done was to put some kind of pressure onto the staff side. Wilson warned of pushing too hard:

> In view, however, of the small size of the Union, there hardly appears to be any justification for taking action which would be likely to break up the Shop Committees and ultimately the Industrial Council.[57]

Progress then was slow. At a local level, the Devonport union applied to the local Whitley Council for recognition and this was referred to the trade union side of the Admiralty Industrial Council.[58] By October 1928, the Industrial Council had rejected the application and, as a consequence, a major conference on the whole issue of Whitley representation was called at the Admiralty in February 1929.

This was not in response solely to the lobbies from Devonport and Portsmouth. Much greater pressure appears to have been brought to bear by the Admiralty Established Civil Servants' Federation, an organization which claimed some 4000 members, an estimated 40 per cent of established men in the dockyards.[59] This society was clearly seeking to home in on the 1927 legislation and to develop their bargaining position. A major petition was delivered at the end of November 1928, followed by a deputation to the Admiralty in December. Apart from seeking improved leave and optional retirement at 55, the main claim of the petition was to have access to all the materials sent to and from Whitley Committees. In support of this latter point, the Federation was very clear:

> It was not fitting that the Established men should be thrown back on to the Trade Unions, not only in respect of any movement in connection with wages or other conditions of employment, but even for obtaining information concerning conditions of employment.[60]

The Admiralty's response was sympathetic – one official commented on the 'humiliation' of established men 'beholden to Trade Union representatives'. Much was made of the representative scheme, introduced at Deptford following the General Strike, which ignored union connections. The general desire to extend such a scheme, as a challenge to the principles of Whitley, was expressed. However, this was seen as impossible

> Because of the hostile ['intolerant' crossed out] attitude of Trade Unions to non-Union workmen, and the absolute refusal of those officially connected with Trade Unions to have any dealings with non-Unionists in connection with matters relating to employment.[61]

Despite this, it was agreed that all Whitley papers should be sent to the Federation Secretary, accepting that it was likely to produce a backlash. In March 1929, the Admiralty distributed a general letter saying that any 'properly constituted Association' was to be given the right to regular meetings with the Admiral-Superintendent of their yard, provided he was assured that a 'substantial number of the trade or class' were members of the association.[62] This right, and attendant circulation of Fleet Orders and other documents, was to be extended to at least ten different groups of non-union men.

Inevitably, as the Admiralty had recognized, the unions responded vigorously. The trade union side secretaries of the AIC and the STJC requested a special joint meeting of the two councils to discuss the decision to send papers to the AECSF (and demanded that the agenda and minutes of both councils be withheld from that group until the meeting).[63] This joint meeting took place on 18 April and Admiralty acceded to trade union protests, after making vague noises about their belief in the wide circulation of Whitley documents, and agreed not to distribute material to the AECSF.[64]

However, the Federation did not give up. In March it had requested direct access to local yard committee minutes and other documentation, claiming over 500 members in Devonport, Chatham and Portsmouth. Once again, the argument was that non-affiliated unions or unions 'without political ambitions',[65] as the Plymouth joiners put it, could and should be able to represent particular groups of men. Evidence of pressure from other organizations operating to try and fracture the Whitley framework came when the trade union side of the AIC sent a deputation to the Admiralty at the end of June 1929. E. P. Harries of the Shipwrights outlined their case, saying that the regular meetings between the associations and yard officers had established a rival machinery to Whitley. Kaylor, of the AEU, suggested that the original invitation to the associations 'appeared to be an attempt to organise non-unionists in the Dockyard'. He claimed that some of the associations also had trade unionists among their membership, e.g. Chargemen's Association. A. G. Gourd, of the Workers' Union, provided evidence of attempts in Portsmouth to set up a counter-Whitley machinery and highlighted the threat posed by schemes like that operating at Deptford to the existing system of industrial relations. As Gourd noted, the original Admiralty proposal was an incentive for men to leave unions and join these new associations, whose dues were often less. 'The effect would be to smash the Trades Unions in the Dockyards.'[66] The Admiralty's defence was to say that it was merely offering opportunities for wider consultation and that the Whitley system was not being replaced.

However, the force of union opposition appears to have worked and, two weeks later, the 21 March letter was withdrawn and regular meetings with the associations ended. Whilst there is little doubt that, from both sections of the workforce and from the Admiralty, there had been a concerted move to undermine formal trade union recognition, the wider political currents had not run in their favour. The price of challenging the consultative framework of Whitley, and the official union involvement, was ultimately too high. That attempts were made is indicative of the strength of hostility towards trade unions by both employers and elements of the workforce.

Other ways in which the Admiralty sought to flex its employer muscles against the workforce were caught up in a general industrial hostility towards political activism, particularly towards a perceived threat from communism. This was part of an overriding fear during the inter-war period but was no doubt compounded by the close proximity of dockyard workers to naval personnel and establishments. Recent history, the Russian Revolution and the importance of naval mutinies in Germany in 1918 had indicated to British authorities the potential for revolutionary behaviour within the armed services and, for many, the Invergordon Mutiny of 1931 seemed to confirm that possibility in Britain. Coupled with the events of the General Strike already referred to, there was ample evidence, for those in authority who wished to see it, of the 'Red Menace' in British naval dockyards.[67]

Certainly, the Communist Party sought in the late 1920s and early 1930s to politicize members of the armed forces, although the extent of its success is questionable.[68] More significant, in the short term, was the General Strike, which led to Cabinet discussions in May 1927 on 'The Employment of Communists in War Department Establishments'. 'Active' and 'passive' Communists were to be dismissed and the Admiralty took the lead in this. A secret memorandum was sent to all dockyards on 15 August 1927. Active Communists, who disseminated 'anti-constitutional and revolutionary propaganda, either oral or written' were to be discharged; passive Communists should be 'eliminated from the Service' when the opportunity arose.[69]

The Admiralty's conception of 'communism' was something of a comic opera scenario. In an internal memo the following year, particular concern was expressed at the dangers of those working with or near explosives: 'Good workmen and apparently loyal they are ready to cause damage which might render the Fleet inactive when the order is given to them by their masters.'[70] It proved, however, difficult to operate, at least obviously, a policy of overt discharges. Attempts at Woolwich Arsenal in 1928, which led to AEU protests and much public discussion, indicated that any direct bar on the employment of communists was still controversial and the Admiralty had to deny that there was any hard-line policy.[71] What is clear from Admiralty records is the strong reaction within Admiralty circles towards political activists, defined as 'communists' and the extent to which surveillance was in place by the end of the 1920s. No doubt, when there were discharges from the various yards, Admiral Superintendents and other officials took the opportunity to dispense with the services of such 'troublemakers'.

It was in the early 1930s that the caricature of sabotage by the communists seemed to be proved valid. Claims of deliberate damage began to emerge in 1933, at Devonport and at Chatham. A third incident, involving H.M.S. *Oberon*, was revealed in September 1935, and a hired shipwright, J. H. Salisbury, was interviewed. Salisbury was known to the security services and alleged to have passed details of the sabotage on to the *Daily Worker*, which published them. This was deemed contrary to dockyard regulations and Salisbury was considered 'an untrustworthy person' and thus discharged, 'Services No Longer Required'.[72]

Further incidence of alleged sabotage occurred throughout 1936 and Admiralty officials decided to build them into an action against subversives, despite any significant evidence. Indeed, an internal memorandum of November 1936 suggested there would be dismissals for 'participation in dangerous subversive activities'.[73] In January 1937, when news of five dismissals broke, this had been moderated to 'services no longer required'.[74] The formal Admiralty announcement was that 'the continued employment of these men is not in the interests of the Naval service'.[75] No exact case could be proven, but all five were suspected of communist connections and it is clear that 'Secret Service officers' had been extensively active in the dockyards. There was much publicity and discussion in the press, questions were asked in the Commons and trade unions, particularly the Transport and General Workers, in the shape of Ernest Bevin himself, lobbied the government.[76] Detailed evidence does indicate varying degrees of political activism by the five men but, once more, there seems little indication of extensive support amongst dockyardmen. Threats of 'surveillance' seemed to have increased the dominant conservatism of the workforce and there were few challenges to the dismissals from within the dockyard walls. Coming at a time of increasing employment, due to rearmament, the sabotage incidents could never be firmly implicated on any overtly political individual or group. Thus, from the Admiralty's perspective, they have to be seen as a convenient weapon with which to challenge the potential of activism within the dockyard workforce and to provide a ready excuse for continued vetting and control over its employees. In this way, the use of the 'Red Menace' was an extension, albeit one which drew on wider state forces, of industrial relations within the dockyards.

The Second World War effectively saw an end to the attempts to undermine conciliatory labour relations and, as in the 1914–18 conflict, a combination of relative advantage to the workforce and a sense of national duty produced relative harmony. Such sentiments seemed to be reinforced by the Labour victory of 1945 and the implementation of nationalization schemes in key industries, such as coal, iron and steel. In this context, Whitleyism seemed to offer a valuable illustration of the way in which labour relations could develop within a state-controlled industry, and thus there seems to have been a reluctance to challenge once more the authority of the unions within such a structure. In contrast to the ending of the First World War, there was no wholesale rundown in the dockyards and few diplomatic limitations on construction programmes in the following years. There was some dislocation of labour, as already noted, with the dismissal of temporary workers and the cancellation of some construction orders. For some yards, Chatham in particular, there was never a buoyant order book in the post-war era, although the demise of this dockyard can be seen as part of the Admiralty's long-term agenda.[77] For other dockyards, major repair and refitment programmes and then, by the 1950s, significant construction work, secured employment for many workers.[78] All these factors appear to have tipped the balance of power once more in favour of the workforce. By 1950, the role of the unions as representative of the men and women who worked in the Royal Dockyards was firmly established. The influx of new workers, often with more direct experience of trade unionism, but also with less deferential attitudes towards authority generally, helped to reinforce this new-found confidence. This is not to argue that management and the Admiralty lost control of the yard workforce. In many senses, the channelling of industrial relations through the Whitley system continued to defuse any real potential for challenging the dockyard system. Whilst trade union membership was continuing to grow in the post-war years, it was also effectively accommodated into these conciliatory structures. For a decade or so, it produced relative calm and impressions of mutual agreement, since the majority of yard workers felt secure and comparatively well-rewarded. It was not until the 1960s, and the first of what was to be a series of studies on the management and organization of the dockyards, that this pattern of labour relations was seriously threatened.

Notes

1. See Portsmouth Royal Dockyard Historical Trust (PRDHT) Oral History Archive on interviews with ex-dockyard employees. The archive is lodged with Portsmouth City Museums and Records Service.
2. See S. and B. Webb, *The History of Trade Unions* (first published 1920; reprinted, New York, Augustus Kelley, 1965), pp. 646–8; G. D. H. Cole, *Workshop Organisation* (Oxford, Clarendon Press, 1923; 2nd edn, London, Hutchinson Educational, 1973), ch. XIII; H. A. Clegg, *A History of British Trade Unions Since 1889. Vol. II: 1911–1933* (Oxford, Clarendon Press, 1985); J. W. Stitt, 'The role of the Whitley Councils in British labour relations, 1917–1939', *Essays in Economic and Business History*, **8** (1990), 343–54.
3. PRDHT Oral History Archive. The archive contains a number of interviews with women who worked in Portsmouth Dockyard, particularly during the Second World War.
4. See details in Clegg, *A History of British Trade Unions Since 1889*, pp. 206–7.
5. *Parliamentary Debates*, vol. 152, col. 1292, 10 February 1938.
6. *Hampshire Telegraph (HT)*, 10 March 1922.
7. *Portsmouth Evening News (EN)*, 4 January 1922.
8. P. K. Cline, 'Eric Geddes and the "experiment" with businessmen in government 1915–22', in K. D. Brown (ed.), *Essays in Anti-Labour History* (London, Macmillan Press, 1974).
9. *Parliamentary Debates*, vol. 139, col. 1763, 17 March 1921.
10. *Parliamentary Debates*, vol. 188, for debates on this decision.
11. P. M. Kennedy, *The Rise and Fall of British Navy Mastery* (London, Macmillan, 1983).
12. W. D. McIntyre, *The Rise and Fall of the Singapore Naval Base, 1919–1942* (London, Macmillan, 1979).
13. B. Porter, *The Lion's Share: A Short History of British Imperialism 1850–1983* (London, Longman, 1975), pp. 301–2.
14. *Parliamentary Debates*, vol. 152, col. 851, 24 March 1922.
15. E. H. Lorenz, *Economic Decline in Britain: The Shipbuilding Industry, 1810–1970* (Oxford, Clarendon Press, 1991).
16. See A. Day, ' "Driven From Home": the closure of Pembroke Dockyard and the impact on its community', *Llafur*, **7**(1) (1996), 78–86.
17. See, amongst others, Lorenz, *Economic Decline in Britain*.
18. J. M. Haas, *A Management Odyssey: The Royal Dockyards, 1714–1914* (Lanham, MD, University Press of America, 1994), p. 2.

19. G. A. H. Gordon, *British Seapower and Procurement Between the Wars* (London, Macmillan, 1993).
20. *EN*, 21 November 1923.
21. *Parliamentary Debates*, vol. 286, col. 1090, 28 February 1934.
22. *Parliamentary Debates*, vol. 331, col. 1292, 10 February 1938.
23. Public Records Office (PRO), ADM 116/4722, Report on Dockyard Schools 1941–42 and the unpopularity of shipwright apprenticeships.
24. PRO, ADM 116/4533, Control of Labour 1939–42.
25. See Galliver's chapter in this volume for a discussion of labour migration during the 1890s.
26. See details in H. Parris, *Staff Relations in the Civil Service: Fifty Years of Whitleyism* (London, George Allen & Unwin, 1973), pp. 25–8.
27. S. and B. Webb, *The History of Trade Unions*, p. 647.
28. *The Dockyard Industrial Review*, **1**(1), 4th quarter, 1924.
29. *The Dockyard Industrial Review*, **1**(2), 2nd quarter, 1925.
30. *The Dockyard Industrial Review*, **1**(3), 3rd quarter, 1925.
31. See, for example of arbitration procedures, PRO ADM 116/32322 on selection of men for discharge between 1920 and 1926. See also ADM 116/3848, Minutes of Admiralty Industrial Council, 1934–39.
32. PRO, ADM 1/3382 and ADM 1/3390, Employment of Women in Devonport Dockyard. See also National Maritime Museum, CHA/F/29 and CHA/F/30 Chatham Letter Book 1816–17 (references kindly supplied by Philip MacDougall).
33. G. P. H. Cole, *Workshop Organisation* (Oxford, Clarendon Press, 1923).
34. W. G. Gates, *Portsmouth and the Great War* (Portsmouth, 1919).
35. PRDHT archives, photograph book of women workers in Portsmouth Dockyard in 1917.
36. B. Drake, *Women in Trade Unions* (London, Virago Press, 1984).
37. R. Croucher, *Engineers at War 1939–1945* (London, Merlin Press, 1982).
38. S. Walby, *Patriarchy at Work* (Cambridge, Polity Press/Oxford, Basil Blackwell, 1986).
39. This view is corroborated in the interviews with women who worked in Portsmouth Dockyard during the Second World War. See PRDHT Oral History Archive.
40. S. Boston, *Women Workers and the Trade Unions* (London, Lawrence and Wishart, 1987).
41. P. Summerfield, *Women Workers in the Second World War* (London, Croom Helm, 1984).
42. Drake, *Women in Trade Unions*, see Appendix.
43. H. Smith, 'The problem of "equal pay for equal work" in Great Britain during World War II', *Journal of Modern History*, **53**, December 1981.
44. PRO, ADM 1/16717 Rates of pay for women in Devonport Dockyard in Naval Stores Department. Also ADM 1/17986 Claim for revision of standard rate for women replacing unskilled labourers.

45. PRO, ADM 1/10831, Minutes of Shipbuilding Trades Joint Council Meeting, 21 June 1940.
46. PRO, ADM 1/11268, Minutes of Proceedings in the Industrial Court re Bonus for Woman Workers.
47. PRO, ADM 116/4533, Control of Labour 1939–42 – Extended employment of women in engineering, 24 May 1940.
48. *Chatham News*, 27 September 1919.
49. *EN*, 19 October 1920, Report on 'Rights to Strike'.
50. J. Altfield and J. Lee, 'Deptford and Lewisham', in J. Skelley (ed.), *The General Strike, 1926* (London, Lawrence and Wishart, 1976), pp. 261–82.
51. See Topping's signed confession, 20 May 1926, in PRO ADM 116/2312.
52. For full details see file on Deptford strike, PRO ADM 116/2310.
53. Clegg, *A History of British Trade Unions Since 1889*, p. 423.
54. PRO, ADM 116/2626, Notes for 4 March 1929 – Admiralty meeting with all Superintendents of Home Dockyards on issues of trade union representation within Whitley.
55. PRO, ADM 116/2626, Letter from Royal Dockyards Ship Joiners Association to the Admiralty, 30 July 1928.
56. PRO, ADM 116/2626, Vincent Baddeley (Admiralty) to Sir Horace Wilson, Ministry of Labour, 28 June 1928.
57. PRO, ADM 116/2626, Wilson to Baddeley, 6 July 1928.
58. PRO, ADM 116/2626, See exchange of correspondence July to October 1928.
59. PRO, ADM 116/2626, Internal Admiralty memo, 8 January 1929.
60. *Ibid.*
61. *Ibid.*
62. PRO, ADM 116/2626, Admiralty letter, 21 March 1929.
63. PRO, ADM 116/2626, Letter to Admiralty, 22 March 1929.
64. PRO, ADM 116/2626, Admiralty internal memo, 29 April 1929.
65. PRO, ADM 116/2626, F. Williams (Secretary of Devonport Branch of AECSF) to Construction Department Manager, Devonport Dockyard, 20 April 1929.
66. PRO, ADM 116/2626, Report of deputation from TU side of Admiralty Industrial Council, 27 June 1929.
67. For state perceptions of the 'Red Menace', see, amongst others, R. Thurlow, *The Secret State: British Internal Security in the Twentieth Century* (Oxford, Blackwell, 1994), ch. 4. David Turner's work on the Admiralty's complex 'dealings' with communism in the inter-war period will be a valuable addition to this literature.
68. See N. Branson, *History of the Communist Party of Great Britain, 1927–1941* (London, Lawrence and Wishart, 1985), ch. 3.
69. PRO, ADM 178/163, Secret Admiralty memo to all Admiral Superintendents, 15 August 1927.
70. PRO, ADM 178/162, Internal memo, 23 March 1928.

71. PRO, ADM 178/162, See Admiralty internal memos, October/November 1928.
72. PRO, ADM 178/162, Note by Secretary to the Admiralty – 'Untrustworthy Persons', 1936.
73. PRO, ADM 178/162, Department of Naval Intelligence memo, 19 November 1936.
74. PRO, ADM 178/162, Department of Naval Intelligence memo, 15 January 1937.
75. *Daily Herald*, 13 January 1937.
76. PRO, ADM 116/162, Letter to Stanley Baldwin, 14 January 1937.
77. The decrease in importance of Chatham Dockyard stemmed from a number of factors, not least its geographic position, which made it inaccessible for larger vessels, and the Admiralty's decision to limit its constructive role mainly to submarines.
78. P. MacDougall, *Royal Dockyards* (Newton Abbott, David and Charles, 1982), pp. 186–7.

8 NEITHER COLONIAL NOR HISTORIC: WORKERS' ORGANIZATION AT ROSYTH DOCKYARD, 1945–95[1]

Alex Law

As Britain's youngest and Scotland's only naval dockyard, Rosyth's development differed from the historic English yards in significant ways. Although a dockyard had been proposed at Rosyth as early as 1903, Admiralty prevarication delayed its opening until 1916, when the Royal Navy limped into the still unfinished yard in the aftermath of the Battle of Jutland.[2] But only nine years later Rosyth was abruptly closed under naval economies.[3] By the mid-1920s the model workers' housing scheme of Rosyth's 'Garden City' was transformed into 'the town that was murdered', a full decade before the more famous case of Jarrow.[4] However, after re-armament for World War Two reopened the dockyard, Rosyth prospered, eventually outlasting all but one of the traditional English dockyards into the 1990s. Alongside this fitful historical development, labour organization at Rosyth represented a further contrast to the English yards. Situated on the River Forth at the southern edge of the militant West Fife coalfields, the newer workforce at Rosyth did not fully inherit the quiescent labour traditions of the older southern dockyards. A seven-week strike in 1972 and a rash of disputes between 1978 and 1981 certainly seemed to bear out Rosyth's reputation for strong workplace organization and labour combativeness. Yet in the late 1980s all this changed. Rosyth was now presented as a model for co-operative labour relations under a new human resource management regime introduced by the yard's commercial managers, Babcock Thorn Ltd.[5]

An adequate understanding of this turnaround rests in having a sense of continuities and discontinuities of the deep-seated bureaucratization of workers' organization at Rosyth. Yet while an idea of bureaucratism may be necessary, it is an insufficient guide on its own: bureaucratization is not congenital. Here some idea of dockyard workers' organization capacities

151

will help to make sense of the processes and structures underlying bureaucratization.

In general, organizational capacities presuppose unequal structural capacities within the relations of production, conferring particular powers on capital and labour. At their most basic level, workers' structural powers derive from the social relations of 'collective wages labour'; for capital, including state capital, they derive from effective possession of the means of production.[6] In this sense, a 'structured antagonism'[7] also exists within the dockyards: dockyard workers exchange their capacity to labour in return for wages; dockyard management, for their part, need to control, co-ordinate and convert combined labour power into actual labour performed. Mediating the structured antagonism, trade unions, like Janus, face two ways: externally, to the employer, the state and political parties and, internally, to the membership and other workplace unions. Hence, organizational capacities refer not only to the institutional forms workplace relations take through collective bargaining but also include changing material, cultural, ideological and political resources.

Three organizational capacities, in particular, will be considered for Rosyth: 'Whitleyism' as a particular form for regulating the effort bargain; 'lobby politics' as a form of political bargaining; and the 'service ethos' as a repertoire of accommodative symbolic and material resources. Whitleyism refers to the routines and outlook derived from the Whitley system of centralized bargaining, institutionalized in various committees locally and in detailed procedures for grievances and discipline. Dockyard lobby politics have their roots in centuries of deferential petitioning of the Admiralty, employing the moral economy terms of loyalty and service. Modern lobby politics, however, depend upon corporate appeals to the national interest with the overall aim of exerting persuasive pressure on MPs and Parliament. The policy process is viewed as rational, neutral and open to specific, defensive campaigns at moments of perceived danger to the interests of dockyard workers. Historically, dockyard work cultures emphasized 'competitiveness, diligence, permanence, loyalty, localization and relative relaxation with regard to the pace of work'.[8] Southern dockyard life fashioned through inter-generational trade and kin continuities a hierarchical system of imposed and informal rewards and penalties, centred around a permanent core of 'established' workers and a wider group of less secure 'hired' workers. A dockyard service ethos developed out of this sense of employment continuity and a meritorious dockyard promotion apparatus functioned to reward seniority and sustained an ideology of service: to the Crown, dockyard and workplace community.

As a way of showing the specificity of dockyard organizational capacities, a contrast will be drawn next between the home-based historic dockyards and the overseas colonial ones. Between these two basic models, the case of Rosyth sits uneasily. Nonetheless, by the 1960s, Rosyth, always unlike the colonial yards, was becoming more like the historic yards. The following section identifies the formation and consolidation of dockyard organizational capacities at Rosyth after 1945. Here the rise of labour militancy at Rosyth in the 1970s and union resistance to commercial management in the mid-1980s will be treated as the severest test for dockyard organizational capacities. Finally, a brief comparison of labour under commercial management will assess the extent of the shift in organizational capacities.

Rosyth Dockyard: Between Historic and Colonial

Until the late 1950s a global network of overseas and home dockyards spanned the nodal points of the British Empire. At the core of the imperial naval-industrial complex, two basic kinds of dockyard could be distinguished. On the one side were the micro-state colonial dockyards at Malta, Hong Kong, Singapore and Gibraltar and, on the other, the historic metropolitan dockyards on the south and east coasts of England: Portsmouth, Chatham, Plymouth and Sheerness. Table 8.1 gives an indication of the scope and scale of the post-war decline of the global dockyard network. Of the eleven yards operating at the start of 1950, only two, Rosyth and Devonport, survived into the 1990s.

Within the international dockyard complex, uneven combinations of social scale, ideology, work cultures and organization made for varied forms of organizational capacities. Yet, Baldacchino suggests that the high levels of group solidarity and militancy found among dockyard workers in Malta might be a worldwide phenomenon.[9] However, workers in the historic English dockyards this century earned a reputation for accommodative, dependent, divisive and bureaucratic union organization. Social scale, politics, employment relations and ideology are important for organizational capacities: whether dockyard workers are in the realm of Lilliput or at the metropolitan heart of Empire matters. While it has been noted that some Maltese workers developed a positive anglophilia under

Table 8.1 *Opening and Closure Dates and Employment Levels at Major British Dockyards Worldwide*

Yard	Opened	Closed	Employment levels		
			Peak	1980	1995
HOME DOCKYARDS					
Rosyth	1916	1925–38	7000	5900	3300
Devonport	1690	–	16,400	12,700	4700
Chatham	1559	1984	14,500	6000	–
Portsmouth	1212	1983*	17,200	7400	
Sheerness	1665	1960	3300	–	–
Pembroke	1809	1925	3600	–	–
OVERSEAS DOCKYARDS					
Gibraltar	1740	1983	4000	1300	
Singapore	1937	1969	3200	–	–
Hong Kong	1856	1959	4200	–	–
Malta	1814	1959	10,800	–	–
Simonstown	1861	1957	600	–	–
Bermuda	1798	1950	1200	–	–
Haulbowline (Queenstown)	1806	1925	2000	–	–
Total	13	12	88,000	33,300	8000

* Portsmouth was reduced from full dockyard status to Fleet Maintenance and Repair Organization status in 1983.
Source: Adapted from D. K. Brown, *A Century of Naval Construction: The History of the Royal Corps of Naval Constructors, 1883–1983* (London, Conway Maritime Press, 1983), p. 272.

the fortress economy, the dependent, small-scale and concentrated nature of Maltese society magnified social, cultural and class differences. Micro-state life gave colonial structures on the island, particularly the dockyard, an all-pervasive presence over the economy, politics and even residential areas and language. Employment security in the dockyard was all the more important since there was no 'physical hinterland for the indigenous

Maltese to retreat to'.[10] Prevented by the Admiralty from occupying any post above supervisor, Maltese workers were cut off from the competitive promotion system. Moreover, union organization at colonial and historic yards differed quite markedly. In Britain, fourteen shipbuilding and engineering unions were represented on the various dockyard committees; at Malta there was only one, the General Workers Union. Politically, the GWU was virtually indistinguishable from the left-wing Maltese Labour Party, while dockyard unions in Britain policed the trench between 'economics' and 'politics' vigilantly, engaging only sporadically in defensive parliamentary lobby politics.

In conditions quite different from Malta, Rosyth also stood apart from the historic southern dockyards. From a virtually derelict site in 1938, abandoned thirteen years earlier under the inter-war cuts, Rosyth remained open and even flourished during the long years of Cold War 'normality'. Yet, initially, traditional dockyard forms of worker acquiescence in the overall goals of the organization had little purchase at Rosyth. First, closure in the 1920s had given the lie to dockyard labour market traditions of service, security and stability. Second, dockyard managers and workers often occupied quite alien national and class-bound cultures. Third, redundancy or the threat of redundancy, in common with the southern yards, was a recurring feature at Rosyth down to the 1960s. Until then Rosyth lived a precarious existence employing a mere tenth of the total workforce in the four British dockyards; Portsmouth and Devonport had around a one-third share each and Chatham about a fifth. Then, in 1963, Rosyth's fortunes were transformed when it became the refit yard for Polaris submarines. By 1980 Rosyth was the biggest single-site employer in Scotland. Table 8.2 shows that employment levels were over one-third higher in 1980 than in 1950. In contrast, employment levels were halved over the same period at Portsmouth while at Chatham they declined by a third.[11] A further indication of the changing character of the work undertaken at Rosyth was that the rising number of technical and professional non-industrial workers increased from one in ten of the total workforce to around one in four by 1980.

The Wartime Origins of Labour Organization at Rosyth

Due to inter-war neglect an entirely new workforce had to be created at Rosyth after 1939. Recruited late into the rearmament drive, industrial

Table 8.2 *Employment at Rosyth Dockyard 1939–95 (percentage increases in parentheses are relative to the year 1950)*

Year	Industrial	Non-industrial	Total
1939	–	–	730 (17)
1945	–	–	6100 (142)
1950	3900	400	4300
1960	4100 (105)	400 (100)	4500 (104)
1970	4300 (110)	1200 (300)	5500 (128)
1980	4400 (112)	1500 (375)	5900 (137)
1987	4163 (110)	1629 (407)	5792 (135)
1991	3352 (86)	1733 (433)	5085 (113)
1995	1921 (49)	1362 (340)	3283 (76)

Sources: CED HQ Bath, in *The Speed Report*, Vol. II: F-1; Rosyth Dockyard Campaign Committee, *Rosyth Dockyard* (Dunfermline Town Council, 1947), p. 6; *Spotlight*, December 1972; company sources.

workers at Rosyth tended to be local, and traditional dockyard labour relations tended to be weak. Women workers and dilution were introduced at Rosyth to a greater extent than for other dockyards and outside industry. By 1944, for example, 25 per cent of the Rosyth workforce was composed of women workers compared to between 12 and 16 per cent at southern yards.[12] While many workers were transferred from England these were mainly 'mobile', non-industrial civil servants. Although pay was determined centrally, labour management functions in the dockyards were decentralized to the level of autonomous professional departments (Constructive, Mechanical, Electrical). Such autonomy largely depended on labour continuity and identification with organizational goals: at Rosyth, however, *discontinuity* was at a premium. A critical 1941 report by the Ministry of Labour identified unusually high levels of absenteeism, idleness and 'subversive elements' at Rosyth.[13] Experimentation with a participatory worker discipline regime failed because recalcitrant workers 'treated it with contempt' and management resented trade union incursions into their control prerogative.[14] Nevertheless, unions at Rosyth, including those influenced by Fife Communists,[15] were committed to the underlying principles of Whitleyism: industrial peace through participative negotiating machinery.

While Whitleyism developed by fits and starts at Rosyth, the tradition of lobby politics took off rather more smoothly. Where lobbying had been tried, and had failed, to prevent closure in the 1920s, the rhetoric of 'national unity' during the Second World War structured the possibilities for a renewed emphasis on lobby politics at Rosyth. As the unions argued, 'Today we are stronger, more united as a result of our bitter experiences in the lean years. No longer can we tolerate the irresponsibility which has in the past characterized the Admiralty's handling of Rosyth.'[16] In August 1944, Rosyth shop stewards initiated a campaign for retention and extension of the dockyard.[17] Behind them the stewards drew in a veritable 'popular front' of support across Scotland, ranging from landowner Lord Elgin to William Gallacher, the Communist MP for West Fife. A range of arguments were made for the retention of Rosyth as a major British dockyard: strategic, industrial, infrastructural and social.[18] Above all, however, it was argued repeatedly that Rosyth was the 'only real link which the Scottish people have with the Royal Navy, and it is in the interests of the Nation [sic] that this tie be strengthened rather than weakened or severed'.[19] Gallacher typified such national-populist appeals when he argued at a meeting in Dunfermline that it was

> scandalous to suggest a country like Scotland, a country that pioneered naval construction and training should be without a naval establishment ... Imagine closing Chatham and Portsmouth and make Rosyth a fully developed naval base ... the English lads would not stand for it. Rosyth must be built up into a fully developed naval establishment ... in the name of Scotland.[20]

Within the workplace, however, the dockyard service ethos had little resonance among industrial workers at Rosyth; until the 1950s few local Rosyth workers had acquired established status. It was precisely the cleavage between established southern non-industrials and non-established local industrials which made it difficult to implant the service ethos at Rosyth. Non-industrials sold their labour power under advantageous terms: they started work at 8.17 a.m. while industrials began their shift at 7 a.m.; they were better paid and had more generous leave, superior working conditions, sickness and pension entitlements and better promotion and transfer opportunities. The gulf in employment conditions was exacerbated by the wide cultural chasm between mainly local industrial labour and dockyard managers drawn invariably from the south. By the 1950s, however, the range of dockyard promotion, employment benefits and 'establishment' status was being opened up increasingly to locally recruited labour.[21]

As the complex of benefits and promotional opportunities became available, labour relations at Rosyth lost much of their distinctiveness from southern dockyards. In short, inherited dockyard traditions such as Whitleyism, lobby politics and the service ethos were reshaped, adapted and modified to suit conditions at Rosyth.

Whitleyism and Work Organization

By the 1960s, then, traditional dockyard organizational capacities were taking root as a strange sense of 'normality', based upon the seemingly permanent character of the Cold War, settled upon Rosyth. A benign internal dockyard state[22] was secured firmly around the seniority functions of the internal labour market and the routines of collective bargaining and grievance procedures. Corporate-welfare functions further bolstered the internal dockyard state. Uniquely at Rosyth, for example, a Whitley committee allocated 3500 houses to dockyard workers on the basis of documentary evidence of marriage, profoundly shaping the structure of the local residential community. Moreover, the Civil Service 'marriage bar', in excluding married women from the dockyard, helped mould a sexual division of labour which only began to flake away at the edges in the 1970s.

As a 'model employer', union membership, consultation and representation was formally encouraged. Trade union density was high, sustained by recruiting hundreds of 'new starts' and apprentices at specially arranged induction meetings. A highly structured Whitley system connected numerous committees and sub-committees from national to local level. Enforcement of bargaining rights depended on an intimate knowledge of the procedures outlined in the voluminous MOD manuals and various local and national agreements. All key negotiations on pay and conditions took place nationally at the Shipbuilding Trades Joint Council (STJC). Locally, the shop stewards fed on the scraps of Whitleyism, bargaining over the details of centrally determined policies. One senior Rosyth steward later said that the Whitley system was 'decrepit with nothing much to argue about'.[23]

Yet Whitleyism supported a bloated workplace bureaucracy. With the introduction of any new bonus scheme, the unions fought, often with success, for increasing numbers of senior stewards to be 'made up' to full-time status. So where Whitleyism attempted to impose a uniformity on labour relations it was always caught in a certain tension with the peculiarities of individual union organizations. Full-time positions often came to be regarded as the private responsibility of their long-serving incumbents. By the 1980s there were over 30 industrial shop stewards working full-time on union duties and around 300 lay shop stewards representing about 4000 manual workers. At that time there were ten individual shop steward committees for the industrial workforce, ranging from those representing mass memberships like the 1500-strong Transport and General Workers Union (TGWU) to the couple of dozen represented by the Furniture Timber and Allied Trades Union (FTAT). Each individual shop steward committee fiercely defended its own organizational integrity, autonomy and specific trade identity according to its own rule book and traditions.

Labour organization and consciousness also varied greatly between different work groups. Dockyards typically divide into shop workers and afloat workers. Repair and refit work carried out on board ships was done by gangs of craft workers from the same trade and therefore the same union. Working in close co-operation, afloat gangs were able to form closely-knit, sectional identities and carved out large measures of work group autonomy and control over the labour process. Such self-sufficiency bred a deeply sectionalist consciousness among afloat workers, aware that their own industrial strength was usually enough to preserve the advantageous terms of the effort-bargain against managerial encroachments.[24] For workers engaged on nuclear refits the position was even clearer. Working in the nuclear complex created a sense of separateness; a physical separateness represented by the erection of a fence marking off the nuclear area from the rest of the yard and an ideological sense of separateness derived from the strategic nature of the work done 'behind the fence'. A tacit understanding of the vulnerability of nuclear refits to industrial disruption ensured that nuclear workers received the best working conditions and monetary benefits. One indication of the ways in which the nuclear area was protected was that a number of more militant shop stewards failed to get security clearance for access to work 'behind the fence'.

Although craft prerogatives were as jealously guarded in the shops as afloat, the division of labour under factory conditions was more detailed, with workers operating individual machines under closer supervision and stricter job definitions. In general, labour organization in the shops was less robust and more passive than afloat sections. One outstanding exception to this was the Pipe Shop which had a reputation throughout the dockyard for militancy. Coppersmiths, a trade largely specific to the dockyard, had few avenues of promotion, had a lower-than-average age profile and acquired a strong sense of group identity from being a relatively small trade union of around 100 AUEW-TASS members working in a single workshop.[25] Their reputation for militancy grew in the 1970s, particularly after a young shop steward from a Fife mining/Communist Party family background became first a senior steward and, later, convener.

The consolidation of Whitleyism at Rosyth in the 1950s institutionalized dockyard labourist consciousness. On the one hand, Whitleyism took care of industrial issues; on the other, lobby politics dealt with political matters. Even the convener of the coppersmiths eschewed 'politics' and stressed direct workplace organization.[26] Highly sensitized to threats of political 'subversion', dockyard workers were 'positively vetted' by the Admiralty. In a Communist Party stronghold like West Fife the Admiralty could well expect to be employing left-wing militants. As part of the Civil Service Cold War purge of active left-wingers among the workforce in March 1950, a welder, John Copeland, was suspended from Rosyth by the Admiralty.[27] Copeland, secretary of the Lochore branch of the Communist Party and the Communist candidate at the Fife County Council elections in 1949, pleaded 'guilty to the fact that I am a Communist' and claimed that 'security' was being used to remove working-class militants from the dockyards.[28] An Admiralty statement said:

> The First Lord has decided that Copeland is employed in connection with work the nature of which is vital to the security of the state ... Mr Copeland has admitted that he is an active member of the Communist Party and it is therefore necessary to remove him from his present duties.[29]

More usually, the labourist divorce between 'politics' and 'economics' went unchallenged in Rosyth. An exception to this was a layer of left-wing TGWU and EETPU shop stewards who were active in the Labour Party.[30] On occasion this wider sense of socialist politics within the TGWU transcended the Whitley/lobby politics dichotomy and translated into workplace-based action. A ringing example of this was the blacking of tailshafts for the Chilean submarine *O'Brien* in 1974 in protest against the Pinochet regime in Chile. After docking at Scott's yard in Greenock the *O'Brien* sent tailshafts to Rosyth to be repaired, protected and shipped back to Chile as spares. On arrival at Rosyth local TGWU stewards in PSTO(N), the stores organization, refused to release them and demanded from the MOD 'that no future Chilean Navy work will be done in

Rosyth Dockyard until the fascist Junta is removed, a freely, democratically-elected government put in power, and human rights restored in Chile'.[31] After years of blacking, the MOD eventually relented. The Materiel Manager wrote to the TGWU, 'Your action has resulted in specific assurances that no materiel supplies will be made from Rosyth to the Chileans in the foreseeable future or work undertaken at Rosyth on their behalf',[32] and repeated an earlier request for the TGWU to lift the blacking: 'I wonder if, in the light of the above, you are now able to seek your membership's agreement to lift the blacking imposed so long ago on these MOD(N) shafts in order that they may now be transported to Portsmouth'.[33] Eventually, in December 1978, the TGWU agreed to lift the blacking. Although internationalism at Rosyth could be traced as far back as 1919 when a group of Portsmouth engineers based at Rosyth agitated over the 'Hands Off Russia' campaign,[34] such examples of strong class-based organizational capacities were exceedingly rare.

1972: Rank-and-File Eruption and National Divisions

Whitleyism proved highly effective in channelling local discontent into the formal regulatory machinery. Only in 1962 did the first post-war strike at Rosyth take place, when over 1000 workers at Rosyth struck against the government 'pay pause' for public sector workers.[35] Strikes would not become a regular feature of labour relations at Rosyth for another decade. Then, in 1972, two serious disputes occurred. By the early 1970s, discontent was building up in the dockyards over low pay and the bonus system and the dockyards were affected by the wider industrial militancy in Britain. In May 1972, nine TGWU members of a Port Auxiliary Service (PAS) crew refused to work two tugs to clear a path for the Polaris submarine HMS *Repulse*, which was being undocked after refit. The nine were soon joined by the other PAS crews. An overtime ban had been imposed by the PAS crews since January because a claim for an allowance for handling nuclear work was being dealt with too slowly. Against threats that the SSBN HMS *Renown* would not be refitted at Rosyth if the dispute continued, management offered a cash settlement and a revised shiftworking agreement. After the PAS crew returned to work on 3 July the dockyard newspaper stressed the need for conciliation on all sides: 'The return to duty of the PAS and the offer made by management may be the basis of a goodwill for which there is always room in this sort of situation'.[36]

Yet the dockyard axioms of goodwill, compromise and reasonableness were to be put immediately to an even sterner test with the rejection of the annual pay award as 'insulting'.[37] Labour–management relations quickly deteriorated at Rosyth and pressure grew to escalate the dispute: mechanical fitters and constructive trades organized an overtime ban; one-day token strikes were held in all dockyards in June; management efforts to lay off 250 workers at Rosyth in July because of the PAS dispute were successfully resisted by the unions; the government again threatened not to risk putting *Renown* into Rosyth; management docked 1.25 hour's pay from the wages of 2000 workers who attended a mass meeting, the unions withdrew from the Whitley committees in response and management declined permission for further shop steward meetings.[38] As the Trade Union Advisory Committee expressed the mood: 'We are fighting the government here. They are using us as whipping boys. They want to put the boot into us. But the attitude of the workers is hardening.'[39] Yet the Trade Union Advisory Committee proved more equivocal in practice and resumed their Whitley positions a few days later. As a spokesman put it, 'We are sensible and reasonable people ... We might be doing our members a disservice by suspending negotiations.'[40] Until late August a combination of lobby politics and token action prevailed at Rosyth with the result that the offer was increased from £1.50 to a still unsatisfactory £1.75.

Then a qualitative shift in the dispute occurred when an unprecedented 4000 industrial workers at Rosyth walked out on unofficial strike on 22 August. Against national union instructions that dockyard workers should 'continue to exert moral pressure on management by limited stoppages, working to rule etc.', the local TGWU District Officer conceded that 'some of the members decided that was not strong enough'.[41] Typically, the action was unco-ordinated as, one-by-one, shop steward committees led individual memberships out on strike.[42] Even a management statement admitted that 'production work at Rosyth has virtually come to a standstill.'[43] Large numbers of pickets, involving up to 1000 workers, successfully picketed the dockyard gates on a daily basis.

Despite persistent appeals, however, little was done to overcome the strike's principal weakness: the limited action at the southern dockyards. Although it was made official in early September the Rosyth unions' call for all-out strike action from the southern yards continued to meet with little response. Two Rosyth shop stewards toured the southern yards in an attempt to spread the action and reported that, while the response at Chatham was 'poor', things were improving at Portsmouth and

Devonport.[44] Devonport had already taken sporadic action in support of the wage claim and finally struck on 25 September – one month after the strike at Rosyth began.[45] Action spread to other MOD establishments; 500 TGWU members struck at Faslane, 200 at Coulport, and establishments at Arrocher, Livingston, Lathalmond and several in England were also affected.[46] Regular meetings were held in Stirling with union representatives of 25 other government establishments in Scotland, including the Faslane and Coulport bases. While the unions claimed that 17,000 workers were on strike across the country in late September, both the southern yards and the Royal Ordnance factories gave only limited support.

Such belated support failed to affect the course of the dispute. Throughout the seven-week strike, fewer than 10 per cent of industrial government workers in Britain joined the action. Nationally, the union leadership in the Joint Co-ordinating Committee decided unilaterally to refer the claim to arbitration, a decision immediately denounced as a 'sell-out' by the 50 Rosyth strikers in London for the meeting. A mass meeting at Dunfermline Athletic's football ground jeered and heckled TGWU National Secretary, John Cousins, over the 'sell-out'. Cousins claimed that the failure of the southern workers made such a decision inevitable.[47] But even at Rosyth things began to fray at the edges. Isolated and frustrated, the strike at Rosyth seemed doomed to certain defeat. One indication of this was the Boilermakers' narrow vote to return to work two weeks before the strike ended. A call for a return to work at Rosyth in the first week of October was backed at a mass meeting amid bitter recriminations against the MOD, the trade union leaderships, strike-breakers and, of course, against the passivity of the southern yards. On the day of the march back to work, placards were carried declaring 'Southern Yards Let Us Down' and workers refused to start work until 'scabs' were moved to different sections.[48] As the normally moderate union secretary of the Industrial Whitley Committee, Jim McCusker, put it:

> We have been promised all sorts of support from our Trade Union representatives, at national level from our Executive Committees, from the Trade Union side of the General Co-ordinating Committee. These promises have never been fulfilled. We condemn and deplore their attitude. We condemn them for their lack of leadership. They should be condemned for failing miserably.[49]

Against a government determined not to risk another defeat by public sector workers as heavy as that inflicted by the miners' strike in February 1972 and trade union officials who seemed unsure of how to conduct the strike nationally, local initiatives proved incapable of generalizing the dispute much beyond Rosyth, even to the other dockyards, let alone to the hundreds of thousands of industrial workers in other government establishments.[50] Shop stewards at Rosyth suspected that the government had served 'D' Notices to suppress information about a strike in one of the most sensitive industrial sites in the country.[51] Although the Arbitration Committee awarded an across-the-board rise of £2.60 per week, with percentage increases for women and apprentices, the memory of the 1972 strike among Rosyth workers would remain one of defeat and betrayal.

The Acid Test of Commercial Management

During the late 1970s and early 1980s, as the unions recovered from the 1972 strike, industrial action again became a familiar feature of labour relations at Rosyth.[52] This account, from the management point of view, of the £50 million refit of the Polaris submarine *Renown* in Rosyth between July 1978 and February 1980 shows some of the many sources of labour unrest and their consequences:

> The refit got off to a bad start when an industrial dispute over quality control documentation escalated to such an extent that all work stopped, other than that essential for nuclear safety. Work resumed after three weeks' delay and for the next two months progress was up to schedule though already there was cause for concern about the coppersmith effort ... The portents for the New Year were not encouraging as industrial problems in the pipework area resulted in a considerable backlog in the welding of pipework ... It seemed likely that the refit was already running four weeks late when a non-industrial pay dispute brought all work to a stop for about six weeks. Industrial morale, already badly hit, was further worsened by problems over their pay award. All this led to a re-scheduling allowing eight weeks delay.[53]

This rising tide of dockyard militancy came against an increasing sense of the incoherence of dockyard management organization. In virtually every decade over the course of a century, attempts to reform dockyard management structures had been proposed and, except for a shift from professional departments to functional management in the 1960s, quietly shelved.[54] Three main problems were identified in previous studies;

ambiguities in the dockyard–Navy relationship, constraints of Civil Service status of dockyard organization and inadequate accounting procedures. Organizationally, the dockyards formed part of a 'one body' model, always subordinate to the needs of the Navy. Costs were relegated below a higher appeal to service interests, with naval staff acting as sole customer and the dockyards as a near-monopoly supplier. The obscuring of the customer–supplier relationship was compounded by Civil Service traditions of 'promotion from within'. Organizational incestuousness caused what the Speed Report called 'undue turbulence in the top posts' and effectively kept out managers with relevant industrial experience. In 1980 this meant that

> 60% of the senior managers have been in post for under two years and nearly 40%, including the Chief Executive himself, have moved in the last 12 months. Less than 10% have held the same post for more than four years.[55]

Such a high turnover rate diminished management's authority in its dealings with subordinate managerial grades, trade union representatives and the workforce. The failure to act on the recommendations of earlier reports, particularly after the Mallabar report in 1971, led to what Speed termed a 'crisis in the dockyards':

> ... the dockyards are failing to meet the increased needs of the Royal Navy. Management recognises this but lacks authority to respond to the growing difficulties. The workforce is discontented about pay and fearful of the future. Local trade union representatives are dissatisfied with the lack of authority of management to settle difficulties locally and local problems are exacerbated by delay. Job satisfaction among non-industrials is reduced by diffused responsibility and they are disgruntled by the narrowing of differentials.[56]

Such were the internal symptoms of organizational malaise. Speed's proposals for organizational reform were stillborn due to the 1981 Defence Review and the Falklands War of 1982. The former cut the number of fully-operational dockyards from five to two, closing Chatham and Gibraltar, reducing Portsmouth to a repair and maintenance base and concentrating refit capacity at Rosyth and Devonport.[57] However, when Michael Heseltine took over from John Nott as the Secretary of State for Defence in January 1983, he commissioned a report on the dockyards from his 'special personal adviser', Peter Levene.[58] Four weeks after his initial appointment and brief visits to each dockyard, Levene recommended that commercial managers be brought in to run the dockyards.

Naturally, the trade unions were expected to lead the opposition to any form of commercial management. *The Economist* said:

> The plan sounds more radical than it is ... The navy will not object ... The main problem will be with the trade unions ... One of the attractions of the scheme is that dockyard labour problems can be dropped in the laps of the commercial operators who run the yards.[59]

From the outset the prospective bidders for the tender were acutely aware of this. The Managing Director of Babcock International said that 'the biggest task will be to convince the trade unions that we are responsible management organisations'.[60] Kennedy, a defence economist, argued that this process would be 'easily exploited by unions with sixteen years' experience of running rings round overdue reforms'.[61] Far from being a bulwark against change, the unions' initial response to Levene was 'constructively' measured in the forlorn hope of opening up a dialogue. The Rosyth trade unions commissioned a study to counter 'the current vogue where decisions are based on narrow ideological grounds'. In its preface, Rosyth union leaders appealed for full participation in the decision-making process:

> This document is not a policy document. Any reader will note that several of the suggestions in the document are anathema to some within the trade union movement but we let them stand to demonstrate our willingness to participate in a full debate and to show that we are ready to negotiate on measures to improve our efficiency.[62]

Such efforts at consultation were studiously ignored by the government. Trade union requests for information through the conventional Whitley system of negotiations and direct appeals to the Secretary of State fell on deaf ears. Whitleyism as a system of corporate industrial relations in the dockyards was clearly finished. Levene's proposals were excluded from the normal channels of consultation on the pretext that his status as a 'personal adviser' put his advice beyond established procedures.[63] The duration, method and biased content of the consultation process were criticized both by the trade unions and the Defence Select Committee. The Defence Committee concluded that the MOD's handling of the consultation process was 'inept and insensitive' and that there was a 'strong reason to suspect that "consultation period" is in any case a misnomer, and that the Government had already decided for its preferred option'.[64]

The banning of trade unions at GCHQ in early 1984 indicated the level of hostility of the Thatcher government to public sector unions.[65] This disintegration of participative forms of Whitleyism into the seemingly harsh and unyielding environment of 'new realism' returned lobby politics to the centre of the STJC strategy. In this it largely succeeded. The success of lobby politics was reflected in two highly critical Parliamentary Committee reports. When the government decided to press ahead anyway the unions drew ever closer to the Labour Party as the agency for resisting commercial management. Union success at this stage came from the substantial delay to the Dockyard Services Bill which took 25 sittings to eventually clear and so jeopardized the government's implementation timetable. Jack Dromey, TGWU secretary of the STJC, hailed the delay as a 'major blow' to the government.[66] An amendment to the Bill by Lord Denning allowed the unions a provision to obtain a declaration from the High Court if they were dissatisfied with the government's consultation process. Commitments were also given by the opposition parties to return the dockyards to the public sector after the impending General Election. Delaying the introduction of commercial management until the election when, hopefully, a Labour government would keep the dockyards in the public sector became the main plank of the union strategy.[67] Unfortunately, on Friday, 3 April 1987, the last working day before vesting day, Judge Millet at the High Court dismissed the unions' argument about inadequate consultation. Commercial management was introduced into the dockyards on 6 April 1987.

Throughout the campaign the Labour Party and the trade unions persisted with the core themes of Tory ideological dogma versus rational managerialism, the elevation of private profit above national security and the indecent disregard of the Tories for parliamentary institutions and the 'due process'. In a distant echo of the lobby politics of 1925 and 1945, in 1985 a broad alliance was formed to protect the Rosyth (and Devonport) yards, ranging from Lord Denning to Ken Gill, Communist trade union leader and unilateral disarmer. This was mainly achieved by employing the rhetoric of defending the national interest and endorsing the procedural role of Britain's national institutions – the House of Commons, the House of Lords and the High Court. All the established symbols and myths of British, mainly English, maritime history and national archaism were drawn on freely. One campaign leaflet from 1985 illustrates how pride in the dockyards' role in Anglo-British naval history was represented by national trade unions (see Figure 8.1). Under a depiction of a warship flotilla the battle honours of the distant and near past ring out.

DEFEND THE DOCKYARDS

ROYAL NAVAL DOCKYARDS TRADE UNIONS

Five reasons commercial management will not work . . .

**ENGLISH CHANNEL 1588
TRAFALGAR 1805
JUTLAND 1916
ATLANTIC 1942
FALKLANDS 1982**

Britain's navy has been well served by the Royal Dockyards. Now the Government wants to hand them over to commercial management. That would break up a winning team after 400 years of proven success at the most critical time in our history. Help the Royal Dockyards to work better – but please don't kill them off.

ROYAL DOCKYARDS FOR THE ROYAL NAVY

Figure 8.1 *'Defend the Dockyards' leaflet*

The unions frequently emphasized that the yards were *Royal* Dockyards and that the workforce were *loyal*. Dromey even stressed that in the Queen's Speech announcing the Dockyard Services Bill she had called the yards 'my dockyards'.[68] It was from such imagery that Lord Denning's support was drawn. For him it was a constitutional issue over whether the Crown could compulsorily transfer the workforce of the dockyards to a new employer without their consent. He related anecdotal evidence from Devonport, 'I have been there and I know that from generation to generation for the last two hundred years they have been in the service of the Crown, and proud they are of it.'[69] Even the Royal Prerogative could not deny the rights of 'free-born Englishmen' to be consulted about which employer they should choose to 'serve', with Denning citing Lord Aitken from a 1940 case: 'That right of choice constitutes the main difference between a servant and a serf.'[70]

In the dockyards, industrial action was expected to play a purely supporting role to the main lobby politics strategy at national level. Yet industrial action at Rosyth threatened repeatedly to escape nationally circumscribed limits. Strikes, demonstrations, delegations, 'guerilla actions', 'blackings', overtime bans and general non-co-operation and hostility to management maintained the momentum of the campaign in the workplace between 1984 and 1987. Local management, under pressure to improve efficiency, adopted a more austere form of labour relations. For instance, they refused to officially recognize the Rosyth unions' anti-privatization committee because it fell outside of the Whitley machinery, and in 1986, in an unprecedented move, 86 ex-apprentices were refused employment by the MOD as craft workers, resulting in a deep distrust and hostility.[71] Any work associated with private refits was blacked by the industrial unions. In June 1985 mass walkouts took place in support of stores workers refusing to handle equipment for the private refit of HMS *Euryalus*. In October the entire craft section of the AUEW membership was suspended after refusing to perform remedial work on the propellers of the privately refitted HMS *Redpole*. Yet, even at the height of the blackings, attempts were made by longer-serving conveners to shore up Whitleyism. Bureaucratically inured over the years, such conveners wanted to return the genie of workforce activism to the Whitley bottle until the centralized leadership granted permission for its use. In one case the TGWU convenor issued a call to union members for a return to 'orderly workplace relations' after unofficial meetings were held by shop stewards to discuss blacking work on HMS *Whitehead*.[72]

Locally organized demonstrations and harassment of, and walkouts against, private companies had become part of the national strategy to 'scare off' interested companies in late 1985. The government was increasingly concerned that 'while companies were interested in the government's proposals, few were pressing for the contract'.[73] Although the announcement in December 1984 to allocate the lucrative Trident refits to Rosyth ensured serious interest was more easily retained than at Devonport, only three out of the original twelve potential bidders remained by late 1986. Demonstrations within Rosyth and pickets of contractors displayed the depth of workforce opposition to private contractors. Threats of physical obstruction by dockyard workers prevented interested contractors from touring the yard. When representatives of Babcock International and Thorn EMI attempted to tour the Rosyth workshops on 2 April 1986, a noisy human barrier of 2500 workers surrounded the visitors and forced the visit to be abandoned.[74] Demonstrations were also organized against government ministers and departmental officials when they visited Rosyth or the locality. When Michael Harte, the senior civil servant preparing the introduction of commercial management, visited Rosyth, industrial workers staged 'guerrilla action', stopping work for an hour at prearranged, staggered times, to ensure that the yard was 'in a state of total disarray' and production was 'disrupted for the day'.[75]

A series of walkouts and one-day token strikes to coincide with key government announcements were solidly supported by the industrial workforce. The first strikes were called in August 1984 to protest against what were to be the first 500 redundancies in the yards and predicted job losses of 25 to 30 per cent following commercial management. As part of the national strategy, strikes were designed as set pieces primarily for propaganda purposes; they were not designed to hit production:

> In taking industrial action at this stage, we are not seeking to put at risk the functions of the Yard. Our objective is to bring home to the government our intention to bitterly resist their proposals and to show to [the] public and Parliament what is happening.[76]

Traditional dockyard forms of union campaigning were packaged with a thoroughness and professionalism hitherto unknown. Apart from the study into alternatives to Levene commissioned by the Rosyth unions, the Queen Mother was petitioned, all the main party conferences and MPs at Parliament were lobbied, a music festival was organized, a series of public meetings and a conference with Fife Regional Council were held, regular collections took place outside local football grounds and leaflets were distributed in the local communities.

Yet the inoffensive cultivation of public opinion came unstuck when Norman Lamont, the recently appointed Minister for Procurement, visited Rosyth in early December 1986. His visit came only days after he had steered the Dockyard Services Bill through Parliament enabling privatization to go ahead. A demonstration of 1000 industrial workers blocked all the exits to the Main Office Block, trapping Lamont inside the building for 30 minutes. Eventually, the police forced a passage through the demonstrators to effect his release.[77] During the mêlée which followed, windows were broken, the Managing Director's official car was damaged and policemen and demonstrators were injured. Eleven workers were later suspended by the MOD with seven eventually dismissed after being convicted in court of very serious charges of affray.[78] Nationally, the union leadership were embarrassed by the publicity over the Lamont disturbances and worried about the impact on sympathetic MPs and Lords. Although neither local nor national union leaderships had been present at the Lamont demonstration they determined that no similar incidents recurred.

Organizational Capacities and Bureaucratization

From such levels dockyard unrest quickly subsided as the local dependency on centralized leadership and lobby politics was restored. This return to workplace normality prepared the way for a three-year 'honeymoon period' after the new commercial managers, Babcock Thorn Ltd (BTL), took over in April 1987. In that time pay levels were improved, a new code of behaviour for employees was introduced, a new industrial relations organization and bargaining machinery were created and a general mutuality developed between the new managers and the trade union convenors.[79] Clearly, a modified service ethos was being reconstructed, albeit on the basis of the 'risks and rewards' of 'competitive markets'. The decentralization of bargaining finished off what remained of Whitleyism as a set of rigid, routinized bureaucratic reflexes at once preserving and limiting labour's organizational capacities. New organizational capacities for labour around the twin poles of bargaining independence and a corporate responsibility to make the dockyard efficient and competitive were in the process of creation. Lobby politics was held in abeyance since key bargaining matters were being decided locally for the first time, although lobby politics would be resurrected with a vengeance for the campaign to refit the Trident submarines at Rosyth between 1991 and 1993.

Not only were organizational capacities reshaped but leading individuals from both management and unions were replaced in the process. In the early years of commercial management there was a rapid turnover of full-time shop stewards and conveners. Some found a place as union negotiators in the new structures, many of the longest-serving union conveners elected for voluntary redundancy in the first year, while some shop stewards, most active during the anti-privatization unrest, were promoted to staff BTL's new industrial relations organization. Thus the unions lost the carriers of the old organizational capacities and, to a lesser extent, the potential carriers of new ones. Around a numerically smaller layer of convenors who became active in the late 1970s and early 1980s, and thus less encumbered by the old organizational order, BTL attempted to 'professionalize' industrial relations around emerging capacities of mutuality and strong, independent, but 'responsible', bargaining. This enhanced role for local union convenors was positively embraced as the few remaining dissenters became marginalized.

The rise and decline of dockyard militancy thus becomes more explicable against the dynamic but contradictory forms of organizational capacities. Rosyth was neither a colonial dockyard nor an historic royal yard. Nevertheless, Rosyth unions inherited traditional dockyard organizational capacities modified to local circumstances. Whitleyism rigidly regulated the centrally determined terms of the effort bargain and in the process legitimized the bureaucratization of workplace trade unionism, while lobby politics separated out 'politics' from 'economics'. Paradoxically, while political alliances in Scotland were mobilized early to lobby for Rosyth's survival in the 1940s, the unions struggled to have Whitleyism adopted in the first place because for local management it represented union strength and interference. But by 1972 the habituation to committee life and the incorporating force of the service ethos was temporarily transcended at Rosyth by a wider sense of horizontal comradeship in a rank-and-file rebellion. The 1972 strike happened at a precise conjunctural moment: first, tight labour markets and a strategically vulnerable product market, the Polaris refits, gave Rosyth workers heightened structural power; second, centrally determined bargaining failed to reflect this in higher wages; and, third, shop stewards and members alike were influenced, externally, by the wider labour unrest in the country and among the Fife miners in particular. Yet even here dockyard organizational capacities – of dependency on a centralized leadership, of bureaucratization locally, due to Whitleyism, and of accommodation through the service ethos – remained pervasive at the southern yards; a dockyard-wide comradeship could not be sufficiently mobilized by Rosyth shop stewards alone.

Later, militancy was always contained within precise limits. Between 1978 and 1981 the overlapping waves of industrial action flowed from two sources: centrally-led token actions over wage controls and sectional disputes over the effort bargain.[80] Although Whitleyism and the service ethos were eclipsed as incorporating forms between 1984 and 1987, local actions remained subordinate to the continuing force of lobby politics and centralized control of the campaign. The logic of lobby politics was not seriously challenged within Rosyth, indeed it was taken up with vigour locally. Some autonomy was permitted locally but only where national strategy allowed for it. National strategy used the arguments of loyal dockyard 'service' to build lobby politics alliances. As Lord Denning put it, British dockyard workers were pictured as loyal servants, not serfs, and, he might have added, certainly not colonials.

More recently, the 'inner dockyard state' has been sacrificed to an internal dockyard market and a new managerialist ethos. Intense competition for, and the ultimate loss of, Rosyth's core product, nuclear submarine refitting, framed a changed set of organizational capacities in the first half of the 1990s. Discontinuities, represented by mass job losses, wage freezes, work intensification and flexible secondary labour markets, contradict the current fashion for human resource management theory and the 'new' organizational capacities of mutuality, local empowerment and responsibility at Rosyth. Shorn of Whitleyism and the service ethos, and as lobby politics gives way to the despotic culture of human resource management, dockyard labour has become increasingly like 'outside' industry, with all the possibilities and limitations that that implies.

Notes

1. I would like to thank Peter Kennedy, Ken Lunn, Paul Thompson and Brian Woods for useful suggestions.

2. For the political, technical and bureaucratic disputes behind the delays to Rosyth's construction see G. Harrison, *Alexander Gibb: The Story of an Engineer* (London, Geoffrey Bles, 1950), pp. 57–81.
3. Despite being Britain's most modern dockyard, S. V. Ward argues that Rosyth was sacrificed and the southern dockyards kept open in a social, political and cultural context which tended to work against Rosyth and favoured the more traditional yards. The 1925 closure was foregrounded against an Admiralty engaged in a desperate struggle to resist proposals to commercialize dockyard operations, earlier industrial unrest at Rosyth during the war, the wider management structures of the Admiralty, local workplace and community traditions, and cultural attitudes towards the Navy. *The Geography of Interwar Britain: The State and Uneven Development* (London, Routledge, 1988), pp. 84–7.
4. For Jarrow's dependency on Palmer's, the Admiralty shipbuilder, see E. Wilkinson, *The Town That Was Murdered* (London, Victor Gollancz, 1939). The centrality of the 'housing question' at Rosyth is brought out by the *Report of the Commissioners for Scotland: Commission of Enquiry into Industrial Unrest, No. 8 Division* (1917), para. 8; the *Second Report from the Select Committee on Public Accounts* (HC 155, 1926), para. 2553–2581; S. Gleave, *The Influence of the Garden City Movement in Fife, 1914–23, with Particular Reference to Rosyth* (St Andrews University, unpublished M.Phil. thesis, 1987); D. Whitham, 'National policies and local tensions: part 1, state housing and the Great War', in R. Rodger (ed.), *Scottish Housing in the Twentieth Century* (Leicester, Leicester University Press, 1989), pp. 94–9.
5. J. Gennard and J. Kelly, 'The role of human resource management at Rosyth Royal Dockyard, 1987–1990', *Human Resource Management Journal*, **1**(4) (Summer 1991), 77–89.
6. While not all of their arguments are accepted, particularly the game-theoretic aspects, the organizational capacity argument made here reworks, in part, two suggestive approaches: E. O. Wright's, in *Class, Crisis and the State* (London, New Left Books, 1978), and S. Lash and J. Urry, 'The new Marxism of collective action: a critical analysis', *Sociology*, **18** (1984), 33–50.
7. P. K. Edwards, *Conflict at Work: A Materialist Analysis* (Oxford, Basil Blackwell, 1986).
8. N. Casey and D. Dunkerley, 'Technological work cultures: conflict and assimilation within a mid-nineteenth century naval dockyard', in K. Thompson (ed.), *Work, Employment and Unemployment: Perspectives on Work and Society* (Milton Keynes, Open University Press, 1984), p. 149.
9. G. Baldacchino, *Workers Cooperatives with Particular Reference to Malta: An Educationalist's Theory and Practice* (The Hague, Institute of Social Studies, 1990), p. 116, note 9. Baldacchino bases this claim about dockyard militancy on a misreading of R. Sandbrook, 'Worker consciousness and populist protest in tropical Africa', *Research in the Sociology of Work*, **1** (1981). Here

Sandbrook discusses *dockworkers*, that is, port workers handling cargoes, and not *dockyard* workers engaged in ship repair or refits. E. L. Zammit records that numerous protests, demonstrations, industrial actions and outbreaks of violence occurred at Malta Dockyard between 1917 and 1971, when the dockyard was nationalized under partial workers' control, in *A Colonial Inheritance: Maltese Perceptions of Work, Power and Class Structure with reference to the Labour Movement* (Malta, Malta University Press, 1984), p. 47. This is not to argue that all colonial dockyards were as militant as Malta. For example, at the dockyard in Hong Kong mass dismissals were resisted by 'squat-down' strikes, demonstrations and an occupation of the yard in March 1958 but, after concessions by the British authorities to raise the level of gratuity pay and help find alternative employment, the rundown was orderly. See *Hong Kong Annual Report 1958* (London, HMSO, 1959), pp. 39–40; *Hong Kong Annual Report 1959* (London, HMSO, 1960), pp. 39–40; K. Harland, *The Royal Navy in Hong Kong since 1841* (Liskeard, Cornwall, Maritime Books, 1984), p. 54.
10. R. G. Sultana and G. Baldacchino, 'Introduction: sociology and Maltese society: the field and its context', in R. G. Sultana and G. Baldacchino (eds), *Maltese Society: A Sociological Inquiry* (Malta, Mireva, 1994), p. 15.
11. CED HQ Bath, in *The Royal Dockyards, A Framework for the Future: Consultative Document on the Dockyard Study (The Speed Report)*, vol. II: F-1.
12. P. Inman, *Labour in the Munitions Industries* (London, HMSO, 1957), p. 149.
13. J. C. Stewart, *The Sea Our Heritage* (Keith, Rowan Books, 1993), p. 151.
14. Inman, *Labour in the Munitions Industries*, p. 287.
15. For the role of Communist militants at Rosyth balancing between support for uninterrupted war production and defending workers' conditions see B. Selkirk, *Life of a Worker* (Dundee, privately published, 1967), pp. 41–2, and M. Docherty, *A Miner's Lass* (Cowdenbeath, privately published, 1992), pp. 155–7.
16. *Rosyth and the Future?* (Rosyth Dockyard, The Shop Stewards, n.d. [1945]), p. 3.
17. The Rosyth stewards demanded a modernization programme for the yard, government control and a fairer distribution and planning of industry in Britain, a fairer share of Admiralty work and facilities for the trade unions 'to examine all aspects of production and a greater say in determining the programme of work at all times'. *Rosyth and the Future?*, p. 7.
18. See Rosyth Dockyard Campaign Joint Committee, *Rosyth Dockyard* (Dunfermline, Dunfermline Town Council, 1947).
19. *Rosyth Dockyard*, p. 8.
20. *Rosyth and Inverkeithing Journal*, 26 December 1945. In fact when Chatham and Portsmouth were run down in the early 1980s little resistance took place beyond ritualized forms of token campaigning and lobbying.
21. A process largely accomplished by February 1969 when, as part of a trade-off for dockyard reductions, establishment was extended to all industrial

employees with five or more years' service. As David Owen, Under-Secretary of State for the Royal Navy, put it in a message to dockyard workers, 'We want to work in the closest partnership with the Trade Unions with the object not only of making the dockyards more productive and efficient but, at the same time, seeing that those who work in them obtain a fair share of the benefits which these improvements should bring.' *Extracts from the Defence White Paper 1969 relating to Dockyards*, 20 February 1969, mimeo, p. 3.
22. Burawoy uses the notion of an 'internal state' where workers acquire rights to prevent arbitary exercises of managerial authority while leaving management's overall control function unchallenged. M. Burawoy, *Manufacturing Consent: Changes in the Labour Process under Monopoly Capitalism* (Chicago, University of Chicago Press, 1979).
23. Interview with ex-Convenor of Coppersmiths, 12 December 1995.
24. Interviews with Small Ships Fitters, 3 November 1995, 23 January 1996; Large Ships Shipwright, 30 November 1995.
25. Interview with ex-Convenor, 12 December 1995.
26. Interview with ex-Convenor, 12 December 1995.
27. Political suspensions were not confined to Rosyth. A similar case arose at Devonport dockyard when a dilutee electrical fitter with nine years' service in the dockyard and ten years in the Navy was suspended in October. See *Glasgow Herald*, 31 October 1950.
28. *Glasgow Herald*, 18 March 1950.
29. *Ibid.*, 12 April 1950.
30. One of these, senior TGWU shop steward and dockyard lagger, Alec Falconer, became the left-wing Labour MEP for Fife and Mid-Scotland in 1984.
31. TGWU letter, 15 December 1978.
32. PSTO(N) letter, 16 October 1978.
33. PSTO(N) letter, 29 August 1978.
34. J. Holford, *Reshaping Labour: Organisation, Work and Politics – Edinburgh in the Great War and After* (Beckenham, Croom Helm, 1988), p. 170.
35. *Dunfermline Press*, 10 February 1962.
36. *Spotlight*, July 1972 (Newspaper of Rosyth Dockyard).
37. *Dunfermline Press*, 7 July 1972.
38. *Ibid.*, 21 July; 28 July; 11 August; 18 August 1972.
39. *Ibid.*, 7 July 1972.
40. *Ibid.*, 18 August 1972.
41. *Ibid.*, 25 August 1972.
42. Interview with Alec Falconer, 24 March 1996.
43. *Spotlight*, August 1972.
44. Interview with Alec Falconer, 24 March 1996; *Dunfermline Press*, 29 September 1972.
45. K. V. Burns, *The Devonport Dockyard Story* (Liskeard, Cornwall, Maritime Books, 1984), p. 120.

46. *Dunfermline Press*, 1 September 1972; 22 September 1972.
47. *Ibid.*, 29 September 1972.
48. *Ibid.*, 13 October 1972.
49. *Ibid.*, 13 October 1972.
50. Interview with Alec Falconer, 24 March 1996.
51. *Dunfermline Press*, 13 October 1972. The 'D' Notice system is a voluntary code operated between government and the various branches of the media. Notices were issued by a committee composed of members of the media and MOD officials to editors, publishers and the BBC for their general guidance on material sensitive to 'national security'. As Harold Wilson said, ' "D" Notices were loyally observed, almost without question, by the press and other media, and most were scrupulous in asking clearance for any story they proposed to publish which might come near the scope of a Notice in force' (*The Labour Government, 1964–70*, Harmondsworth, Penguin, 1974, p. 479). On the lack of coverage of the Rosyth strike see, for example, a report by Chapman Pincher in the *Daily Express*, 11 September 1972, which discusses selective walkouts at Devonport and work-to-rule action at the southern yards, amid 'fears that Communist militants could take advantage of the situation', without anywhere mentioning the far more serious strike at Rosyth, by then in its third week. However, the local press covered the dispute prominently over the course of the strike.
52. See for example *Dunfermline Press*, 4 August 1978; 6 July 1979; 18 December 1980; 5, 12 June 1981; 7 August 1981.
53. D. K. Brown, *A Century of Naval Construction: The History of the Royal Corps of Naval Constructors, 1883–1983* (London, Conway Maritime Press, 1983), pp. 21–2.
54. See *Eighth and Ninth Reports from the Select Committee on Estimates: His Majesty's Dockyards* (HC 245, HC 259, 1950–1); *Ninth Report from the Select Committee on Estimates: Her Majesty's Dockyards* (HC 263, 1961–2); *Fifth Special Report from the Estimates Committee* (HC 101, 1962–3); *Government Industrial Establishments* (Cd. 4713, 1971); *The Royal Dockyards: A Framework for the Future: Consultative Document on the Dockyard Study, Volume I, Report*, and *Volume II, Annexes* (1980) (hereafter *The Speed Report*); *Defence Committee: The Royal Dockyards and the Dockyard Study* (HC 362, 1980–1).
55. *The Speed Report*, vol. I, p. 29.
56. *The Speed Report*, vol. I, p. 7.
57. This, and cuts in the surface fleet, resulted in the dismissal of Keith Speed as Under-Secretary for the Navy.
58. *The Observer*, 31 March 1985.
59. *The Economist*, 16 March 1985.
60. *The Engineer*, 7 November 1985.
61. G. Kennedy, *The Privatisation of Defence Supplies* (Glencorse, The David Hume Institute, 1986), pp. 28; G. Kennedy, 'Royal dockyards: time for action', *Fraser of Allander, Quarterly Economic Commentary*, **11**(1), August 1985, 67–71.

62. Rosyth Naval Base Trade Unions, *Giving the Royal Dockyards a Chance* (Rosyth, 1984), p. vii.
63. *Fourth Report from the Defence Committee: The Future of the Royal Dockyards* (HC 453, 1985), Q. 200.
64. *Twenty-Second Report from the Committee of Public Accounts: Control of Dockyard Operations and Manpower* (HC 342, 1985), pp. xii–xiii.
65. A token one-day national strike in defence of trade union rights at GCHQ called by the TUC was well supported at Rosyth. See *Dunfermline Press*, 3 February 1984.
66. J. Dromey, 'Ministry of Defence Joint Industrial Whitley Council', *TGWU Reports and Accounts 1986*, p. 101.
67. Interviews with Convenor of Shipwrights, 3 November 1995; ex-Convenor of Coppersmiths, 12 December 1995.
68. Dromey, 'Ministry of Defence', p. 101.
69. *Parliamentary Debates*, 9 June 1986, col. 39.
70. *Ibid.*
71. *FACT*, no. 18 (Rosyth industrial unions bulletin).
72. *This Week*, 21 June 1985 (Rosyth management bulletin).
73. M. Harte, 'The introduction of commercial management into the Royal Dockyards: Devonport and Rosyth', *Public Administration*, **66** (Autumn 1988), 319–21.
74. *Dunfermline Press*, 4 April 1986.
75. *FACT*, 29 October 1986.
76. STJC circular, 15 August 1984.
77. *The Scotsman*, 7 December 1986.
78. A weekly levy was collected from the workforce to pay the wages of members suspended because of the Lamont disturbances. Later, in May 1987, the Civil Service Appeals Board found that the dismissals were unjustified and the new commercial managers offered the workers their jobs back as part of a general amnesty for previous conduct, helping to 'set the scene for a smooth transition period', according to the Chairman of the industrial unions at Rosyth, *Dunfermline Press*, 8, 15 May 1987; Interview with sacked worker, 24 November 1995.
79. Gennard and Kelly, 'The role of human resource management'.
80. *The Royal Dockyards* (HC 362, 1980–1).

9 THE WAY FORWARD? THE ROYAL DOCKYARDS SINCE 1945

Kenneth Lunn

Introduction

The fate of the royal dockyards since 1945 has, in many respects, reflected the complexity of political, economic and social change in Britain during these years. The analysis of the nature of such changes requires detailed consideration of a range of factors, all of which have impinged to some extent on the existence of the yards. International relations, technological developments and ideological considerations have all combined to produce the kind of chequered history which Law's detailed study of Rosyth has suggested. Management and control of the dockyards has significantly altered, particularly in the last fifteen years and the nature of the work experience and of labour relations have been affected as a result.

At the end of the Second World War, the future of the dockyards was less certain than may have been supposed. Although the repair of war damage, decommissioning of former civilian ships and the perceived need to maintain a strong naval force were all vital issues, there was also a desire on the part of the state to return as swiftly as possible to 'normality' and to pay attention to other economic priorities in public spending.[1] The two yards deemed to be the most vulnerable, Pembroke and Rosyth, had only been re-opened because of the hostilities, and workers in both yards feared permanent closure as part of a post-war rationalization.[2] In Pembroke's case, the inter-war status of 'care and maintenance', in effect closure, was re-invoked in 1947, although the yard remained in Admiralty hands until 1964.[3] Rosyth, for the strategic and political reasons outlined by Law in the previous chapter, remained open and subsequently took on a major role in support of British defence policy over the next 50 years.

The other British dockyards concentrated, in the immediate post-war years, on decommissioning and a programme of repair and maintenance.

Although there was some initial employment dislocation, as temporary wartime workers, particularly women employed in the industrial sector, were replaced by men returning from other wartime service, it was some time before employment levels returned to 'normal'. This did not, however, prevent speculation about the viability of all the yards, despite expansion plans for Devonport and Portsmouth.[4] Chatham's future seemed even less certain, given that its main post-war task was the maintenance of ships until they were scrapped.

What secured, at least in the short term, the future of the yards was British foreign policy in the 1950s. Drawn into the continued support of distant overseas interests, particularly in the east, and involved in many of the international conflicts of the early 1950s, dockyardmen benefited from the desire of both Labour and Conservative governments to maintain a high profile in terms of world politics. Defence spending in these years was estimated to be 8 per cent of GNP, compared to 6 per cent for France and 4 per cent for West Germany.[5] Whilst this may have resulted in long-term imbalances in the British economy, it provided security of employment for most dockyard workers.

Some recognition of these financial and foreign policy problems was apparent with the publication of the 1957 Defence White Paper, which outlined what has been called a 'landmark' in British defence policy. This confirmed an intention to devote resources to nuclear defence, reduce conventional services and attempt to contain overall defence spending.[6] There were a number of implications which directly impinged on the dockyards. First, as part of the 'rationalization' programme, Sheerness Dockyard was closed in 1960, a reminder of the potential vulnerability of defence establishments to government policy changes. Secondly, the balance of naval construction between the royal yards and the commercial sector was finally tipped heavily in favour of the latter. As Lunn and Day have argued elsewhere in this volume, there was an increasing tension throughout the twentieth century over the balance of warship construction within the royal yards and in the commercial sector. Even at the peak of the Dreadnought programme in the build-up to the First World War, the private yards were producing the majority of these battleships.

Arguments for and against such a strategy raged in the inter-war period, as both sectors tried to justify their existence. By the 1960s, the balance had tipped firmly in favour of the commercial yards. The years 1967 and 1968 saw the last launches of vessels built within the confines of the three major yards, Portsmouth, Devonport and Chatham.[7] However, it was a combination of international relations and technological developments in weaponry which gave new roles to those yards which remained. Rosyth, Chatham and Devonport were extensively developed in the 1960s and 1970s as bases for the maintenance and operation of nuclear submarines and, in Devonport's case, the construction of a frigate complex, opened in 1977, provided additional employment opportunities.[8] Portsmouth, after apparent neglect in the 1960s, announced a modernization programme of some £60 million in 1970, with specialization in destroyers.[9]

Defence expenditure, particularly with its commitment to a so-called independent nuclear deterrent consisting of the Polaris nuclear submarine programme and its replacement, Trident, was, however, increasingly under review. Despite the economic difficulties of maintaining a complex and costly defence strategy, the trend within post-war politics was to adopt what Baylis has defined as a gradualist approach notwithstanding the apparent need for dramatic reductions.[10] Indeed, the Labour government in 1978 initiated a so-called re-armament boom.[11] It took the election of the Thatcher government to fracture this 'consistency' of approach[12] and even then it was a question of switching resources from conventional forces to support a growing nuclear commitment.[13] Previous attempts at initiating change to the overall structure and organization of defence establishments, such as the Mallabar Committee, set up in December 1968, had suggested the need for a more commercially-minded approach, but no government had been able or willing to try to create a political consensus around how this might be achieved.[14] Only the Thatcher government was prepared to tackle the issue.

The Defence White Paper of June 1981, 'The Way Forward', outlined a strategy which claimed to introduce efficiency and economy into defence provision and to provide more professional and competitive management. Despite the interlude of the Falklands War, which could be read as evidence of why 'over-capacity' was an essential feature of the dockyard structure, a long-term programme of reducing provision and changing management was initiated. Chatham was closed in 1984. Portsmouth, reprieved from a similar fate by the conflict in the Atlantic, was retained only as a naval base and repair yard. Devonport and Rosyth were left to compete for the refitting and location of nuclear submarines and other more conventional maintenance work. As Law's study has shown, the management of these two yards was put into private hands in 1987,[15] although the yards themselves are still owned by the state. At the time of writing (February 1997), Portsmouth's operation, where all in-house services are subjected to 'market testing' comparisons with private contractors,[16] is likely to be placed under similar managerial control. All this has meant considerable reductions in the dockyard workforces and a very different pattern of work and labour relations from that which was in place in 1945.

Employment and Trade Union Politics

For those who worked in the dockyards, or whose living was largely dependent upon their existence, this somewhat chequered post-war history had a particularly powerful impact. From the immediate post-war years, and even at the height of the 'Never Had It So Good' era, there was an air of fragility to dockyard employment which permeated the local consciousness. The legacy of inter-war closures and reductions still persisted. Discussions about diversification into alternative commercial work, such as the construction of merchant ships, which had been explored in detail in the 1920s, were re-introduced. As early as 1946, dockyard town MPs were lobbying for this kind of alternative to try and counter the feared reductions in the workforce.[17] Despite a few minor concessions, however, the Admiralty and successive governments have been reluctant to open up the dockyards for anything other than naval work,[18] and the impact of the recent 'Peace Dividend'[19] has largely been negative, at least for the workforce.[20]

In terms of industrial relations, the early post-war years seemed relatively peaceful. The spirit of wartime co-operation, and also the growing confidence of unions through wartime consultation, seemed to give a new lease of life to Whitleyism. Combined with a Labour government committed to state-owned enterprises and to direct involvement of trade unions in their management,[21] this provided an incentive to operate within the framework laid down in 1919. For a while, it appeared to work effectively and in 1946, largely through the efforts of the engineering unions in a wider context, dockyard industrial workers secured a five-day week.[22]

The 1950s saw the consolidation of employment, at least for the industrial workers within the yards, although rates of pay and conditions still lagged behind those of the private sector. Even within dockyard towns, where the local economy had been constructed around these enterprises to the exclusion of much else, alternative employment opportunities were beginning to make a significant impact. Apprentices were often able to find better-paid work outside the yards on completing their training, and there were difficulties in recruiting school-leavers into the apprenticeship system. The less-obviously transferable skills of trades such as smiths, boilermakers and founders were spurned, while ship fitters and electrical fitters, occupations which seemed to offer job mobility, were the most popular choices.[23] For many workers, however, the opportunity of a 'job for life' and a pension was still seen as an attractive proposition. In addition, industrial relations, provided work was available, seemed to offer a shining example of consultative negotiation. Certainly, management felt this to be the case, as seen through the words of a senior yard official in 1955:

> Thanks to the practical characteristics of the Whitley organization, and to the team spirit, balanced outlook, and moderation shown by both sides of the committees, the great majority of the numerous local labour and production problems can be resolved in a satisfactory way, without the need for reference to a higher tribunal in Admiralty.[24]

Indeed, these characteristics were displayed to the full a couple of years later, during the national shipyard strikes in 1957. There was much panic in the Admiralty that the stoppages would spread to the royal dockyards. With some 200,000 private sector workers out in pursuit of a 10 per cent wage increase, a special meeting of the Admiralty Shipbuilding Trades Joint Council was called to discuss the threat to their concerns. With the engineering unions also brought out in pursuit of similar claims in the private sector, there was considerable unease. However, union leaders representing with the yards' workforces, already negotiating for a 9 per cent increase through the Whitley machinery, were able to reassure Admiralty officials that they would not be coming out in sympathy with the commercial shipyard dispute.[25] As it transpired, the 9 per cent was refused, but dockyard union leaders continued with the negotiating process rather than turn to other forms of industrial action.

It is this aspect of industrial relations which has been one of the key dimensions to the history of dockyard labour. As a number of contributors to this volume have outlined, the particular characteristics of employment and of work control have given the dockyards a rather different framework of labour relations. In many cases, it has produced a conflict with organized labour outside the dockyard sector, despite a common membership of many unions. Galliver's study in this volume on the period 1880–1914 has been particularly revealing in this respect. By the inter-war period, as Lunn and Day have indicated, there was a growing rivalry between the public and private sectors for the construction of naval vessels. Given the problems of the shipbuilding industry at this time, these tensions were often played out in rival claims about relative efficiency and ability and led to entrenched and oppositional camps being created. Royal dockyard men resented the 'theft' of their work by private yards while those in the private sector were quick to link the security of employment enjoyed by many dockyard employees with their alleged lack of support for trade unionism and their absence of sympathy for fellow workers. This situation repeated itself in the immediate post-war years, through competition for refitting and repair work and allegations of favouritism towards the state sector. Thus, the 1957 strike was further evidence of these divisions within shipbuilding and repair and indicative of the different cultures and traditions which had developed over the years.

Early in 1962, when there had been a one-day token stoppage called by the Confederation of Shipbuilding and Engineering Unions against the government pay-pause policy,[26] the gulf became obvious. The majority of dockyard industrial employees were not involved in the strike call. In Portsmouth, the Amalgamated Engineering Union had requested its members to come out but the Transport and General Workers Union, with by far the larger industrial membership (some 6000 compared to the AEU's 1000) had left the decision to the local executive, who declined to call on its members to support the action. It was believed that some of the workforce had taken a day's leave of absence without pay, in apparent accord with dockyard regulations, but, overall, only 250 out of some 15,000 industrial employees were absent that day. At a rally in the city, union officials representing workers from the non-dockyard sectors were bitterly critical of the lack of support, reinforcing the splits between the various sectors and the subsequent growing divisions in the labour movement, both at national and local level.[27] This situation goes some way to explaining the problems of co-ordinating support for a fully-fledged opposition to the reforms of the 1980s and 1990s, something which Law's work on Rosyth has already indicated.

It would, however, be wrong to see the royal yards' workforce as being totally subservient to, and isolated from, other industries and from the wider patterns of industrial relations within the British economy. Indeed, much of this volume has been concerned to indicate patterns of militancy and self-awareness, albeit shaped by the particularities of the dockyard.

Whitleyism may have reinforced patterns of deference, but it also opened some channels of communication with unions outside the yards. Indeed, as Galliver suggests, such influences were already in operation by the late nineteenth century. In the post-war period, the continuing movement of labour between the public and private yards encouraged this perspective. In addition, it was increasingly the white-collar sector of the workforce which took the lead in industrial activity, a reflection of changing trends within the British economy and the labour force as a whole.[28]

By the 1960s, the lead in breaking from traditions of negotiation came from the non-industrial workforce. In September 1962, telephonists belonging to the Civil Service Union began an unofficial go-slow action in demand for transfer to non-industrial status and a concomitant pay rise (including a call for equal pay for male and female operatives). This action came about over frustration at the apparent inability of the consultative machinery to produce any response to this request.[29] Later in the same month, scientific assistants in government employment, including dockyards and other establishments, took part in a one-day stoppage over pay.[30] Although most of those involved were members of the Institute of Professional Civil Servants, the strike was an unofficial one. The dockyard no-strike attitude was still maintained, at least by management. A spokesman for the Admiralty Superintendent of Portsmouth Dockyard claimed, 'It is not a strike. The men are only taking part of their annual leave. They had to apply for it and it has been granted only where they could be spared.'[31]

A growing unease with the ability of Whitleyism generally to deal responsively with many of the demands for pay increases and to act as an effective voice for many sections of the workforce in the dockyards was becoming apparent by the late 1960s. In the 1970s, the yards were the setting for a number of significant confrontations, largely over pay and conditions but also over regrading (which often involved the former).[32] A study of Devonport yard has noted the increasing tendency to resort to more militant forms of action: there was a major stoppage of a week in late September 1972, following a series of token strikes over pay. The base was brought to a standstill by this action.[33] Over the next few years, there were a number of official and unofficial disputes, patterns mirrored in the other yards, which seemed to indicate a new phase to labour relations within the sector. This reflected, no doubt, the general pattern of confrontational politics within Britain in these years and was perhaps an indication of the changing balance within the yard workforce. It is clear that much of the action was prompted by groups of non-established men and by those not brought up within the craft union association of dockyard tradition. Fears about job security had also begun to present a renewed threat. In the late 1960s, as part of a general attempt to reduce defence spending under the ministerial leadership of Denis Healey,[34] there had been much informal discussion about the closure of Devonport, since it had not yet been revamped to take on nuclear submarines. It was only with the intervention of the then Navy Minister, David Owen, who was MP for Plymouth Sutton, that a rethink preserved the yard's future.[35] Under new proposals, it was now Chatham that was to be closed – a decision that was rescinded soon after but spelt out the likely direction of future cutbacks. In 1971, the Mallabar Committee recommended retention of all four yards with reduced capacity. It was against this background of uncertainty and a growing lack of belief in the outcome of any Whitley-based negotiations that the militancy of the yards in the 1970s developed.

The Thatcher Era

The previous chapter by Law has outlined the broad nature of the changes implemented in the 1980s and 1990s, their impact on the size of the workforce and on the consequent restructuring of labour relations in the dockyards. Attention is drawn to the strength of feeling in Scotland about the lack of support and solidarity displayed in English dockyard towns in attempts to resist the changes. The argument that many of the Rosyth workforce came from, or were influenced by, an activist labour tradition rather than that of the established and traditional yards, and therefore were more committed to challenging the new management scheme, is difficult to refute. Studies of the closure of Chatham and the reduction in status of Portsmouth indicate considerable hostility to the measures at a local level but also a recognition of the *realpolitik* of the situation. Protests and lobbying reflected the extent of the attempts to alter these decisions. It did appear that centuries of channelled complaint and protest had determined the limited nature of the responses to government policies. Putting these events in context, most of the Conservative attempts to restructure other sectors of public services and nationalized industries were met with broadly similar patterns of muted or ineffective challenges. However, in the case of the dockyards, the legacy of subservience and acceptance became apparent. The history of the politics of defence may also have intruded. As Smith has written of the 1980s, with the exception of some fierce discussion over the implications of the nuclear issue, argument over defence policy was seen as 'rarely penetrating into domestic debate'. Historically, accountability has been lacking. 'Parliament is less involved in defence issues, and the executive controls the agenda.'[36]

What was left, then, was a moral critique of the reductions after their implementation. On the day that Portsmouth had its status reduced, some (anonymous) members of the workforce placed an obituary in *The Times*. 'H.M. Royal Dockyard Portsmouth passed peacefully away at 12 o'clock last night after nearly 800 years of faithful service. It will be sadly missed by many.'[37] Similarly, Kate Losinska of the Civil and Public Servants Association, speaking at the 1986 Trades Union Congress, made the point that recent events and public displays of loyalty by the workforce had served for nothing. 'It is strange that this Government who depended so heavily on the Dockyards and the Ordnance factories to win the Falklands campaign should now kick them in the teeth.'[38] Such public sentiment, however, did not effectively challenge government strategy towards the public sector, which was concerned not merely with a drive towards efficiency but also sought to attack the alleged power of trade unions in this field. As Drewry has written of the general drive towards Civil Service reforms:

> They also gained impetus from the government's determination to diminish the power of the trade unions – including, of course, the civil service unions, with which the Thatcher government came quickly into conflict. The early phase of the reform programme featured rhetoric about 'deprivileging' the civil service and plans to cut civil service numbers and peg back pay increases.[39]

In effect, the trade union movement had much to defend amid the challenges posed by the Thatcher governments, and protection of the management structures of the royal dockyards was only one small aspect of the larger scene. The TUC was aware of the proposed changes, having passed an emergency resolution at the 1984 Congress opposing plans 'to privatise the warship yards'[40] and had initiated discussions on a campaign to reverse the decision. Specific interventions in the dockyards came in the privatization debate in 1985 and, the following year, there were a number of contributions which sought to expose and to challenge the plans for privatization of management.[41] However, the inability to alter the course of the government was amply displayed by the testimony of a delegate from Devonport who, some three weeks after the implementation of the new structure, drew attention to the announcement of some 3500 redundancies to be implemented over the following two years, 2000 of them to be immediately effective. This ran counter to promises that jobs would not be threatened. The message for other sectors was spelt out:

> We have debated policy on privatisation, so whilst we are doing that let us remember the reality of privatisation as shown so brutally and dishonestly at Devonport. Let us send our support and our solidarity to a somewhat disillusioned but still proud and loyal labour force at the dockyards.[42]

The question remains, however, about the degree of support for the campaign to defend the yards. There are a number of issues which hint at a less than committed position within the labour movement generally. Law has already suggested a lack of motivation in the English yards compared to Rosyth. There must, however, also be suspicion of a general lack of information about the extent of the privatization proposals, again as indicated in Law's study. Here, the tradition of relatively less accountability in defence debate may have been a determining factor. What is also apparent is the division within the labour movement with regard to the dockyard employees and their position as trade unionists. When the TUC was exploring the possibilities of launching a campaign in 1984/85, its Nationalised Industries Committee had informal discussions with representatives from the Confederation of Shipbuilding and Engineering Unions. In March 1985, after a joint meeting with the CSEU, which explored whether to meet with the government and to take up the issue with the Labour Party, it was decided that no action be taken. 'The view of the CSEU was that such a meeting with Government would be unproductive and that there was little enthusiasm in the warship yards' workforce for a campaign against privatisation.'[43] Having fought an unsuccessful defence a few years earlier against the de-nationalization of British Shipbuilders, it seems that the CSEU had little expectation of success in this situation and perhaps little sympathy for the naval yards at this point.

One other intangible factor is the extent to which the labour movement in general supported aspects of dockyard work. There has been a long history of hostility to elements of British imperialism and to the production and maintenance of weapon systems within some strands of the movement.[44] The increasing reliance on nuclear weapons had heightened this opposition and had sometimes made it difficult for

Labour Party candidates in dockyard towns to balance personal and party politics with the economic and political needs of the local economy. Given the increasing involvement of dockyard workers with nuclear weapons, and an unease within the wider labour movement towards some aspects of British foreign and defence policy, a degree of detachment, if not overt hostility, may have contributed to less than robust support for the continued existence of the dockyards.[45]

Conclusion

What remains then, at the end of the twentieth century, is a significantly reduced conventional naval defence force and its support mechanism of royal dockyards. Construction has long disappeared from the scene and most of the sites are now far better known for the development of the heritage industry than for their involvement in naval repair and maintenance.[46] For those who continue to find employment in the yards which still exist, dramatic changes in job security, management and consultation and the work itself have taken place. The apparent strength of trade unionism, once so entrenched through the Whitley system, has arguably been exposed, principally by a series of governments ideologically committed to undermining the role of unions as anything other than friendly societies.

The communities built around, and dependent on, the yards have suffered from their loss or reduction,[47] although some of this fragmentation may already have been underway due to diversification in the local economies and the erosion of the social and cultural aspects of workplace communities in post-war Britain. In this sense, the restructuring of the British economy and society has, in the last quarter of the twentieth century, had a powerful impact not just upon the old industrial sectors but also on towns which felt themselves to be exempt from those exigencies. The lack of effective opposition to the reductions has in many ways reflected the wider response to Conservative changes. Indeed, it may be argued that they took place with some degree of political consensus, at least with regard to the broader principles. What has been most dramatic in the case of the dockyard towns and their workers is that, having devoted themselves to the service of the state, and acquiring values and attitudes which distanced them from other areas and groups, they were themselves deemed surplus to requirements. Given the current nature of management under privatization and the level of reductions, it is difficult to see the future of state-owned and state-controlled dockyards as anything other than limited, and the existence of dockyard workers as a continuation of the trend of 'deprivileging', which has now extended to most sectors of the British economy.

Notes

1. For a range of perspectives, see J. Fyrth (ed.), *Labour's High Noon: The Government and the Economy 1945–51* (London, Lawrence and Wishart, 1993).
2. For such attitudes in Rosyth, see A. C. Graham, *Random Naval Recollections* (Gartocharn, Dumbartonshire, Fainedram Publishers, 1979), p. 315, and Alex Law's chapter in this volume.
3. A. Day, '"Driven from home": the closure of Pembroke Dockyard and the impact on its community', *Llafur*, **7**(1) (1996), 68–77.
4. P. MacDougall, *Royal Dockyards* (Newton Abbot, David and Charles, 1982), pp. 187–88.
5. A. Sked and C. Cook, *Post-War Britain: A Political History* (Harmondsworth, Penguin, 1993), p. 141. For detailed statistics on defence spending since 1945, see J. Baylis, *British Defence Policy: Striking the Right Balance* (Basingstoke, Macmillan, 1989), pp. 139–40.
6. M. Chalmers, *Paying for Defence: Military Spending and British Decline* (London, Pluto Press, 1985), pp. 66–7.
7. MacDougall, *Royal Dockyards*, p. 189.
8. K. V. Burns, *The Devonport Dockyard Story* (Liskeard, Maritime Books, n.d.), p. 112.
9. MacDougall, *Royal Dockyards*, p. 193.
10. Baylis, *British Defence Policy*.
11. M. Chalmers, *Biting the Bullet: European Defence Options for Britain* (London, Institute of Public Policy Research, 1992), p. 50.
12. This phrase is from S. Smith, 'Foreign and defence policy', in P. Dunleavy *et al.* (eds), *Developments in British Politics 3* (Basingstoke, Macmillan, 1990), pp. 246–65.
13. See Sked and Cook, *Post-War Britain*, pp. 388–92.
14. Burns, *Devonport Dockyard Story*, pp. 109–10; M. Harte, 'The introduction of commercial management into the Royal Dockyards: Devonport and Rosyth', *Public Administration*, **66** (Autumn 1988), 319.
15. Harte, 'The introduction of commercial management', pp. 319–28.
16. *Portsmouth Evening News*, 'The story of the dockyard', 5 April 1993 (supplement), p. 31.
17. *Portsmouth Evening News*, 28 June 1946.

18. For details of some post-war commercial work see Graham, *Random Naval Recollections*, p. 315, and I. E. King, 'Forty Years of Change at Portsmouth Dockyard with Some Notes on Dockyard Organization' (paper given at The Institution of Naval Architects on 5 April 1955), p. 389.
19. For a discussion of the 'Peace Dividend' see Chalmers, *Biting the Bullet*.
20. For the impact of dockyard reductions see: S. Milne, 'A long, slow climb back up jobs escalator', *Guardian*, 4 January 1984; J. Cunningham, 'The great display case on the Medway', *Guardian*, 6 March 1984; and P. Gripaios and R. Gripaios, 'The impact of defence cuts: the case of redundancy in Plymouth', *Geography*, **79**(1) (January 1994), 32–41.
21. For details see R. Hyman, 'Praetorians and proletarians: unions and industrial relations', in J. Fyrth (ed.), *Labour's High Noon: The Government and the Economy 1945–51* (London, Lawrence and Wishart, 1993), pp. 165–94.
22. *Portsmouth Evening News*, 23 December 1946.
23. *Ibid.*, 20 August 1952.
24. King, 'Forty Years of Change', p. 398.
25. *Portsmouth Evening News*, 18 and 19 March 1957.
26. For details of the 'pay pause' see K. O. Morgan, *The People's Peace: British History 1945–1990* (Oxford, Oxford University Press, 1992), pp. 210–11.
27. *Portsmouth Evening News*, 5 February 1962.
28. For an analysis of public sector unionism see P. Fairbrother, *Politics and the State as Employer* (London, Mansell, 1994).
29. *Portsmouth Evening News*, 11 September 1962.
30. *Ibid.*, 22 August 1962.
31. *Ibid.*, 21 September 1962.
32. *Ibid.*, 'The story of the dockyard', p. 27.
33. Burns, *Devonport Dockyard Story*, p. 120.
34. For details see D. Healey, *The Time of My Life* (Harmondsworth, Penguin, 1990), part 3.
35. D. Owen, *Time to Declare* (London, Michael Joseph, 1991), pp. 150–1.
36. Smith, 'Foreign and defence policy', p. 259.
37. *The Times*, 1 October 1984.
38. Report of the 118th Annual Trades Union Congress, 1986, p. 553.
39. G. Drewry, 'The civil service: from the 1940s to "Next Steps" and beyond', *Parliamentary Affairs*, **47**(4) (October 1994), p. 587.
40. Report of the 117th Annual Trades Union Congress, 1985, p. 314.
41. See details in both 1985 and 1986 TUC Reports.
42. Report of the 119th Annual Trades Union Congress 1987, p. 543.
43. Report of the 117th Annual Trades Union Congress, 1985, p. 314. Further support for this idea was demonstrated by a strike in Portsmouth Dockyard on 8 August 1989 by some 8000 industrial workers. This strike over pay demonstrated a curiously late conversion to industrial militancy, one which was not displayed during the campaign over the yard's reduced status (see *Portsmouth Evening News*, 'The story of the dockyard', p. 31).

44. See Morgan, *The People's Peace*, pp. 180–4, for the origins of CND and its links with the labour movement from the late 1950s.
45. References to opposition to dockyard nuclear work and to some unease within the workforce at this development may be found in the Portsmouth Dockyard Oral History Archive (currently deposited with the Portsmouth Museums and Records Service).
46. On the establishment of the Chatham heritage site see Cunningham, 'The great display case on the Medway'.
47. See comments of Bob Bean, former Labour MP for Rochester and Chatham, whose family worked in the yard for 80 years: 'The Navy has been a hard taskmaster as well as provider. It created a culture, then pulled out, leaving nothing of it. The town has paid for its involvement over the years in blood' (Cunningham, 'The great display case on the Medway').

INDEX

absenteeism 44, 53, 156
accidents 12
Achilles 52, 55
Admiralty Established Civil Servants'
    Federation 142–3
'afloat' gangs 159
alehouses 55
Altfield, J. 140
Amalgamated Society of Engineers
    (ASE) 94, 106, 114, 116, 136
Amalgamated Union of Engineering
    Workers (AUEW) 169, 184
Anderson, Alexander 101
Anson, Admiral-Superintendent 95
apprentices 4–5, 7, 13, 22, 28, 34,
    43, 51, 54, 94, 104–5, 169, 183
  education of 66–70, 76–9
  standards of behaviour of 81
arbitration 134, 163–4
Associated Society of Shipwrights
    (ASS) 90, 107–9, 111–13
associations outside the Labour
    movement 141–3

Babcock International 166, 170
Babcock Thorn Ltd (BTL) 151,
    171–2
Baker, (Sir) John 103, 115
Baker, Richard 23
bakers 33, 50
Baldacchino, G. 153
Barham Commission 67
Barnes, George 94, 99
Barrington, Lord 13
Barrow, John 59

Baylis, J. 181
Beresford, Lord Charles 119
Berry, H. 133
Bevin, Ernest 145
blacking of work 160, 169
blacklisting of workers 23, 118
Block Mills (Portsmouth) xi
boilermakers 93, 139
Boilermakers' Society 113, 163
Bonham-Carter, John 60
Broadhurst, Henry 106
bureaucratization of industrial
    relations 151, 172–3

Caird, C.S. 110
Carter, C. 92
caulkers 43–4, 53
Central Mathematical School 69, 73
Chatham Dockyard 4, 9, 24–6,
    42–3, 52, 47–8, 55–6, 59, 61, 67,
    90, 94, 116, 145–6, 155, 165,
    180–1, 186
Chatham Dockyard Committee 95
Chatham School 69
Chile 160–1
chips, collection of xv, 6–7, 11, 31
Churchill, Edward 22
Civil Service Equal Pay
    Committee 138
Clarke, Sir Andrew 90
class divisions, social 71–5, 155
classification of workmen 58–62,
    109–11
clerical workers 136–7
closure of dockyards 130, 154

193

INDEX

Coffin, Commissioner 24, 27, 30
Cole, G.D.H. 88, 96
colonial dockyards 153–5
Colour Loft work 135, 138
Combination Acts 27, 47, 50–1
'command and control'
    methods 127–8
commercial management 165–72
    passim, 181
Commission on Fees and
    Perquisites 7
Commission for Inquiring into
    Irregularities, Frauds and
    Abuses 31
Commission of Naval Inquiry 6
Commissioners of Naval
    Revision 31, 33, 34
Committee on Dockyard
    Economy 70–2
Committee on Dockyard
    Management 113
communist influence 144–6, 156, 160
community influences in dockyard
    towns 28–9
competitive working
    environment 76–7, 101, 109
conciliation 139
Confederation of Shipbuilding and
    Engineering Unions
    (CSEU) 188
conformity with dockyard value
    system 78–80
conscription of labour 13
conspiracy charges 27
'contracting out' 131–2
convict labour 13
Cooper, William 60
Copeland, John 160
coppersmiths 159–60
Cornelions, A. 92
corporal punishment 10
corruption 24–6
Coulport 163

Cousins, John 163
craft status and traditions xiii, 87
Craig, Sir James 129
Crossick, G. 79

'D' Notices 164
de-skilling 128
defence policy 165, 180–1, 187–8
Defence Select Committee 166
'Defend the Dockyards'
    campaign 167–8
demarcation between trades xii–xiv, 49, 93, 103, 105–7, 159
demonstrations 169–71
Denning, Lord 167, 169, 173
Deptford Dockyard 9, 24, 27, 31, 56, 140
Devonport Dockyard 58, 79, 99, 129, 141–2, 145, 153, 155, 163–9, 180–1, 185–6, 188
Devonport School 68
dilution of skilled labour 135, 156
Diomede 28
discharge
    for affray 171
    appeals against 51
    following cuts in production
        129–30
    for indiscipline 30–1, 33, 50–4, 57, 62
    of suspected communists 144–5
    of trade unionists 114–15
disciplinary procedures 10–11, 156
    in dockyard schools 75
    see also discharge
dissenters, religious 23–4
Dock Labourers' Union 114
Dockyard Branches Convention 111
Dockyard Burial Fund Society 102
Dockyard Ex-Apprentices
    Association 118
Dockyard Grievances
    Committee 116
Dockyard Labourers' Association 91

INDEX

Dockyard Services Bill 167, 171
Dolling, Robert, Revd 111
Drake, Barbara 137
Dreadnoughts 132, 180
Drewry, G. 187
Dromey, Jack 167, 169

Earle, H.T. 106
earnings, *see* wages
Economist, The 166
education, *see* schools
Edwards, Clem 114
Edye, William 78
Egmont, Lord 8
elections 25
electrical engineers 73
Elgin, Lord 157
Eliot, Admiral 90
emigration 5, 27
employment levels in home and overseas dockyards 154, 156
empowerment of the workforce 88
engine fitters, *see* fitters
Engineering Employers' Federation 136, 138
engineering tradesmen 116
Englander, D. 94
equal pay for equal work 135–8, 185
'established' status xii, 102–4, 117, 120–1, 140–2, 152, 157
ethos of dockyards xii, xiv, 32, 157–8, 171–3
Euryalus 169
Ewing, Sir Alfred 89
ex-servicemen, employment of 114
examinations, competitive 76–8, 88–9

Falklands War 181
Faslane 163
Federal Council of Government Employees 90
female labour, *see* women workers
Fife coalfield xv, 151, 173

fines on workers 42–4
First World War xvii, 129, 135–6
fitters 70, 73, 105, 117, 120
Fitzherbert, Thomas 5
Fitzroy, R.O.B. 110
Flexman, John 78
food co-operatives 55
food prices 46, 49–50
foreign policy 129–32, 180
Forwood, Arthur 91–2
French dockyards 13
French Revolution 46
friendly societies 55, 100, 102, 109

Gallacher, William 157
Geddes, Sir Eric 129
General Strike 140, 144
Gibraltar 165
Gill, Ken 167
Gillingham 89
Gould, Richard 103, 108–9, 114–15
Gourd, A.G. 115, 133, 143
Government Communications Headquarters (GCHQ) 166
government employees, *see* privileges
Government Labourers' Union 114–15, 119
government policy, *see* defence policy; foreign policy
Graham, Admiral 109–10, 113
Graham, Sir James 58, 67, 72
Grant, H.D. 110
Grant, Thomas 28
Greene, W. Grahame 115
grievances, redress of xvi, 42–3, 62, 89, 115–16, 133
    see also petitions

Haas, J.M. 11, 131
habeas corpus, suspension of 47
hand-drillers 115
Harries, E.P. 143
Harte, Michael 170
Haulbowline Dockyard 130

INDEX

Hawkins, A.W.   120
Healey, Denis   186
health risks   12
Heseltine, Michael   165
hierarchy of workers   xiii, xiv, 136
'hired' workers   xii, 94, 102–3, 117–18, 120, 132, 152
Hobbs, Richard   60
'horsing'   7, 28
hours of work   6, 33–4, 54, 56
House Establishment School   80
house-carpenters   44, 56–7
Howell, George   111
Hughes, Colonel   90
Hughes, Commissioner   53
human resource management   151, 173

impressment
  for dockyard work   1–3, 13, 27
  into ships   9
industrial democracy   134
inflation   30, 34, 46, 54, 119
inter-trade links   41–2, 45, 47–8, 94
inter-yard links   xvi, 22, 44–5, 49, 90–1, 93
internal labour market   158, 173
Invergordon Mutiny   144
inward-looking nature of dockyard society   102
ironworking trades   55, 87, 104, 107

Japan   131
joiners   43–4, 56–7, 104
Jones, John Gale   47–8
Joseph, Charles, Revd   111

Kelly, E.H.   103
Kennedy, G.   166
Kennedy, Paul   130
Kersey, T.   110
Kingsland, James   91
Knott, John   165

Labour Party   167, 188–9
Labour Supply Committee   137
labourers   57
  see also skilled labourers
Lamont, Norman   171
Large, William   8
Lecras, Commissioner   27
Lee, J.   140
Levene, Peter   165–6
Lewington, William   89–91
Linebaugh, Peter   11–12
lobby politics   xviii, 132, 152, 155–62, 167–73, 186
lodging allowance   54
London Corresponding Society   46
Losinska, Kate   187

McCusker, Jim   163
MacTavish, J.M.   118–19
Maddocks, Richard   3
Maitland, F.L.   54
Mallabar Committee   165, 181, 186
Malta   153–5
management structures   164–5
managerialism   173
Mann, Tom   119
market testing   182
martial law   27–8
Martin, Sir Byam   56
mass production   xi
Matthews, Thomas   43
Mechanics' Institutes   81
Members of Parliament   24–5, 60–1, 90, 94–5, 99, 106, 108–9, 111, 113
merchant ships, construction of   182
Middleton, (Sir) Charles   9, 27–9
migration
  between naval dockyards   xv, 9
  between public and private shipyards   185
  see also emigration
militancy   35, 116–18, 160–3, 172–3, 184–6
Millet, Judge   167

196

INDEX

millwrights   54–5
minimum wages   137
Ministry of Labour   141, 156
Minto, Lord   60
mobility
  of senior managers   165
  of workers   26
  see also migration
Monsell, Sir Eyres   132
moral code and moral regulation   13, 81–2
'moral economy'   xv–xvi, xviii, 152
Morris Award   138
Morriss, Roger   51–2, 54
Mosely, H., Revd   68
moulders   139
mulcting   44, 75
mutinies in the fleet   30, 144

Nassau   42
National Insurance Act   118–19
National Union of Government Ship Joiners, Furnishers and Allied Trades   141
Navy Estimates   129
  debates on   90, 106
Naysmith, David   118
New Unionism   100, 114
non-industrial civil servants   156–7, 165, 185
nonconformists, religious   24
nuclear submarines, refitting of   159, 173, 181, 189

Oberon   145
O'Brien   160
older men, pay of   32
open competition for entry to dockyard employment   78
Osborne, J.   94
Otway, Arthur   90
overtime   6, 43, 46, 95, 118
overtime bans   161–2, 169
Owen, David   186

parish relief   34
paternalism   94, 96
patronage   68
patternmakers   93
pay, see wages
payment by results   2, 141
  see also task work
Pembroke Dockyard   130–1, 134, 179
pensions   8, 31, 34–5, 56, 60, 94, 102–4, 112, 118, 127, 140, 183
perquisites, see wages, supplementation of
petitions   xii–xvii passim, 24, 30, 41, 51–62, 87–91, 102, 109, 152
  advantages of   52–4, 58
  dissatisfaction with system of   95, 99, 101, 116, 120
  ending of system of   133–4
  levels of demand in   92–4
picketing   162
pieceworking   29, 44, 58, 109, 115, 141
  see also task work
Pinochet regime in Chile   160
Plymouth Dockyard   2, 24–6, 28, 30, 32, 50
pneumatic tools   93
Polaris submarines   155, 161, 164, 172, 181
political activism   xviii, 24–6, 46, 100, 132, 144–6, 186
  see also lobby politics
political control of administrative practice   29
Pollard, Sidney   11
poor houses   34
Port Auxiliary Service (PAS)   161–2
Porter, Bernard   131
Porter, G.W.   116
Portsmouth Dockyard   4, 6, 24, 43–4, 53–4, 57, 60–1, 92, 94, 129, 136, 155, 165, 180–1, 186–7
  trade unionism in   99–121

197

INDEX

Portsmouth Trades Council   116
positive vetting   160
Pounds, John   80
premiums for entry to dockyard employment   22
press-ganging, *see* impressment
prisoners, use of   13
private shipyards   13
   comparisons with   93, 118–21, 182
   naval construction by   131, 180–1, 184
privatization   171–2, 187–8
privileges of government employees   22, 82, 99, 101, 187
productivity   11, 109
'professionalization' of industrial relations   172
promotion systems   22, 68, 72–3, 75–8, 105, 152, 165
public meetings   59
public service, sense of   29, 152–3

radicalism   xviii, 46
Rae, Robert   68
Rand, William   42
re-armament drives   132, 151, 155, 181
recruitment methods   xiv–xv, 132, 155–6
   see also conscription; impressment
Redpole   169
religious conformity   23–4
religious education   74
Renown   161–2, 164
Repulse   161
respectability, encouragement of   80
retirement of dockyard workers   7–8, 118, 132, 142
rioting   30
Robertson, Paul   80
Robinson, W.B.   106
Rochester   48
ropemakers   2–3, 9, 12, 42–4, 92, 135, 138

Rosyth Dockyard   xiv, xv, xviii, 130–1, 134, 151–73, 179, 181
   employment levels at   156
Royal allegiance   23, 169
Royal School of Naval Architecture   69

sabotage   145
sailmakers   12, 107
St Vincent, Earl of   32, 50
Salisbury, J.H.   145
Sandwich, Lord   8, 10, 12, 29
'sandwich' training   71
Saturday working   56–7
School of Naval Architecture   67
   see also Royal School
schools in royal dockyards   xii–xviii, 66–82
   hegemonic role of   82, 88
   limitations of   69
   two-tier education in   71–3
Second World War   128, 138, 146
security of employment   xii, 7, 23, 26, 79, 82, 102–4, 118, 184, 186
Seditious Meetings Act (1795)   46–7
servants   7
Sheerness Dockyard   10, 27, 30, 180
Ship Constructive Association (SCA)   104, 106–9, 111–13
Shipbuilding and Engineering Federation of Trade Unions   95
Shipbuilding Trades Joint Council (STJC)   133, 138–9, 143, 158, 167
Shipconstructors' and Shipwrights' Association   107
shipwright modellers   92
shipwrights   xiii, 2, 43–5, 49, 53–7, 69, 87
   demand for   6, 10, 118
   'gentleman' and 'sledgehammer' types   73–4
   migration and emigration of   5, 9, 26

198

INDEX

other trades' hostility towards   105
privileged status of   73, 104–5, 131
union organization amongst   101, 104–13
wages of   4, 8, 14, 30
shoaling   32–3, 35
shop stewards   158–9, 162, 172
Shrubsole, William   10–11
sickness benefits   112
Singapore   130–1, 153
skilled labourers   101
  union organization amongst 113–16
Slaughter, A.G.   120
slumps in trade   35
Smith, S.   187
social control   88
socialism   119
socialization   74, 81
Society of Dockyard Labourers   91
solidarity   41–3, 45, 49, 57, 186, 188
  see also inter-trade links; inter-yard links
Speed Report   165
Spencer, Lord   108
state, the, employment by   xii, 139–40
  see also privileges of government employees
strikes   xv–xvi, 2, 5, 9–10, 30, 42–5, 49, 55, 119–20, 139–40, 161–3, 169–70, 184–5
  abandonment of use of   41, 52, 57, 61–2, 102
  breaking of   4, 9, 28, 35
  in private shipyards   183
'structured antagonism'   152
subsistence money   31
surveillance of subversives   145
sweated labour   137
Sylph   29

task work   2–3, 9–10, 12, 44, 53
technical education   89
technological change, impact of   xiii

terms of employment, reform and standardization of   31–3
Terry, Percy   95
Thatcher, Margaret   181, 187
Thompson, E.P.   13
Times, The   187
Topping, Samuel   140
Toulon   6
Trade Disputes Act (1927)   140–1
trade societies   54
trade unions   xiv, xvii, 77, 87, 90–1, 94–6, 127–9, 132–46
  conditions favourable to   117–18
  diminishing power of   187, 189
  general role of   152
  membership of   136, 158
  in Portsmouth Dockyard   99–121
  recognition of   99, 114, 120, 128
Trades Union Congress (TUC)   108, 111, 187–8
traditional attitudes and practices   xiii, 121, 158
Transport and General Workers' Union (TGWU)   160–3, 169, 184
treason   27
Treasonable Practices Act (1795)   46–7
Trident submarines   170, 172, 181
troops, use of   9–10
Tucker, Rufus S.   46
'Two Acts', the   47–9

Vanbrugh, Philip   10
Venice   6
victimization of workers   140
voting rights and voting behaviour   25

wages
  delays in payment of   2
  differentials in   xv, 4, 33, 45, 58
  equalization between older and younger men   32
  inflexibility of   11

199

INDEX

wages – *continued*
  rates of   6
  reductions in   33–4, 56–8
  supplementation of   6–7, 22, 31
  see also equal pay; shipwrights; task work; terms of employment
Washington Treaty   130
Waters, M.   52, 55, 73, 76, 116
Watts, Sir Philip   104
Webb, Sidney and Beatrice   105, 133
Wells, R.   50
White, Sir William   81, 104
Whitehead   169
Whitley, J.H.   133
Whitley Council system   xiv, xvii, 88, 96, 100, 127–9, 132–5, 139–46, 152, 156–62, 166–73 *passim*, 182–6
  real impact of   134–5
widows   94, 135
Wilkie, Alexander   90, 94, 107–8, 111, 113
Wilson, Sir Horace   141
Winterbotham, William   24
Women Power Committee   138
women workers   xiv, 127–8, 135–9, 156, 158, 180
  belonging to trade unions   136
Woods, Sam   115
Woolley, Dr   75–6
Woolwich Arsenal   144
Woolwich Dockyard   3, 5, 9–10, 24, 43, 56
Wykeham-Martin, Philip   90